BST

7/8/08

Real Estate
Salespeople,
BEWARE!

Real Estate Salespeople, BEWARE!

Protect Your Clients and Increase Your Success on Every Deal

Includes what you need to know about the new Privacy Act

MARK WEISLEDER

ECW Press

Published by ECW Press
2120 Queen Street East, Suite 200, Toronto, Ontario, Canada M4E 1E2

NATIONAL LIBRARY OF CANADA CATALOGUING IN PUBLICATION

Weisleder, Mark
Real estate salespeople, beware! : protect your clients and
increase your success on every deal / Mark Weisleder.

includes index

ISBN 978-1-55022-820-5

1. Real estate business — Law and legislation — Canada. 2. Disclosure
of information — Law and legislation — Canada. I. Title.

KE1987.R4W442 2008   346.7104'37   C2007-905232-0
KF2042 R4 W442 2008

Cover Design: Dario R. Inzirillo, urbanstructure.ca
Text Design: Tania Craan
Typesetting: Mary Bowness
Printing: Marquis

This book is set in Minion.

Passages from the Real Estate Council of Ontario Code of Ethics and the discipline proceedings
related thereto are reprinted with the kind permission of the Real Estate Council of Ontario.

The Ontario Real Estate Association copyrighted forms are used with the kind
permission of the Ontario Real Estate Association.

Although this book discusses legal and ethical situations and principles regarding the
practices of the real estate profession and practitioners, it is not meant to be advice
to the reader about specific legal situations that they may be involved with.
Such readers are urged to consult a lawyer.

The publication of *Real Estate Salespeople, Beware!* has been generously
supported by the Government of Canada through the Book Publishing Industry
Development Program (BPIDP).

Canada

DISTRIBUTION
CANADA: Jaguar Book Group, 100 Armstrong Avenue, Georgetown, ON, L7G 5S4

PRINTED AND BOUND IN CANADA

ECW PRESS
ecwpress.com

To Jodi, Hillary, and Jillian,
for always making me appreciate that "these are the days."

To my late parents, Ida and Harry Weisleder,
for their everlasting wisdom.

To Anne, Marsha, and Louis,
for their love and support.

Table of Contents

Acknowledgements

I would like to thank the following people for all their invaluable assistance in helping me complete this book:

Jack, Adrienne, David, and the rest of the crew at ECW Press, for their continuing creative ideas and education;

Don Bastian, for being my sounding board;

Shaun Belding and Judi Walsh, for their great coaching advice and friendship;

Martin and Ethel Sirotkin, for always being there;

Shelley Koral, Patsy Mackle, Nicholas Baker, and Bob Kinnear at the Ontario Real Estate Association, for their support;

Real Estate Registrar Allan Johnston and President Tom Wright at the Real Estate Council of Ontario, for their invaluable guidance;

Ruby Silvertown of The Travel Network, for sharing how to create a great travel agent experience;

All my colleagues at Bell Canada, for their encouragement and for teaching me what a great customer experience is all about.

The Moments of Truth

In any personal or business relationship, there are moments of truth that determine the success or failure of that particular relationship.

How many of you have said or done something at a wedding to a relative that haunts you for the next several years? How many times has a long-standing business relationship come to an end as a result of one mistake made at a critical time?

The theory in most businesses is that, if you treat customers with superior service at the moments of truth, they will not only remain loyal customers for many years but also refer you to more customers. Unfortunately, if you fail at these moments of truth, not only are you likely to lose these customers, but also they will relate the negative experiences to relatives, friends, and colleagues.

We are all bombarded with advertising today, whether on TV, radio, e-mail, or the Internet. Yet if one of your friends comes up to you and recommends a certain restaurant or retail store, you are much more likely to listen to your friend than to any other of the usual forms of advertising.

This is the power of word-of-mouth advertising. Advertisers know this themselves, and that is why they try to use "guerrilla" marketing tactics by having a certain demographic experiment with and then convey by word of mouth information about a particular product or service. All companies can create this form of powerful advertising every day.

For most businesses, one of the key moments of truth is when a customer calls the call centre or customer service department. Most of us do not like to call customer service. It usually means that something has gone wrong and needs fixing. We dread having to wait on hold or get trapped in an ivr "jail" by either punching buttons or trying to make an electronic voice understand where to direct us. We also believe that most companies will just transfer us to another person who will not help us and only say something like "Sorry, that's our policy."

However, those businesses that do get it, that do care, that make sure their service representatives solve customers' problems every time, on the first call, these are the companies that succeed at this crucial moment of truth, developing long-term, loyal, profitable customers.

In the experience of real estate salespeople, similar moments of truth determine success or failure in the same way. The four key moments of truth are as follows:

(1) signing the listing or buyer representation agreement;
(2) marketing the property;
(3) negotiating the Agreement of Purchase and Sale; and
(4) communicating and following up until final closing.

How do you succeed at the moments of truth? By adhering to the following three principles, which I will refer to in this book as the Three Pillars of Loyalty:

(1) being prepared;
(2) being careful – taking care of your clients; and
(3) practising full disclosure.

In my analysis of all legal and disciplinary decisions affecting salespeople and brokers that are discussed in this book, almost all of them involve an error relating to these loyalty pillars. Most of the errors were not caused because of fraud. They were caused simply as a result of not being fully prepared, being careless, and/or not practising full disclosure.

BRAND IMAGE

Major corporations spend a lot of money promoting and protecting their brand images. They can have enormous value in the marketplace. In the real estate salesperson world, your name is your brand image. It's not the name of the company that you work for, whether it's Remax, Royal Lepage, or Coldwell Banker, although these are all well-known, successful branded brokerages. Referrals will come to you based on the experience that you deliver to your clients as well as on what is said about you in the community.

IT'S ALL ABOUT LOYALTY

I have often read that the two simple rules of a successful business are

(1) keep your existing customers satisfied, and
(2) get new customers.

As I will demonstrate in this book, these rules are related. If you are successful in keeping your existing customers satisfied, they will return to you for repeat business as well as provide positive testimonials and referrals for potential new customers.

To keep your customers satisfied, you must give them a superior customer experience from the moment you meet them until the conclusion of the transaction. This means being loyal to them in providing all of your services.

Using the Three Pillars of Loyalty will assist you in protecting your deals, your reputation, and your customers. You'll be able to establish real relationships with them.

PROTECT YOUR DEALS

The chief goal of many salespeople, unfortunately, is to obtain listings. Salespeople face this pressure every day from their brokers as well as from their own desire to produce income. What they fail to realize, however, is that, once you are fortunate enough to obtain a listing, this is when the work really begins. It doesn't get any easier the more successful you become. Actually, it becomes more difficult since each client will expect and demand your personal attention. Your chief goal should in fact be building long-term relationships with your clients.

The best way to start building these relationships and protect your deals is to be very organized and meticulous in everything you do on behalf of your client. Be prepared to follow through on every commitment you make. Listen to your clients' needs and take action when required. Keep your clients fully informed at all times about the steps you are taking on their behalf. Don't assume anything. Be careful when you review every document relating to a listing or a transaction to ensure its accuracy. As I will demonstrate, it is the little things that make the difference.

PROTECT YOUR REPUTATION

As discussed, your personal brand image will set you apart from other salespeople. Protecting your reputation or brand image should thus be one of your primary goals in all dealings with your clients as well as with other salespeople. If a former client was describing you to one of her friends or relatives, which adjectives would you like her to use? How about professional, hard working, knowledgeable, caring, honest? If you want to hear those words, then that's what must guide everything you do.

As I emphasize throughout this book, when you are considering following any advice of your client you do not agree with, or doing anything you sense is not appropriate, think long and hard about the effect this could have on your reputation if things don't turn out well. All it takes is one problem transaction, complaint, or lawsuit to hurt your reputation, besides causing you great financial and personal stress as you attempt to defend your position.

PROTECT YOUR CLIENTS

In every action you take, focus on protecting your clients. This involves everything you do on their behalf, from gathering all the pertinent facts about a property to marketing the property, completing the Agreement of Purchase and Sale, and then following through on any conditions and potential closing matters. However, this doesn't mean doing anything that may be in violation of the law or the Code of Ethics.

In other words, deliver the right experience at each of the moments of truth.

The goal of protecting your clients becomes another important reason for you to take continuing education

courses, not just to satisfy any provincial registration requirement, but also to stay current on issues that impact your
clients, whether in a positive or a negative manner, and to have
the tools to protect them properly.

WHY I WROTE THIS BOOK

I worked as a private practice lawyer for 12 years in the real
estate industry. I then joined Bell Mobility, where I worked for
13 years as in-house counsel and later general manager of the
customer experience in the Bell retail stores and call centres.
For the past 20 years, I have lectured to salespeople and brokers on topics such as property law, legal updates, privacy law,
and building loyal customers. My original book, *Real Estate
Agents, Beware!*, sold out in its first printing.

My goal was simple. I wanted salespeople to learn how to
build successful practices, without ever having to see a lawyer's
office, unless they were picking up a commission cheque.

In updating this book, I have had the benefit of seeing the
impact of the new Real Estate and Business Brokers Act, which
took effect March 31, 2006, in Ontario and which I will sometimes refer to as REBBA. I have also seen some decisions by the
Privacy Commissioner of Canada that assisted me in interpreting the new privacy rules, which took effect on January 1, 2004.

I have also witnessed the dramatic effect of the Internet on
the real estate brokerage business and the perceived threats as
a result of mortgage fraud and identity theft. The way in
which the Canadian Real Estate Association has chosen to deal
with its MLS trademark has created national attention in the
context of Internet threat and protection of the public.

Yet as will be discussed later, all of these threats can still be
dealt with by following the Three Pillars of Loyalty. In fact, I
intend to demonstrate that proper use of the Internet presents

great opportunities for salespeople to deliver an even better experience for their clients.

This book warns you against approaches and practices that will hurt you as a real estate professional — even to the extent of getting you dragged before your provincial real estate council's discipline committee or before the courts. It also gives you advice that will help you to become respected, trusted, prosperous, and safe. Aren't these some of the words you'd like people to use when they talk about you?

Here's how the book lays these topics out.

- Chapter 1 looks at the overarching principle of staying out of trouble through the use of the Three Pillars of Loyalty, being prepared, being careful, and above all providing complete and conscientious disclosure practices. Real estate may be all about location, location, location, but for you, personally and professionally, it's all about disclosure, disclosure, disclosure.
- Chapter 2 introduces you to the Wheels of Misfortune, the real estate wheel and the insurance wheel.
- In Chapter 3, I help you to avoid the "spokes" of the real estate wheel, the types of activities that can get you into trouble with your real estate council and with legal proceedings.
- Chapter 4 discusses the federal Privacy Act, the recent decisions applicable to the real estate salesperson industry, as well as practical advice on how you can use this as an opportunity to market your services.
- Chapter 5 talks about the perceived threat and the opportunities presented by increased use of the Internet as it relates to the real estate industry as well as the recent phenomenon of identity theft and mortgage fraud.
- Chapter 6 closes with tips on risk management – both for keeping you out of trouble and for knowing how to act and what to do if you do get into trouble. I take you through three types of proceedings: legal, real estate council discipline, and privacy.

When explaining real estate discipline proceedings, I use as a frame of reference the discipline process under the Code of Ethics and REBBA. Yet every province in Canada has a similar code and process, as do most U.S. states. In addition, I refer to actual disciplinary proceedings against salespeople in Ontario, which again are similar to the issues raised in proceedings in other provinces.

When the term "salesperson" or "real estate salesperson" is used in this book, I am referring to real estate salespersons, brokers, brokers of record, or registrants, as they may be referred to under REBBA or under similar legislation, who are considered professionals in their field.

Under the new REBBA legislation, there is new terminology that differentiates between a "client" and a "customer" and the agreements that salespeople should be signing with each. Typically, when a business calls someone "my client," it usually signifies a closer relationship than if you call someone "a customer." We must, however, always practise the Three Pillars of Loyalty, no matter whom we are representing, to ensure success.

Whatever province you practise in, if you follow the guidelines explored in this book, you will protect your deals and ensure your success in this wonderful profession you have chosen.

CHAPTER 1

The Loyalty Pillars: It's All about Disclosure, Disclosure, Disclosure

Whenever somebody in one of my real estate seminars asks me an opinion on whether something should or should not be disclosed in a transaction, I usually say, "If you do disclose this, the chances of your being sued will be zero. If you do not disclose this, you may very well not be sued, but there is always the chance. The question that each of you here must ponder is, 'Do I really want to risk a lawsuit?'"

Trouble may come at you from lawsuits brought against you by a seller or a buyer or another salesperson. But it can also come at you from your provincial real estate council, either through one of their routine checks or because of a complaint filed against you with the council by one of the aforementioned parties.

Obviously, you should try to avoid lawsuits and professional discipline proceedings at any cost. In some cases, as we will see, this may mean saying goodbye to your potential seller or buyer at the beginning of the relationship or partway through the process. Doing so may cost you a commission in the short term, but the peace of mind that you will gain by not having to go through a legal or discipline proceeding will be well worth it.

To put a twist on an existing expression, we should treat our clients, especially in a real estate transaction, as though they were our closest and dearest friends. Putting it another way, if you were the one buying or selling this property for yourself, what would you want to be disclosed to you? Invariably, when I ask salespeople attending my seminars whether they would want to know the information themselves, almost all of them raise their hands.

To put it simply, ask yourself the following question: "Would it matter to me if I were buying this property myself?" If the answer is yes, then disclose the information. Do not confuse full disclosure with privacy legislation. In Chapter 4, "Casting Light on the New Privacy Act," I discuss how full disclosure may or may not be impacted as a result of the new privacy legislation in Canada. For the most part, the principle remains unchanged: Tell your clients everything that you would like to know if you were buying or selling the property yourself.

In some cases, you cannot disclose important material facts. For example, when you are acting in multiple representation you must make it clear at the outset to both parties that you cannot tell the seller how high a buyer may go or the motivation of any buyer in entering into the transaction. However, you are still complying with the concept of full disclosure. You are disclosing fully in advance to your client what you will not be disclosing, which should protect you from any potential lawsuit or discipline proceeding.

Full disclosure means revealing to your clients the services you will provide and any information about the transaction that affects them. What you will say to third-party salespeople or customers who are on the other side of a given transaction is also encompassed under full disclosure principles.

Real estate professionals are subject to statutory regulation (for example, by the Real Estate and Business Brokers Act in Ontario), as well as by codes of ethics that are adopted under the applicable legislation or by their local real estate board bylaws. There are also duties owed to seller and buyer clients that have been established through case law precedents over the years. By following the principles of full disclosure set out in this book, salespeople will be able to satisfy virtually all requirements of any statute, Code of Ethics, and case law decisions.

LOYALTY PILLAR – PREPARATION – GATHERING INFORMATION

The first loyalty pillar, being properly prepared, is how you must approach the information-gathering process. To make full disclosure in a given transaction, you have to make sure you are gathering all the relevant information as soon as possible in that transaction. Get into the habit of gathering this information the same way every time. It's not easy to document everything you do, but as you'll see later in Chapter 6, "Risk Management," you will have a stronger case, in any legal proceeding, if you can show your normal practice of care in these matters by producing two or three prior clients who can verify that you did follow this procedure during your business relationships with them. This will make it more difficult for a current client to deny that you followed that process with them as well.

In most cases, the first experience you will have with your client is when you sign up a potential seller to a listing agreement to sell their property. Proper preparation is key. It is crucial to convey right away to your client the impression that you are very organized and detail oriented and are always there to protect their interests. Before this meeting takes place, you should provide a list of all documents for your seller client to have ready so that the listing process can proceed quickly and efficiently.

Your first step is to review the listing agreement with your client immediately, so that the client is aware of all the terms and conditions, including any provisions regarding multiple representation, or dual agency.

As will be discussed in Chapter 4 on the new Privacy Act, this is also an excellent opportunity for you to review your company privacy policy with your client, to ensure that you have permission to market the fact that you have successfully sold their property once the transaction has been completed. (See Privacy Principle 8 in that chapter.)

The initial meeting is also a good time to verify the ID of the potential seller, especially if this is someone you have not acted for before. As will be discussed in Chapter 5 on identity theft, salespeople have to be extra vigilant not to be drawn into suspicious transactions. Make sure that the person you are dealing with matches the information in the deed and tax bill.

Your next step is to ask the seller to produce whatever documentation they may have about the property so that you can complete the listing information form. This documentation includes the deed, survey, mortgage, and/or tax bill associated with the property. If a survey is available, you may want to walk the property with your client to determine whether or not the survey is up to date, so that you will be able to deal with any survey request that may come with a potential offer on the property.

It is also a good idea to look for the lawyer's report that accompanied the purchase of the property. We live in a time when real estate prices have been gradually rising. It is quite possible that at the time the property was purchased, title or other issues affecting the property were brought to the attention of the buyer, enabling them to get out of the transaction. The buyer may have waived these rights due to the fact that the property had increased in value. It's likely that the buyer-now-turned-seller has forgotten the details of those problems. It may not be clear whether title insurance will cover these problems today if they are not disclosed. It is thus important for you to obtain the lawyer's report and review it with your client to determine whether there is anything in it that will have to be disclosed to any potential buyer. The lawyer's report will also disclose whether or not there is an up-to-date survey for this property. This could save the seller many hours in trying to locate a survey that may not in fact exist.

At the initial meeting with your client, obtain all contact numbers, including phone, cell phone, fax, and e-mail addresses where you can reach them. It becomes much easier to demonstrate that you have satisfied your disclosure obligations if you can prove that you did in fact relate the information using some form of communication. If you are in possession of a hand-held pocket computer or similar mobile e-mail device, you can enter the information into it right at the meeting. This also gives you the opportunity to demonstrate to your client your ability to get in touch with them at any time to keep them updated on the status of their listing. In fact, there are now applications available for these wireless devices that permit you to download all MLS listing information directly to the device. If a client should ask you the details about what a particular listed property is selling for, you can tell them on the spot not only the asking price for the property, but other details such as square footage and lot size, without having to drive back to your office.

You may also want to review your proposed marketing plan for the property as to where and how you will advertise, the types of flyers and brochures that you will use, and how many open houses you will run. You may want to discuss how you can use the Internet to market the property, as I will discuss more fully in Chapter 5. You may also develop and share expertise in how to show or stage the property to prospective buyers so that it generates the most interest.

Taking the above-mentioned steps, as part of your initial preparation, will instill confidence in your clients that you have all the necessary tools to provide them with a first-class customer experience.

The same preparation is needed when you meet with your buyer clients for the first time. You should go through a complete fact-finding exercise to determine the kind of home they can afford, the area they want to live in, or the need for schools in the immediate vicinity, for example. Are they currently renting a property? If so, you will need to advise them as to how much notice will have to be given in order to properly terminate their lease. Asking questions also demonstrates your caring for the client, that you are trying to find a home that is best suited for their needs.

For example, how many of you ask a buyer what he or she likes best about their current location and what they will miss the most? In addition, what would be their top-three "wish list" for the new location that they currently do not enjoy? Right away this gives you a better idea of what to look for and helps you to narrow your search. This will help you to find the right property faster.

Advise buyers about all the applicable and available government programs to assist with their initial costs, whether through their RRSP or any Land Transfer Tax Rebates. Educate your buyers, especially first-time buyers, on all closing costs so that they are certain to have the available funds to complete any transaction.

As will be discussed in Chapter 3 in the obligations regarding multiple offer situations, it is extremely important that you properly prepare a buyer and a seller for the multiple offer negotiation process in order to properly manage expectations. The multiple offer process is essentially unfair to buyers, who may be asked to just fax in their offers and hope that the seller gives them proper consideration. They may have to pay for a pre-offer inspection in order to provide an unconditional offer to purchase, without any guarantee or assurance that the seller will sign it back. As long as the buyer is properly advised and prepared in advance, he won't blame you, as the buyer salesperson, for the outcome.

Weisleder's Wisdom on . . . BEING PREPARED

1. Make sure your seller has all documents ready for your listing presentation.

2. Have your marketing plan ready for discussion right away, including brochures, flyers, scheduled open houses, and use of the Internet.

3. Ask buyers what they like best about their current location as well as their wish lists for the new location.

4. Advise buyers about all applicable government programs to assist with costs, whether RRSP, first-time buyer booklets, or anticipated closing costs.

5. Advise both sellers and buyers what to expect with the multiple offer process in order to properly manage expectations.

LOYALTY PILLAR – BEING CAREFUL – TAKING CARE OF YOUR CLIENTS

I will discuss later in this chapter the importance of surveying your customers and its relationship to loyalty. Many companies also survey former customers to find out why they have left in order to learn how to improve their service to prevent additional customers from leaving. In a cross-industry study compiled by the American Quality Standards Association in 2003, the following were the top five reasons why customers left businesses, together with the corresponding percentages:

They died	1%
They moved away	2%
They received a better price elsewhere	11%
They weren't satisfied with the product or service	16%
They perceived indifference among employees	70%
Total	**100%**

There are important lessons for major companies to learn from these numbers. In most cases, it is not because of price or deficiency of your product or service that causes customers to leave you. It is because they think your company doesn't care about them. It goes back to being used to hearing "Sorry, that's our policy, we can't do that." It's clear that, if you can demonstrate that you do care about your customers in everything you do, you are already 70% of the way toward building loyal customers.

As we will learn in Chapter 3, many claims are brought against salespeople not because of bad intentions or fraudulent behaviour but mainly because of carelessness in

(1) finding out the facts relating to your property that must be included in the MLS listing;
(2) making notes of clients' requests;
(3) diarizing important dates;
(4) providing updates to your clients;
(5) completing the Agreement of Purchase and Sale;
(6) following through on commitments made;
(7) waiving conditions in a timely manner; and
(8) having all advertising reviewed in advance.

By just taking a little extra time to ensure everything is being done accurately and completely, you will continue to demonstrate that you truly care about your customers.

Weisleder's Wisdom on . . . BEING CAREFUL, TAKING CARE OF CLIENTS

1. The main reason people leave companies is because they think the company doesn't care about them.
2. Most claims against salespeople are caused by careless errors.

3. Always take your time when completing anything on behalf of your client.
4. Follow through on all commitments you have made.

Not only will this assist you in creating long-term loyal clients, but you will also learn to count many of these clients as future close friends.

SELLER PROPERTY INFORMATION STATEMENT

There has been much debate over whether a seller should sign a Seller Property Information Statement (spis) (see Appendix A). This is, in effect, a type of disclosure that a seller makes about their property — whether they are aware of any defects in the structure, roof, or basement in their property. Some real estate boards in Ontario require that an spis form be completed by all sellers and delivered to buyers before an offer is presented. Other boards may not require this, but there is a suspicion that if you do not provide the statement, you must have something to hide. The statement itself is not meant to be a warranty, but allows the seller to indicate property defects if they have knowledge of them.

In my view, the spis statement should always be completed by the seller, and the sooner the better. A good time to complete this is at the listing process, when you are gathering information about the property. You can tell a lot by a person's body language. As you go through the statement, watch how the seller reacts when you ask if they are aware of any moisture in the basement or any roof leakage. If you sense that the seller might be lying to you, you should ask yourself whether this is the kind of seller you want to work for. After all, getting out now will save you time and money spent on advertising, conducting open houses, and marketing the sale of this particular property.

Usually, this type of seller will ask you to mislead the buyer. If a legal proceeding is brought against the seller, you can be certain you will be added to the claim, because "you must have known that something was wrong and did nothing to prevent it." Even if you are ultimately vindicated, you will still be dragged through the entire legal process, which means discoveries, cross-examinations, documents, a trial . . . and a lot of stress.

Furthermore, real estate professionals are always wary of clients who use their services and then try to go behind their backs to avoid paying commission, perhaps trying to wait until the holdover period expires. If you suspect that your client is likely to try to cheat a potential buyer, you should immediately be concerned whether he will try to do the same thing to you. And if something does go wrong, this seller will be the first one to blame you. He'll say that he did disclose everything to you and it was your advice not to disclose this to the potential buyer.

You should obtain an SPIS statement for your own protection. It is your proof that you asked the seller questions about the property. With it, you can answer any question that is raised by a potential buyer or purchasing salesperson. The SPIS is also one of the key documents a lawyer may require in order to properly defend you in an action that may not be commenced until months or years after a transaction has concluded.

Should You Give the SPIS Out?

There is much discussion as to whether you should give the seller property information statement to a potential buyer, since there have been some legal decisions that have relied on this statement as evidence against a seller when problems arose after closing that were not disclosed on the statement.

In my view, the courts are not turning this statement into a seller warranty. The language on the form makes it abundantly clear that when a seller signs the statement, it is for information purposes only and cannot be relied on by a buyer as a warranty for any other purpose. Furthermore, if the seller does not know any given answer, there is no obligation to do any further inspection. The seller can just click the box marked "unknown." However, this does not give the seller the right to actively conceal a defect in a property that could not be discovered in a normal home inspection. Sellers do have legal obligations to disclose these kinds of latent defects, especially when they may render a property uninhabitable by a buyer. If no such disclosure is made, the seller will likely be found liable for negligent or fraudulent misrepresentation after closing, whether or not they supplied an SPIS form, which could lead to a legal claim for damages.

For these reasons, I believe that real estate salespeople should recommend to their seller client that the SPIS form should be completed and given to every potential buyer, especially if they are told in advance by the seller that there are defects in the property. All defects should be disclosed in advance. Some defects may be more material than others, but the logic is still the same: You do not want to risk a lawsuit by not disclosing this information. I would also add that if a buyer raises a concern about any potential defect during the negotiations, and if the matter can be answered by the seller, then it should be included in the relevant space on the SPIS form. There is nothing wrong with adding an explanation or qualification to any item found on the form. In fact, this should be encouraged, because it serves to bring all potential problems to the attention of the buyer before the agreement is signed.

If you look at the case law, there have been many legal arguments and debates over what is a latent defect and what is a patent defect and whether or not a defect makes a property inhabitable or not and whether or not you should disclose the defect. You will also learn about the concept of *caveat emptore* or "buyer beware." Legally, buyers are deemed to accept patent defects, which are visible on a normal inspection, under the principle of *caveat emptore*. If a latent defect renders a property uninhabitable, then it must be disclosed. A grey area is whether latent defects that do not render a property uninhabitable need to be disclosed. There may be a conflict between legal principles laid down by the case law and your obligations as a salesperson under the Code of Ethics.

If you ask a lawyer for advice, the best answer you'll get is "You have a 90% chance of winning a lawsuit on this point, even if you do not disclose the information." Usually, the answer will be 60%–80% chance of winning. The point everyone forgets is that, when buyers sue sellers, the only winners are the lawyers. They are the only ones who get paid 100% of the time. Now, if you ask a lawyer what your chances are of getting sued if you disclose everything, the answer will be 0%, and no lawyer has to be paid anything. I would rather you never had to play the percentage game. If it would matter to you, then disclose everything — and never get sued. It's that simple.

The new Code of Ethics under REBBA has specific reference to the SPIS form. It is the new Section 20.

Seller property information statement

20. If a broker or salesperson has a seller as a client and knows that the seller has completed a written statement that is intended to provide information to buyers about the real estate that is available for acquisition, the broker or salesperson shall, unless the seller directs otherwise,

(a) disclose the existence of the statement to every buyer who expresses an interest in the real estate; and,

(b) on request, make the statement available to a buyer at the earliest practicable opportunity after the request is made.

The new act thus makes it a requirement to disclose the existence of the SPIS if it is completed and to make it available upon the request of any buyer. However, there is a qualification that states "unless the seller directs otherwise." Therefore, even if you do complete it, if your seller directs you not to provide it to any buyer, then you do not have to do so.

As indicated previously, given that completion of the SPIS is more for the protection of the listing salesperson than anything else, it's still worth completing in all situations, and the sooner the better.

Physical and Psychological Defects or Stigmas

Is there any difference between disclosing a physical defect in a property, such as moisture leaking into a basement, and disclosing a psychological defect, such as a suicide having been committed at the property? I believe there is no distinction whatsoever. Psychological defects or stigmas are probably matters that you would like to know about if you were buying the property for yourself.

I have seen a clause that some buyers try to use in this regard:

> The Seller warrants, to the best of his knowledge and belief, that the said property does not contain any hidden defects and that there have been no deaths, suicides, illegal activities, or murders on this property at any time, and that there are no neighbourhood conditions that could affect the Buyer's use, enjoyment, or perceived value of the property.

The clause is difficult because it's very subjective. What does "neighbourhood conditions" mean? Does it include a group home down the street or on the next block, or perhaps subsidized housing? What if there was a suicide on the property, but it happened four years ago and there have been two ownership changes since? I would not advise any seller to sign this kind of clause, but it does illustrate that people are concerned with psychological issues, which, unlike a leaky roof, have no direct physical impact on a property. We can find out how much it costs to fix a leaky roof. It is much more difficult to determine how much, if any, value is lost to a property as a result of a psychological stigma associated with it.

There was a case in British Columbia a few years ago in which a buyer signed, in November, an offer to purchase a beachfront property. The buyers inquired about the park next door and were advised by the seller that it was a "public beach." When they moved into the property the following May, they were shocked to learn that it was in fact a nudist beach. They then sued for damages. (I know what you are thinking: Wouldn't a nudist beach *add* value to the property?)

The result, after three years of proceedings, including an appeal to the British Columbia Court of Appeal, was that the seller was successful. The seller did not have to disclose this information to the buyer.

The real result, however, was that the seller and the buyer both had to deal with the lost time and stress associated with these proceedings for a three-year period, and the only winners were the lawyers, whose fees totalled more than $100,000. I discuss the legal process and the effects of actual legal proceedings in more detail in Chapter 6, "Risk Management," under the heading "Legal Proceedings."

Will this court decision become an iron-clad precedent for any future situation involving a stigma defect? I doubt it. More importantly, do you want to worry about this for three to four years of your life? The answer must be no. In the United States, in several jurisdictions, it is now becoming law that sellers must disclose information such as suicides or murders on a property itself. I expect that this requirement will extend to relevant neighbourhood conditions that impact value. I also expect that registries will soon be available that list properties with this type of information, in the same way that "grow op" properties will soon be listed. It will be up to salespeople to be aware of all these registries and to make sure they are checked every time you are working for buyers.

My advice, therefore, is to disclose everything that you know to be true, including any of the examples listed above, but do not permit the insertion of the stigma clause itself into any Agreement of Purchase and Sale. Basically, I do not like any warranties given by a seller. I prefer that the buyer satisfies himself about the condition of a property by obtaining a home-inspection report.

A home inspection is the most useful way that a buyer can obtain their own full disclosure about a property. When you act for a buyer, you should always recommend that the buyer obtain a home-inspection report, and you should make the transaction conditional on the buyer being satisfied with the contents of the inspection report, in their sole and absolute discretion. (I discuss the actual wording of the condition in greater detail later in this chapter.) However, you must be very careful when you make this recommendation. Here are some issues to consider:

- Since the buyer will be choosing the inspector, find out who is being chosen to conduct the inspection and complete the report. Are they a certified engineer or builder who can provide a useful opinion?
- Is the home inspector or home-inspection company covered by insurance in the event there is an error in the report that costs the buyer money in repairs after closing?
- If the company is covered by an insurance policy, is there any language in the home-inspection contract that limits the liability of the inspector should anything arise?
- As with most recommendations you make to a client, you should be providing at least two or three reputable names for the client to choose from.

There are regions in Ontario where it has been difficult for home inspectors to obtain insurance protection. Many other inspectors have express language in their agreements that any liability will be limited to the amount of money the buyer paid for the inspection report, which is usually around $500. In most cases, this amount will be insufficient to satisfy any repair damages that may ensue as a result of not finding a problem in the inspection that is discovered later, after closing.

There are also concerns whether having a home inspection completed will negate any representations made by the seller in the SPIS form. In my view, this should not be the case. If a property defect is obvious, then buyers will be deemed to have known about it whether or not they conduct an inspection. So always recommend an inspection. On the other hand, if the defect is concealed by the seller, then the seller will still be responsible, despite an inspection having been conducted by a buyer.

There is a growing practice in residential and commercial transactions for sellers to obtain a full inspection report in advance of listing their property and making it available to potential buyers.

For the residential property, the inspection would be limited to the physical condition of the property as in a usual home-inspection report. In a more complicated commercial transaction, there would be a more detailed structural report prepared by an engineering firm, an environmental report prepared by an environmental consultant, and a financial report, which would comment on the lease income for the property as well as due diligence on the seller's financial records.

Obtaining a home inspection in advance permits buyers to make an offer on the property without the need to make the transaction conditional on obtaining the home inspection in a residential transaction or conditional on structure, environment, and financials typical in commercial transactions. This also brings more integrity to the entire process. Many commercial salespeople have told me that this process has also generated much more interest in a property on the part of potential buyers, especially institutional investors. From a residential standpoint, this provides the added benefit of not requiring multiple purchasers in a bidding situation from having to conduct costly inspections in advance. They can rely for the most part on the inspection report prepared by the seller.

Although there may be legal issues as to whether the seller must pay extra to have the inspection report create a legal relationship between the successful buyer and the home inspector, the principle remains the same: Making complete disclosure as soon as possible will not only provide reassurance to any proposed buyer, it should also protect the seller from any unwanted legal proceedings after the fact.

There are now some real estate professionals who will offer to pay for this seller home inspection in exchange for the seller agreeing to list the property with them. This is a very smart practice. Not only does it serve to distinguish this listing professional from others in the area, it gives the listing salesperson the benefit of knowing in advance the potential problems with the property, and they can thus provide the necessary advice to the seller client to make full and complete disclosure.

I have also heard of salespeople who have set up a "committee" of professionals to assess the key items that matter most in an inspection: the roof, the wiring, the plumbing, the furnace, and the basement. They have a roofing specialist, a basement waterproof expert, an electrician, a plumber, and a representative from the local gas utility company for the furnace all attend at the property to provide their opinions. The process may take a little longer and may result in a longer condition period; however, this inspection may indeed serve to give a buyer much more comfort. Since these five items cause the most potential costs to repair long term, I believe that this detailed type of inspection will give buyers more certainty. This is an example of taking the initiative to provide a better, more practical, and more satisfying client experience. This is what differentiates salespeople in the market — making the extra efforts to satisfy their clients.

To properly prepare a buyer, you must make it a point to explain the home-inspection process to your client and then let them make all decisions relating to the contract with the home-inspection company as well as the contents of the report. If necessary, also recommend that they obtain legal advice.

It is also imperative that you explain to a buyer client the need to obtain title insurance as part of any transaction. The policy is purchased through the client's lawyer. The main purpose of title insurance is to protect a buyer against title defects or related issues that may not be uncovered by a lawyer who is doing searches for the buyer prior to closing. These include problems with the tax bill owing, zoning irregularities, renovations completed without a building permit, and encroachments onto a neighbouring property. In many cases, these issues cannot be uncovered by a lawyer no matter how careful they may be due to the fact that the survey may be out of date or the municipality's records about the property may not be accurate. They may also include matters that the sellers are not even aware of, so they may not have had any duty of disclosure. Title insurance provides an easy no-fault solution to most of these problems and thus provides peace of mind to most buyers.

Furthermore, a title insurance policy will protect a buyer after closing from the current disturbing trend of third parties attempting fraudulently to take over title to a property without actually paying for it and then borrowing money with new mortgages being registered as security on these same properties. It is a variation on the identity theft problem that is becoming so prevalent today, discussed further in Chapter 4 on privacy and Chapter 5 on the Internet. This can unfortunately occur to anyone, even if you have owned a property and lived there for the past 30 years. The way this is accomplished is that a third party attends the local registry office or goes through the electronic registration system, and registers a false forged deed that transfers title from the real registered owners to the fraud artist. They even pay the required land transfer tax owing. They then approach a bank and apply for a loan, using the same property as security. The bank lends the money and registers a mortgage against the property. The fraudster then disappears, and two months later the bank comes to the real owners looking for their money, or else they will be commencing power of sale proceedings. You can imagine the emotional turmoil that this can create. Title insurance will protect the innocent homeowner and will pay all legal expenses to correct the matter, which can sometimes be substantial.

Although banks and lawyers are much more vigilant in their loan application programs as a result of these events, it still makes sense for buyers to obtain title insurance. In Canada, title insurance companies have now opened up this protection to existing homeowners as well. I recommend that every homeowner contact their lawyer with a view to insuring their titles, to prevent being part of this kind of unwanted legal proceeding in the future.

Your obligations for full disclosure do not end once an Agreement of Purchase and Sale is signed. They continue until a transaction is completed. In the case of *Yorkland Real Estate v. Dale*, the salesperson did not disclose to her seller client, once an offer was signed, that she had been contacted by a different buyer who was willing to pay more for the property. The salesperson did not bring this information to the seller, and instead acted on the sale of the property from the initial buyer to the new buyer. Not only did this salesperson forfeit her commission on the first transaction, she also had to pay to the seller the commission that she earned on the resale as well. All of this could have been avoided if the salesperson had brought this to the attention of the seller in the first place and just obtained permission to act on the resale transaction.

As many salespeople are aware, it is very important as a marketing tool to keep your clients informed about market developments and trends even after a transaction has been completed. It demonstrates your willingness to share important information in the marketplace that may concern them and will also keep your name "top of mind" the next time they require real estate services or when they are asked for a referral by someone else. Newsletters are a common way to do this. In Chapter 4 on privacy, I discuss the way that you can obtain your client's consent in order to continue this kind of marketing once the transaction is completed.

Disclosing Your Services

Full disclosure also means telling the seller or buyer all the services that you will be providing to them, whether you are acting as a listing or buyer salesperson. In both cases, care must be taken to review the listing and/or buyer representation agreement at the time you start working with the seller and/or buyer.

You should also be very clear as to how you intend to market the property. Will you be advertising the sale in a newspaper? Will you be sending out flyers? How many open houses will you be conducting? Will your seller agree to your marketing the property over the Internet, including a video display? Some sellers may be nervous about this information being made available to anyone who can access your website. This is why it is important to review this with them in advance. All of this is important information to the seller. You do not want them to have false or unrealistic expectations about the services you intend to provide. Making certain that they have a full understanding of the scope of your duties will help you avoid complaints later on if, for example, the property is not selling as quickly as anticipated.

In Chapter 2, I will introduce the Insurance Wheel of Misfortune, which highlights the basis of the claims that salespeople have been making to their insurers as a result of commencement of legal proceedings against them. Over thirty percent of all claims are a result of some kind of non-disclosure or miscommunication by the salesperson. Simply put, this large percentage of claims can be avoided if you adhere to the principle of full disclosure in everything that you do.

Weisleder's Wisdom on . . . DISCLOSURE

1. Be prepared and do your homework before you sign your listing agreement.

2. Make sure the seller has all necessary documents ready before you arrive at the listing.

3. Fill out the SPIS form with your seller. Unless the seller directs otherwise, give out the SPIS form to any buyer upon request.

4. Advise your seller to obtain a home-inspection report as soon as the property is listed and provide potential buyers with a copy of this report.

5. Disclose any physical and/or psychological defects to all potential buyers.

6. Be wary immediately of any seller who refuses to disclose pertinent information to a potential buyer.

7. Encourage home inspections for any buyer, as well as title insurance.

8. Check out the background of every home inspector and the home-inspection agreement itself.

9. Disclose all the services you will be providing as soon as possible.

10. Remember that your disclosure obligations continue until the final completion of any transaction.

UNDERSTANDING CONDITIONS

Most consumers believe that if they make a real estate transaction conditional on anything, it is the same as an option to get out of the deal if they are not satisfied for any reason. This is a very dangerous assumption. Interpreting conditions and demonstrating good faith in exercising conditions have been and continue to be the subjects of many legal proceedings.

It is imperative, therefore, that salespeople understand not only how to compose a condition, but also how to explain the effects of conditions to their buyer and seller clients. When salespeople complete the standard Agreement of Purchase and Sale, the condition clause is usually the only clause they must draft themselves that is not about just filling in factual details, such as property location, price, or closing dates. This is why you must be extra careful in completing any conditions on behalf of your clients, whether you are acting for buyers or sellers.

As I always say when giving seminars on these topics, I am not a fan of litigation. I believe in settling matters and then moving on. The reason I am a fan, even an advocate, of conditions is because they give buyers the time (a) to satisfy themselves regarding any concerns that may affect the property, usually having to do with obtaining sufficient financing; and (b) to complete the purchase and/or home-inspection condition to satisfy themselves as to the physical condition of the property itself.

In most cases, these conditions are for a short time frame, anywhere from three to seven days. Having a property "off the market" for this period of time will normally not materially affect the value of the property. Quite the opposite is often true, as we have seen properties escalate in value in the Toronto area on an almost monthly basis.

Under such circumstances, if a buyer is unsatisfied with the condition, the seller should always let the deal terminate and just move on. I know this is not the attitude many sellers or lawyers take. Many sellers are understandably upset when a buyer attempts to cancel the transaction as a result of the failure to satisfy the terms of a condition. Some sellers claim they want to see a copy of the inspection report, while others want to see proof that the buyers acted in good faith. Can't you just feel the protracted legal proceedings forming?

The case of *Marshall v. Bernard Place Corporation*, which was confirmed on appeal in Ontario, is an excellent example. It includes a superbly drafted condition, and it illustrates that no legal position is guaranteed and that most cases result in victories mainly for lawyers, not their clients.

This particular case involved the purchase of a renovated midtown home for $1,510,000. The deposit was substantial: $150,000. The Agreement of Purchase and Sale contained the following home-inspection condition:

> This Agreement is conditional upon the inspection of the Property by a home inspector of the Buyer's choice and at the Buyer's sole expense, and receipt of a report satisfactory to him, in his sole and absolute discretion. Unless the Buyer/Cooperating Broker gives notice in writing, delivered to the Seller/Listing Broker on or before Wednesday August 19, 1998, that this condition is fulfilled, this Agreement shall be null and void and the deposit shall be returned to the Buyer without interest or deduction. The Seller agrees to cooperate in providing access to the property for the purpose of this inspection at reasonable times upon reasonable notice given by the Buyer. This condition is included for the sole benefit of the

Buyer and may be waived at his sole option by notice in writing to the Seller/Listing Broker within the time period stated herein.

The inspection was conducted, and the buyers were not satisfied with the report. They advised the seller on August 17, 1998, that they would not remove their condition and asked for the return of their deposit. The property could only have been off the market for about seven days at most while the inspection was being conducted.

The seller took the position that since the report showed only minor deficiencies, the buyers were not acting in good faith in attempting to satisfy the condition and accordingly were in breach of the agreement itself. They refused to return the deposit, and the matter proceeded to litigation.

Many lawyers were very interested in this case. In fact, the amount of money necessary to correct the deficiencies was very low indeed, about $1,000. In virtually any home inspection, the inspector can make recommendations about needed repairs that will cost at least $500–$1,000, even for minor deficiencies. Most lawyers would probably tell you that the seller had a very good legal position. But this is not what the judge determined, and his judgment was confirmed by the Ontario Court of Appeal.

The main rationale on which the court based its decision was the wording of the clause itself. Since the wording gave the buyer the "sole and absolute discretion" to make a decision based on the inspection report, they had the right to come to the conclusion that they had reached. The outcome of the case may have been different if the buyers had not conducted a home inspection at all, but had just stated that they were not satisfied with the condition of the home. In that instance, the court may have deemed this to have been acting in bad faith. Nevertheless, even though the sellers seemed to have an excellent legal position, the result, after four years of legal proceedings (including pleadings, motions, examinations, production of documents, the trial, and the appeal), ended up costing in excess of $100,000 in legal fees and probably stressed out both sides for the entire four-year period. All because the property was "off the market" for a period of seven days. Or was it "the principle of the matter, not the money"?

The situation described above underscores my point that if you are advising a seller under circumstances where the buyer is attempting to cancel a transaction as a result of a condition, tell them the following: "Let it go. We will get another offer with a buyer who is willing to conclude a transaction. Move on." In the same vein, you should not get too fussed up about the wording of the condition. Some sellers try to remove the words "sole and absolute discretion" as a result of the above-noted decision. Others demand to receive a copy of the inspection report. In my view, it is not necessary to spend a lot of time on this kind of negotiation. You want to find buyers who want to complete the transaction with sellers. This is what will give the sellers peace of mind from the time they sign the agreement right through to the closing of the transaction. You do not want to be connected to buyers who are just looking for a way out of the deal. If they can't find an excuse in the wording of the condition itself, they will look for any excuse not to complete the transaction, including objections as a result of the searches conducted by their lawyer. That is not the kind of experience sellers need, especially when they may need the funds from this sale to purchase another property.

I understand some sellers will be concerned that if their property is "sold subject to condition" and then it is later discovered that the condition was not waived, it may lead to negative remarks being made by other salespeople that "there must be something wrong with the property," and this will make it more difficult to subsequently sell the property to another buyer. Nevertheless, it is still easier to overcome this type of concern by potential buyers than it is to deal with the effects of protracted legal proceedings.

However, when you act as a buyer broker, you must be very careful when drafting your conditions. You cannot assume that your sellers will be accommodating. They may decide to refuse to refund the deposit based on your not acting in good faith or perhaps failing to carry out the terms of the condition.

Questioning Conditions

To avoid problems, it is important for you to understand what should be included in a condition. A properly worded condition should always be at the sole and absolute discretion of the buyer, with the buyer having the sole right to waiver, and be able to answer the questions: Who? What? How? Where? When?

> What is the subject matter of the condition?
> How is the condition to be satisfied?
> Where is the condition taking place?
> When do you have to notify the other side as to whether you have satisfied the condition?
> Who will be giving the notice?
> For whose benefit is the condition?
> Can the condition be waived?

In the condition noted above in *Marshall v. Bernard Place Corporation*, all these questions have been answered, as follows.

> • *What is the subject matter of the condition?*
>   This Agreement is conditional upon the inspection of the Property by a home inspector of the Buyer's choice and at the Buyer's sole expense . . .

> • *How is the condition to be satisfied?*

. . . and receipt of a report satisfactory to him, in his sole and absolute discretion.

• *Where is the condition taking place?*
   The Seller agrees to cooperate in providing access to the property for the purpose of this inspection at reasonable times upon reasonable notice given by the Buyer.

• *For whose benefit is the condition? Can it be waived?*
   This condition is included for the sole benefit of the Buyer and may be waived at his sole option by notice in writing to the Seller/Listing Broker within the time period stated herein.

As we learned from the Marshall decision, it is extremely important for you to make the condition in the sole and absolute discretion of buyers. Nevertheless, the buyers must be told that in order to avoid any potential problems, they must still try to satisfy the condition, which in the case of a home-inspection subject matter means they should get a home inspection done. If they do complete the inspection, this clause should give them the ability to get out of the transaction without further incident, so long as they are not satisfied with the report itself.

The reason that the benefit of the condition and the waiver must be inserted for the sole and absolute benefit of the buyer is to enable the buyer to always have the right to waive the condition, even if the condition itself is not satisfied. If this is not done, the seller may try to take the position that the condition was in fact a condition precedent and thus cannot be waived by the buyer alone. The seller could attempt to take this position if the condition was not satisfied but the property had in the interim increased in value, in order to try to get out of the deal. For this reason, it is always necessary to ensure that you indicate that the condition is always for the sole and absolute benefit of the buyer and can be waived by the buyer at their sole option.

The other popular condition that is used in most transactions is the one related to financing. Again there is confusion as to how a buyer is to satisfy this condition. So long as the buyer makes a legitimate attempt to obtain financing (i.e., goes to a bank for approval), then if they are denied financing, they can terminate the agreement. The clause should still contain the words "sole and absolute discretion," as stated above. There is some confusion as to whether a seller can offer to satisfy the condition by taking back a mortgage from the buyer on similar financial terms. The case law is plain that unless this option is clear from the wording of the condition itself, then this option is not open to a seller under these circumstances. If you are acting for a seller in this situation, remember my advice to just "let it go."

It is also very important to pay attention to whether the wording of the condition is changed during the offer negotiation. In a recent case, the words "subject to satisfaction with the entire property" were replaced with the words "subject to the satisfaction with the structure on the property." This subtle change had a material effect. The buyer was concerned with the septic system on the property, but the revised clause only permitted the buyer to cancel the transaction if there was something wrong with the structure of the house on the property. The buyer claimed that this was not explained, and the buyer salesperson had to pay the damages. This again demonstrates the second loyalty pillar: Be careful in everything you do, including reviewing any changes made to any offer on any signback.

• *Who gives the notice? When do you have to notify the other side?*

Unless the Buyer/Cooperating Broker gives notice in writing, delivered to the Seller/Listing Broker on or before Wednesday August 19, 1998, that this condition is fulfilled, this Agreement shall be null and void and the deposit shall be returned to the Buyer without interest or deduction.

This clause could be written in different ways. It could indicate that if the condition is not waived by August 19, then the agreement shall be firm and binding on both parties. Either method is satisfactory. Some drafters like to use the phrase "within five business days of acceptance" as the time period to satisfy the condition. I do not like these words, for they invite confusion. It may not be clear when exactly a contract is in fact accepted, due to many signbacks that can occur. Also ambiguous is what a "business day" means. Does it include Saturday if, for example, your bank happens to be open on Saturdays? When a definite date is chosen, there can be no confusion.

Waiving Conditions

Claims and complaints have been made against real estate salespeople as a result of improperly waiving a condition on behalf of a client. This situation can have disastrous results for a buyer. For example, if a buyer does not obtain financing and wants to terminate a transaction, but the salesperson mistakenly waives the condition, then the seller is clearly within their rights to force the buyer to complete the transaction. Failure to complete may result in the buyer forfeiting any deposit and being responsible for any damages that the seller may incur in reselling the property. RECO discipline proceedings may also arise over this same issue.

In the case of *Nykor v. Cil*, decided July 5, 2001, in Ontario, the salesperson was held liable under court proceedings for damages that were caused to his buyer client as a result of waiving a financing condition prematurely. The salesperson had to indemnify the buyer for all damages that the buyer had to pay to the seller.

A similar RECO case decided that the action by the salesperson in waiving the condition without consent from the buyer constituted a violation of Obligation 39 of the REBBA Code of Ethics relating to unprofessional conduct. The administrative penalty levied against the salesperson in this disciplinary decision, which also involved other Code of Ethics violations, was $5,000.

However, we should distinguish this situation from one in which a buyer instructs you to waive a condition even though it has not yet been satisfied. An example would be if the buyer was not yet approved for financing, but was confident that they would be approved since they expected assistance to come from another family member.

In another RECO discipline hearing, dated December 7, 2001, the allegation was that the salesperson had somehow acted unfairly toward the seller by permitting the buyers to waive a condition about financing when the salesperson knew that the financing had not yet been arranged. Here's an important statement that came from the decision, which found in favour of the salesperson:

> In the final analysis, a salesperson will not ordinarily be responsible for a client who, on his own initiative and after due consideration of all material facts, makes the decision to waive a condition included in the Agreement of Purchase and Sale for his benefit.

What can you learn from this? When your client is instructing you to waive a condition without its having been satisfied, you must document these instructions, preferably in a written communication to your client, confirming that you have indeed discussed all "material facts" relating to the decision that has been made. Better still, always have the client sign the waiver.

In a rising market, many buyers will instruct you to waive the condition about a home inspection in order to provide a clean offer. This usually involves multiple offer situations. However, there are other ways to protect the buyer, such as arranging for a home inspection before you submit the offer in the first place. Most sellers will be agreeable to this arrangement. If, however, your buyer has not had a home inspection and instructs you not to include one, or to waive one that has either not yet been completed or satisfied (due to problems that have been identified on the report itself), it is imperative that you document all of these instructions right away. This written record will be critical in any subsequent legal or discipline proceeding.

Speaking of documentation, first and foremost, every salesperson must maintain a diary of all significant dates relating to a transaction — one of the most important being the date that a condition expires. Since you may be involved with many different real estate transactions at a given time — closing some deals, negotiating others — it is easy to become confused or forget about these important condition expiry dates. This may cause you to rely on a verbal statement prior to waiving a condition on behalf of your client. Given today's access to e-mails, faxes, and electronic calendars, these verbal statements can easily be avoided. This is all about the second Pillar of Loyalty, being careful in properly diarizing all of your important dates.

Prior to waiving any condition on behalf of your client, you should be obtaining written confirmation that the condition has in fact been satisfied. Preferably, this communication should come from your client. It can also come from the buyer's bank, if it's regarding a condition related to financing. One way to easily document these instructions is to have your client e-mail you the instructions, or you can send your client a short e-mail confirming the instructions. As discussed under the heading "Gathering Information" in this chapter, if you have the client's contact information, especially in a wireless mobile device, you can very easily document these instructions in writing.

The bottom line is, if you take the initiative to forward the waiver on behalf of your client, you must take extra care to make sure that you have confirmation that the condition is in fact satisfied before you waive the condition itself. The consequences of a mistake will be costly legal proceedings as well as a potential discipline action by your provincial real estate council.

Weisleder's Wisdom on . . . CONDITIONS

1. When drafting a condition, be able to answer the questions: Who? What? How? Where? When?

2. Insert the words "sole and absolute discretion" and ensure that the condition is "for the sole and absolute benefit of the buyer."

3. When acting for a seller, do not get too hung up on a condition; if a buyer wants to cancel for any reason, let it go.

4. Make sure you are careful that any changes made to the wording of the conditions in any signback are explained to your buyers or sellers.

5. Advise buyers that they must always try to satisfy any condition in good faith.

6. Always keep a record of key condition dates.

7. Always have written confirmation from your client before you waive a condition.

GETTING PAID – HOLDOVER CLAUSES – SURVEYING YOUR CLIENTS

Probably no issue causes salespeople more anxiety and concern than clients who make use of their services and then look for a way to avoid paying commission. The listing agreement clearly provides that the owner will pay commission for any sale of the property that occurs during the term of the listing. There is also a holdover clause, which typically lasts an additional 60 to 90 days, specifying that if the seller signs an offer with anyone who was introduced to the property during the term of the listing, then commission is also payable, unless the seller has relisted the property with another salesperson.

Historically, sellers have tried to prove that if the salesperson did not find the buyer, then the salesperson should not be entitled to commission, even if it was during the listing period itself. For the most part, court decisions have favoured salespeople on this point. Most sellers in the market now understand this issue. However, when a seller waits out the holdover period and then signs with a buyer who was introduced to the property during the listing period, they have often been successful in resisting claims made by the salesperson.

It is a different matter when you look at buyer representation. The buyer representation agreement also contains a clause that if a buyer purchases any property during the term of the buyer representation agreement, then the buyer salesperson gets paid commission, even if they did not introduce the buyer to the actual property. Most members of the public are not as familiar with this provision. For this reason, it is very important to review the buyer representation agreement carefully with the buyer at the time that it is signed, so that there is no confusion or misunderstanding.

To properly manage your risk, conduct this explanation the same way every time, with all of your future sellers and buyers. You should also make a simple note confirming the discussion, either on your own checklist of matters to review with your client, or as a separate note inserted into your diary or daily planner. Both of these methods can later be used to defend any claim by your client that you did not explain the document to them in the first place.

Recent decisions involving buyer representation agreements have led to satisfactory results for the salesperson, when the proper documentation was obtained and then found to have been properly explained. What the cases do not mention, however, is the time it takes when you are involved in a legal proceeding. I want you to be aware of what you will be in for if you bring a claim against a client for commission. I understand the indignation you feel, that someone has cheated you out of a commission. It's costing you money. However, once you read and truly understand what you will face in a court proceeding, I think you may want to think it over some more.

Consider the case of *CB Commercial v. Swedcan*, in which a commercial realtor was denied commission. The facts of the case were not disputed. The salesperson had a listing agreement with a holdover clause. The salesperson brought in an offer with four days left in the listing period. The seller refused the offer, then signed with the same buyer nine days after the listing expired. This was well within the holdover period. However, the listing agreement also contained the following clause:

> The listing salesperson agrees to provide the seller with notice of all customers that had viewed the property prior to the expiry of the listing period.

The listing salesperson did not provide an actual list to the seller of all customers that had viewed the property, but relied on the fact that the offer itself constituted notice to the seller of the identity of the buyer. After four long years, the matter was decided in favour of the seller, and no commission was paid, due to a strict interpretation of what the notice should have actually contained. If you had asked most lawyers whom they thought would have won the action, most would have said the salesperson. Yet that is not how it turned out.

What I consider even more compelling is that the salesperson involved in the proceedings now says that he doubts he would ever go through the process again, even if he was certain of a victory, primarily because of the stress associated with the process.

As I discuss in Chapter 6, the legal process is all-consuming, in terms of time wasted and health risked. The time you will dedicate to such an action will be time you are not spending making money. This lost opportunity will more than likely outweigh any monies that you may have lost on the original transaction.

It might help you to look at this issue from a slightly different perspective. I have learned two rules when it comes to customer service.

Rule 1: The customer is always right.
Rule 2: If the customer is wrong, reread Rule 1.

Here are two examples of these rules in action. My wife is in the clothing business. She told me she once shipped a skirt to a customer via Federal Express. The customer's assistant signed for the package, as confirmed by the courier company, yet the customer insisted she never received it. My wife offered to send another skirt and charge the customer half price. The customer agreed and then badmouthed my wife's business to everyone she knew, which cost my wife future business opportunities in that community.

What if my wife had decided never to trust a customer again? Six months later, another customer purchased an outfit, wore it to a party, and then tried to return it, claiming it didn't fit. Without saying a word, my wife refunded the amount in full. This customer has since referred over a dozen new customers to my wife's business.

How does this apply to real estate professionals? They are in a difficult position. The public has an unfair impression that salespeople do not work very hard and can earn very high commissions for just a few days' work. Unfortunately, when something goes wrong in a real estate transaction, this impression makes the salesperson the easiest person to blame. Therefore, it is sometimes easy for a client to justify to himself that he should not pay commission to the salesperson. The more important issue is how the salesperson should deal with this situation. The key to remember is don't rush to sue or threaten to sue your client.

I recall from my days in private practice that I always dreaded receiving a call from a buyer on the day following closing. They never called to thank me for all the work I did on their behalf. It was always about problems with the new house, anything from damages caused during the moving process to the removal of certain fixtures from the property. It was as though they viewed me as a sheriff who somehow had the ability to pick up the phone and solve their problems in an hour.

One client complained that the mailbox had been removed. I asked him what name was on the mailbox. He told me it was the seller's name. When I asked why he needed a mailbox with the seller's name on it, he replied, "It's the principle." The same principle was used to explain another client's anger at light-switch plates being removed — plates which cost probably 50¢ at the hardware store.

Once, a fellow lawyer in our office closed a deal for his own house and came into work stating that the seller had removed all light switches from the wall, so that only a few wires stuck out. They had also taken out all the toilets. Apparently, the seller had heard that the buyer was going to demolish the house. What the seller did not hear was that the buyer intended to live in the house for a year before demolishing it. After almost falling down laughing, I thanked him. From then on, whenever a buyer called me after closing to complain about missing fixtures, I always answered, "Just be happy you have your toilets."

This also demonstrates how important chattels and fixtures are to sellers and buyers. When things are taken out improperly, it leaves bad feelings on both sides, and most often the salesperson is to blame. It is vital that salespeople are very careful in reviewing the status of all chattels and fixtures with buyers and sellers, including making proper descriptions and even taking photographs, to ensure there is no misunderstanding at closing.

To properly protect your buyer clients and to avoid any misunderstanding among sellers, it is crucial that all chattels be listed clearly in any offer. Take the time to list the make and model number for each appliance you are purchasing. Include the colours of all drapes and blinds. The longer you are in business, the longer the list becomes, as a result of sellers removing items such as rosebushes, sheds, and even trees from a property. I once heard about an offer that said "existing washer and dryer." The seller left behind a washing machine with a hair dryer on top.

Many salespeople are now starting to take photos of chattels at the original home inspection. This is a good idea. It can avoid many problems later, especially if there is a long time period between the initial offer and closing. As I will explain later in the chapter on privacy, you should obtain the consent of the seller prior to taking these photos since this is the personal information of the seller.

I give this example to demonstrate how irrational people can be when it comes to buying or selling a home. For many, it is the single most important and expensive contract that they have ever signed or will sign. If problems arise or if they are just unhappy people, they will try to blame someone and perhaps try to justify not paying a salesperson commission.

This may be their justification in waiting out the holdover period to avoid paying you any commission. If this does happen to you, I strongly recommend that before you rush to sue for your money, you take a step back. Go over everything that you have done for this client. Did the client make any complaints while you were working for them? Did you follow through with everything that you said you would do? Were you regularly in touch with the client, updating them as to the progress of their transaction?

In my experience with customer service at Bell Canada, I witnessed many complaints from customers. It seems that everyone has some issue with the phone company. It is also my experience that in most cases, you are much better off trying to settle the matter amicably with the customer by trying to understand their position. I like to refer to this as the LAST principle:

> Listen
> Acknowledge
> Solve
> Thank

Ask your client to explain why they feel you should not get paid any commission. Sometimes this is all that it takes. The key then is to listen. If they do have complaints about you or what you may have done, it is important that you let them explain everything. Don't interrupt. Use words such as "really" or "I see" to show them that you are in fact listening, or just nod your head to encourage them to continue. The main thing is always to look interested in what they are saying.

To demonstrate that you have listened, acknowledge the client by repeating the complaint to them. In addition, say something like, "I understand why that would make you upset." Do not admit that you did anything wrong. While you are listening, try to think of an appropriate response that will help solve their problem. Finally, always thank them for bringing these matters to your attention so that you can benefit from them. If you follow these steps, you have a greater chance of solving the matter in an amicable manner without having to resort to a "demand letter" from a lawyer.

When you solve a complaint in a satisfactory manner, the client ends up being more loyal to your company than a client who never had a complaint in the first place. I am sure that you can draw on your own personal experience that when a company went out of their way to satisfy a complaint that you had raised, you probably stayed with that company longer. The same is true of your clients. If you listen to their complaints and then do something about them, it is very unlikely that these clients will have any cause to even think about doing anything to deny you your commission. Not only that, if you are successful in satisfying their complaints, there is still a very good chance that these same clients will refer your services to others through positive recommendations. In this manner, you can use a negative experience to also grow your business.

I understand that there are some clients who may be completely dishonest, who never had any intention of paying you. You are correct to feel you want to teach them a lesson so that they don't try to do this to you or anyone else again. But also realize that anyone who is completely dishonest will continue to do everything possible to avoid paying you anything. This could include hiring their own lawyer, who will delay the proceedings as much as possible. Undoubtedly, you will become emotionally consumed with the lawsuit. Besides taking away from your ability to earn more commissions, it may also have a negative impact on your reputation, as people will hear that you are in court over non-payment of a commission. People will wonder why someone did not want to pay you, and might start questioning your competence. You do not want clients or potential clients to be thinking this about you or your services.

Even if as a result of your trying to resolve the matter amicably you are not able to do so, it is not a complete loss. You can still learn something from this experience. You will be better able to recognize a similar type of seller in the future, and you will make sure that you are better prepared for every customer interaction. No experience is a failure if you learn something valuable from it.

Surveying Your Clients

How many of you have received a telephone survey after you have purchased a car or stayed at a hotel? The questions on these surveys are pretty much the same. It's how companies determine whether or not they are delivering the right kind of customer experience, the kind that will generate referrals.

The three key survey questions usually asked are as follows. On a scale of 1–10,

1. How was your total customer experience, from the beginning to the end?
2. Will you return to the company for your future purchasing needs?
3. Will you recommend the company to your friends, relatives, and colleagues?

Some companies ask only the third question since it's the one that relates directly to referrals. To generate a 10 on question three, you have to deliver a superior customer experience every time.

What if you asked your own clients the same three questions two weeks after their transactions close? They would be reworded as follows.

1. How would you rate the service you received from the real

estate professional from the time you entered into your listing/buyer representation agreement until your transaction was complete?

2. What is the likelihood that you will come back to the real estate professional for future real estate services?

3. What is the likelihood that you will recommend the real estate professional to your relatives, friends, and colleagues?

Have you ever considered conducting a survey of your clients? You can ask for feedback on all aspects of your services, such as satisfaction with your marketing efforts, open houses, negotiations, and closing. In other words, you can obtain feedback on how you performed at each of the moments of truth.

After each of the three key questions, you can also ask for the reason the client rated you the way he did. You may then have the opportunity to use a positive answer as a testimonial in future marketing activities provided you have the consent of the client. This will be discussed more fully in Chapter 4 on privacy law.

Many successful companies end their surveys with the following question: "Is there anything that we could have done better?" This is a powerful way to improve your level of service. Studies have indicated that over 50% of customers who may have a complaint about your product or service do not actually complain because they think no one is going to care about them anyway. Even though they do not complain, they won't return to you or recommend you to others.

Should you conduct the survey by mail, e-mail, or via telephone? There are many opinions about which method is more effective. Telephone surveys are considered more effective since it's easier to explain the question if there is any confusion. However, you are less likely to invade your client's privacy if you conduct the survey by mail or by e-mail. There are survey companies who can be used to conduct this survey for you, to ensure that all information is gathered in an appropriate and confidential manner and so that you gain the most insight from the responses to improve the way you serve your clients going forward.

Other studies have shown that, when you are successful in resolving a complaint, you obtain an even more loyal client than those who have never complained before.

Think about the last time you had an electrical appliance break down just after the warranty period expired. You dread the whole upcoming process of taking the appliance back to the mall, fighting traffic, looking for parking, finding the store, being directed to the back of the store to the service counter, where you have to wait in line, only to have an argument. How do you feel, that one time in ten, when the service representative says, "That will be no problem, we will fix it for you at no charge." You remain a customer for life and tell others about how you were treated. That is the power of solving a complaint.

When salespeople ask me whether to sue for commission, my advice is now always the same. Go and sit with the client and ask, "What did I do that made you not want to pay me? I want to learn how I can improve myself." Invariably, this approach will lead to a good, honest discussion. In many cases, the client was upset about something you did but didn't bother to complain, thinking that you wouldn't care anyway. Sound familiar? By talking it out, you will have a very good chance of settling the matter right there, but more importantly you will also learn from the experience to become a better salesperson and have the opportunity to repair the relationship with this client.

I have attached a sample survey for your consideration in Appendix B. Consider surveying your clients going forward. You'll be surprised how much you will learn.

If you follow the principles in this book, there should be no reason why a client would ever feel that you do not deserve to be paid. If this does occur, however, remember also to use the experience positively, instead of bristling and heading down the road of uncertain, expensive litigation.

Weisleder's Wisdom on . . . GETTING PAID

1. Review your listing and buyer representation agreements carefully with your clients, especially the holdover clause.
2. Follow through on all your commitments and keep the client informed.
3. Listen for any concerns or complaints raised by your client and then solve them.
4. Resolve any problems using the LAST principle.
5. Do not rush to sue someone when things go wrong; learn from every bad experience instead.
6. Remember, satisfying complaints can lead to further referrals; turn the negative experience into positive results.
7. Survey your clients. You will learn how to make your clients more satisfied than ever before and thus generate even more referrals.

The Wheels
of Misfortune

There are two Wheels of Misfortune, and you never want to find yourself hurt by either of them, whether out of ignorance, negligence, or attempts to get around your provincial council's Code of Ethics. They are the Real Estate Wheel of Misfortune and the Insurance Wheel of Misfortune. Following are two pie charts that have been compiled by the underwriter for the Real Estate Council of Ontario (RECO), showing, by category, the kinds of RECO discipline committee claims made against real estate salespeople and the kinds of errors that lead to lawsuits and thus claims against a salesperson's errors and omissions insurance policies.

In the next chapter, I will discuss some of these "spokes" of the Real Estate Wheel of Misfortune and what you should be aware of when you are doing business as a salesperson. By following key obligations and guidelines, not only will you avoid any unwanted discipline proceedings, but you will also avoid any associated claims against your insurance policy. Note that, while RECO rules and obligations are discussed throughout this book, most provincial bodies dealing with real estate follow similar rules and practices, so the principles are applicable wherever you may practise.

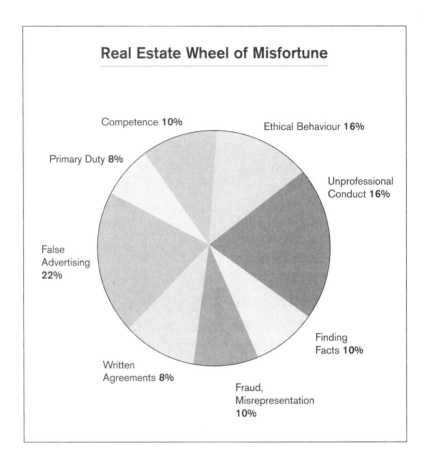

Real Estate Wheel of Misfortune

Competence **10%**

Ethical Behaviour **16%**

Primary Duty **8%**

Unprofessional
Conduct **16%**

False
Advertising
22%

Finding
Facts **10%**

Written
Agreements **8%**

Fraud,
Misrepresentation
10%

Your goal is to conduct yourself as a salesperson, and to do business as a salesperson, so that you never get into trouble with your provincial council's Wheel of Misfortune and so that you are never exposed for ignoring, flouting, or not knowing any of these Obligations.

THE REAL ESTATE WHEEL OF MISFORTUNE

Up until March 31, 2006, salespeople and brokers were governed by a Code of Ethics established by the Real Estate Council of Ontario. The purpose of the code was not only to ensure that salespeople treated each other in good faith but also to protect the public. To ensure compliance with the code, RECO established through a bylaw a process of discipline.

The Code of Ethics initially consisted of 27 rules, which, if breached, could conceivably make a salesperson subject to a discipline committee hearing. For each rule, there were guiding principles to provide examples and amplification of the Code of Ethics. This code and the cases decided under it educated salespeople and brokers in what were acceptable practices in the profession, and it encouraged fair dealings between sellers, buyers, and salespeople in all aspects of their relationships in buying and selling real estate.

Recognizing the importance that the Code of Ethics has on the day-to-day practice of the real estate profession, the government decided to include a revised Code of Ethics directly into the new REBBA, as an attached regulation. This has made compliance with the code an even greater responsibility for all salespeople and brokerages. The new Code of Ethics is reproduced in its entirety in Appendix F of this book.

The concepts of rules and guiding principles have been replaced. The Code of Ethics is now made up of 40 Obligations that salespeople have to their clients and customers. The code also contains details of how the discipline process works, from how the discipline and appeals panels are chosen to the actual hearing details. The 40 Obligations are in many ways a restatement of the prior rules and guiding principles.

All of the discipline cases referred to in this book are based on the original rules and guiding principles of the Code of Ethics that were in place prior to March 31, 2006. With the introduction of the new Real Estate and Business Brokers Act, I have taken the liberty of presenting these same decisions in the context of the new 40 Obligations under the new REBBA. In some cases, while the exact previous rule may not be duplicated in the new Code of Ethics, it is my belief that the

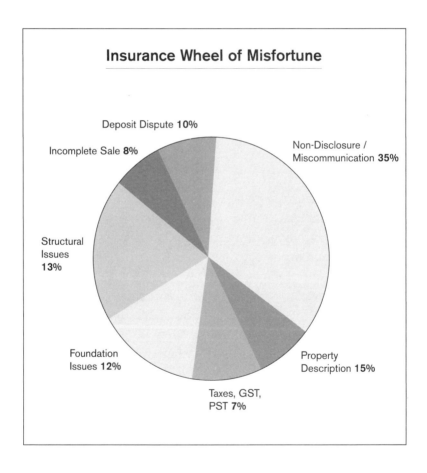

Insurance Wheel of Misfortune

Deposit Dispute **10%**

Incomplete Sale **8%**

Non-Disclosure / Miscommunication **35%**

Structural Issues **13%**

Foundation Issues **12%**

Property Description **15%**

Taxes, GST, PST **7%**

principles to learn from each of the cases will remain the same.

In all areas where salespeople are making errors that end up with legal proceedings, they constantly involve a violation of one of the Code of Ethics Obligations. This applies in all jurisdictions in Canada where salespeople do business. Similar codes of ethics are also found in every state in the United States, illustrating that these principles apply to all real estate professionals who practise anywhere in North America.

THE INSURANCE WHEEL OF MISFORTUNE

On the insurance chart, you can see the types of claims that salespeople have had to report to their insurers in Ontario as a result of claims made against them. These claims fall under RECO's errors and omissions policy. The errors or omissions that are being made are most often a result of not following one or more of the Obligations under the Code of Ethics. In many instances, it is just about not being careful. Yet this behaviour can quickly lead to claims about negligence. In effect, we can see how both Wheels of Misfortune intersect — if you manage to conduct yourself in a manner that keeps you out of trouble with one of the wheels, you will almost automatically stay out of trouble with the other wheel as well.

AN OVERVIEW OF HOW REAL ESTATE COUNCIL PROCEEDINGS WORK

Once a complaint is made against you in writing to your provincial real estate council, either by a member of the public or another salesperson, it will be reviewed to determine whether any further action is necessary. In Ontario, if the complaint refers to a violation of REBBA or the Code of Ethics, then RECO will deal with the matter.

RECO may provide the registrant salesperson or broker who is the subject of the complaint with a written copy of the complaint or RECO's understanding of the nature of the complaint. RECO will also provide a description of the Registrar's Complaints and Inquiries process and require the salesperson or broker to submit a written response to the complaint. Some of the possible outcomes of the complaint could be that the Registrar takes no action or requires that the salesperson or broker attend a meeting, mediation or take additional education courses. When the matters involve more serious violations of the Code of Ethics or REBBA, then the matter could be referred to the RECO Discipline Committee, be prosecuted under the Provincial Offences Act or the Registrar could make a proposal to suspend or revoke a salesperson or broker's registration with RECO. For the Registrar's office, the protection of the public interest is the guiding factor in deciding which recommendation to make.

If the matter proceeds to a hearing, at least three committee members will be appointed to hear the case and make a decision. The salesperson is given 45 days' notice prior to the hearing itself. The salesperson will be issued a copy of all written documentation that RECO intends to rely on at the hearing, including a statement as to which Obligations of the Code of Ethics have been violated and the factual basis for the claims made. The salesperson must file any evidence that they wish to produce at the hearing, whether documentary or testimonial, at least 15 days prior to the hearing. In this manner, there is an attempt to have full disclosure of each side's position to the other side prior to the actual hearing.

RECO will present all evidence at the hearing, including the witnesses that it intends to rely on. The salesperson will have the opportunity to cross-examine any witnesses who attend, as well as to present their own evidence. The decision of the panel is then forwarded to the salesperson within 10 days of the hearing.

To appeal the decision of the committee, under a RECO hearing, you must file a notice of appeal within 30 days of receiving the decision. To win the case on appeal, the salesperson must be able to prove that the committee had no jurisdiction to hear the matter or that there was a denial of natural justice, for example if the committee members were biased against the salesperson.

Failure to comply with the decision of the committee will result in the immediate termination of a salesperson's membership with RECO and could also cause a proposal to the Provincial Licensing Tribunal to revoke the salesperson's registration under the Real Estate and Business Brokers Act. In other words, you are out of business.

In the case of *Luzak v. The Real Estate Council of Ontario*, decided October 9, 2003, the salesperson went through the discipline committee hearing process and was given a penalty of $6,000 and costs of $1,000, which he appealed. The appeal committee that was appointed to hear the matter included a member who also had been on the original panel that heard the complaint. The salesperson felt that this would bias the appeal committee against him and thus requested that a different panel be appointed. RECO denied his request, so the salesperson took the commission to court to argue that this constituted a denial of his right to natural justice.

The court found that the salesperson did not offer any evidence proving that RECO's conduct in not replacing the member denied him the right to natural justice or was unfair to him. He had been duly notified of the complaint made against him, and he had received an impartial hearing. The decision was also noteworthy because it provided a judicial stamp of approval to the entire process by which RECO was set up to enable the real estate profession as a whole to be self-managing. This gives RECO the right to pass bylaws to ensure that its members comply with its Code of Ethics, all for the protection of the public interest.

RECO does not take this obligation lightly, which is why it has strict requirements about the membership qualifications and educational standards for all of its members.

Based on my review of the decisions involving RECO, I can say that it is best for the salesperson to be very cooperative with the process as soon as he receives the initial notification. If the matter can be resolved through meetings, mediation or the requirement to take education courses, it is far more preferable than going through the discipline hearing process. Yet this will ultimately be the sole decision of the Registrar's office.

My advice, if you do proceed to a hearing and a decision is reached, is that you do not appeal the matter. Virtually all appeals are unsuccessful, as it is extremely difficult to prove that the committee was biased against you. The committee members are, for the most part, fellow real estate professionals who understand the business and take their responsibility very seriously. They review all facts presented and consider all arguments before rendering any decision.

AN OVERVIEW OF HOW TO WORK WITH YOUR INSURER

Once you receive a letter or legal claim from anyone that could result in damages claimed, you must immediately inform your insurer. It is best to let them determine the course of action that they wish to take.

If you make any admission of liability before contacting the insurer, there may be grounds for the insurer to deny coverage. Although you may be tempted to try to settle the matter yourself, to make it go away, do not consider this option for the same reason: that the insurer may be able to use this as a reason to deny coverage.

Let your broker know immediately about the complaint or letter that you have received. You may also want to get legal advice before acting. The key thing to remember is not to act quickly in this situation. When someone makes an allegation that you are not competent in your chosen career, it can cause severe personal and professional stress. You are in no position to decide how to proceed. That is why you should contact the insurer first. As long as they are making the initial decisions as to how to proceed, there is virtually no way that they can deny coverage later, unless the complaint is part of the exclusions under their policy.

Once the insurer gets involved, a claims manager or adjuster will take charge of the file and determine how to proceed. This could involve recommending a quick settlement with the person making the claim, if the situation warrants. A decision could also be made that the matter needs to be defended, and the claims manager will then appoint a lawyer to act on the insurer's and the salesperson's behalf.

An ounce of prevention being worth a pound of cure, it is best to find out how to avoid any kind of hearing at all. To do this, you must understand the Obligations of the Code of Ethics, which are explained in the next chapter.

CHAPTER 3

Beware the Spokes of the Real Estate Wheel of Misfortune

This chapter focuses on the key Code of Ethics Obligations that serve as a guide to appropriate professional conduct in the course of carrying out your business. When a salesperson violates one of these Obligations, it results in unfavourable consequences for the salesperson or a member of the public. If you follow the "Weisleder's Wisdom" principles at the end of my discussion of each Obligation, you will avoid being hurt by one of these spokes.

In my experience, almost every legal claim made against a salesperson is caused by crossing the line on one or more of these Code of Ethics Obligations. By avoiding getting hurt by the spokes of the Real Estate Wheel of Misfortune, not only will you be conducting your profession in a safe and respectable manner, you will also be avoiding the disciplinary or legal claims that could destroy your reputation as well as your ability to earn a living. At the same time, you will be practising in a manner that instills trust and confidence in your clients, which will lead to long-term loyal relationships and referrals.

Please note that I do not discuss every Obligation in the Code of Ethics, nor do I discuss them in the order in which they appear in the Code of Ethics. I have tried to get at the most important points, in an order that fits the concerns of real estate professionals wherever they may practise.

The cases referred to in the following pages are based on actual discipline committee proceedings commenced in the province of Ontario, yet the principles to be learned apply equally to all jurisdictions across Canada. All cases can be viewed in their entirety online at the RECO website, www.reco.on.ca, under the heading "Complaints & Enforcements," subheading "Discipline & Appeals Decisions." (This is another reason not to get into trouble with your local real estate council. Your name and thus your reputation will become exposed to everyone who has access to the Internet, to observe the details of your particular decision, for the next five years.)

All of the discipline cases referred to in this book are based on the original rules and guiding principles of the Code of Ethics that were in place prior to March 31, 2006. With the introduction of the new Real Estate and Business Brokers Act, I have taken the liberty of presenting these same decisions in the context of the new 40 Obligations under the new REBBA. In some cases, while the exact previous rule may not be duplicated in the new Code of Ethics, it is my belief that the principles to learn from each of the cases will remain the same.

OBLIGATIONS UNDER THE CODE OF ETHICS
ETHICAL BEHAVIOUR

Fairness, honesty, etc.
3. A registrant shall treat every person the registrant deals with in the course of a trade in real estate fairly, honestly and with integrity.

Best interests
4. A registrant shall promote and protect the best interests of the registrant's clients.

Conscientious and competent service, etc.

5. *A registrant shall provide conscientious service to the regis-trant's clients and customers and shall demonstrate reasonable knowledge, skill, judgment and competence in providing those services.*

Providing opinions, etc.

6. *(1) A registrant shall demonstrate reasonable knowledge, skill, judgment and competence in providing opinions, advice or information to any person in respect of a trade in real estate.*

(2) Without limiting the generality of subsection (1) or section 5,

(a) a brokerage shall not provide an opinion or advice about the value of real estate to any person unless the opinion or advice is provided on behalf of the brokerage by a broker or salesperson who has education or experience related to the valuation of real estate; and

(b) a broker or salesperson shall not provide an opinion or advice about the value of real estate to any person unless the broker or salesperson has education or experience related to the valuation of real estate.

The main guiding principle under the previous Code of Ethics was the golden rule: "Do unto others as you would have them do unto you." This continues to remain a powerful guide as to how you should treat your fellow salespeople as well as your clients and members of the public.

In virtually every discipline decision that has been success-fully brought against a salesperson anywhere, one of these Obligations has been violated. In every decision that you will make, whether it is related to advertising, duties to your clients, disclosure to your clients, or discovery of facts, you will always be faced with the ethical dilemmas as to what should guide your actions. These Obligations become even more important in the real estate profession, where a salesperson's name in the community is one of the primary marketing tools that he or she uses to earn a living.

Major corporations spend a lot of money on their brand image — what sets them apart from the competition. Many corporations have learned the hard way that their business suffers whenever they sacrifice that brand image in order to make a fast profit at the expense of their customers. They may make their financial statements look a little better in the short term, but they lose a lot more — customers, repeat business, referrals, goodwill — over the long term.

Rogers Cable, the leading cable provider in Ontario, once attempted to introduce a service through negative option billing, whereby they provided their customers with five or six new channels for a three-month period in order to try them out. What they did not tell their customers was that they would automatically be charged an extra monthly fee in the fourth month if they did not call in to cancel the service. This was clearly an attempt to raise short-term revenues, banking on the probability that many customers would not think to call and cancel the new service. However, this led to a public outcry so severe that Rogers immediately changed their policy.

The damage caused to the Rogers brand was significant. Over five years after the incident, I noticed the following headline in a newspaper article in Toronto: "Negative Option Billing Rises to New Heights in Toronto." When I saw the headline, I thought that Rogers had made the same mistake involving negative option billing. I was surprised to learn that this article was actually about Rogers' decision to relocate to a new office tower in downtown Toronto. The negative term used to describe this innocent business move demonstrates how a company error can do long-term damage to that same company's reputation and brand image.

The same principle can be applied directly to the real estate business. Do not be tempted to cross the line, in order to make a deal happen, just because the commission can be very lucrative. Look at the long-term cost. When I was in private practice as a lawyer, clients would sometimes ask me to cross the line on a transaction. The only lesson I learned in every such circumstance was that this would probably be the last time I acted for this client. Clients who want you to compromise your ethics only end up blaming you later when things go wrong.

Another brand lesson to be learned is that it is not advisable to attack your competitor's brand. Instead, just show why you are different. Show the benefits your organization brings. Pepsi took on the world's most popular brand, Coke, in the famous "taste test" advertising campaign. For a while they succeeded, so much so that Coke changed their formula. (I am told that this came about after the Coke board of directors took the Pepsi taste test and voted for Pepsi.) Reaction to the new Coke was a disaster. They got the message and reintroduced the original formula, as Coke Classic, and have never looked back.

Toys "Я" Us is one of the strongest children's toy brands in the world. A new company, called SmarterKids.com, entered the market and tried to do things a little differently. They developed a gift centre online so that relatives could avoid giving the same present as other relatives. They permitted a child's profile to be entered so that gifts could be recommended to suit the particular child. This company was successful not because it claimed to be better than Toys "Я" Us but because it demonstrated how it was different.

It is tempting in the real estate business to bad-mouth another salesperson since many salespeople usually compete for the same listings. This is clearly a dangerous practice and a violation of the ethical behaviour Obligation. Consider the discipline case of Holliday, decided August 14, 2002. The complaint was made that this salesperson attacked the reputation of another salesperson. The attacks included the claims

- that, although this other salesperson had a lot of listings, he did not sell many properties because he offered selling salespeople commissions that were too low;
- that the high number of listings carried by the salesperson meant he was too busy to provide proper service to his clients;
- that their actual sales in the area were much lower than those of other salespeople; and
- that this broker would be out of business within six months.

All of these claims were deemed false and misleading. Not only were they deemed to be a violation of Obligation 38, Misrepresentation, but they were also judged a violation of Obligation 3, Fairness, Honesty, in that the actions were not considered fair dealing with other members of the profession and the public.

The power of e-mails and the Internet makes it more important than ever to satisfy your customers' complaints. Consider the following example from outside the real estate business.

Two consultants tried to check into the Doubletree Hotel in Houston after midnight. They were told that they had lost their room, even though the room had been guaranteed in advance by credit card payment. So the consultants decided to strike back. They prepared a short PowerPoint presentation indicating their displeasure and sent copies of it via e-mail to a few of their friends. The presentation contained charts and graphs, which consultants love to use, showing, for example, how much business the hotel would lose based on the negative word-of-mouth advertising that would result from the consultants' negative experience.

Suffice it to say that, within a few weeks, this e-mail had been forwarded throughout the hospitality industry. It has even become part of a course at a major U.S. college as an illustration of how you should not treat a customer. This incident caused Doubletree International to issue a formal statement explaining what had occurred.

The moral of the story? You should always take client complaints very seriously. If you are not listening to your clients and satisfying their needs, complaints will result. Perhaps the complaint may not go as far as a discipline hearing or a lawsuit. But it will definitely be made to other members of the community — and that will tarnish your own personal brand.

So many times we are tempted for the sake of expedience to cross the line. In the discipline case of Ip, decided March 14, 2002, the salesperson signed the names of his clients on documents instead of taking the time to get the clients to do so themselves. The complaint was raised by the broker, who formerly employed this salesperson, due to irregularities in the transaction. The salesperson stated that he was "verbally instructed to do so." He was trying to keep his clients happy, as this is what he "knew they wanted." The sellers even sent letters stating that they were happy with the results obtained. It was nevertheless held to be a violation of Obligation 3, Fairness, Honesty. The fine levied was $2,500, and costs came to $2,100.

Do not be tempted to initial the client signatures during signbacks as offers go back and forth. You may think you are doing your client a favour by initialling documents on their behalf, based on a verbal instruction, but you are not. Without written authorization, you are headed for a problem. What if your client changes their mind after the signing takes place? They will quickly point to the final initial and state that this was not their signature, that they had not authorized the change.

I recall a similar situation when I was starting out in private practice. A client needed a document notarized. It is required that the client sign a document in the lawyer's presence before the notary stamp can be affixed. The client, however, did not want to travel downtown just to sign the document. They asked if they could just tell me they signed it and courier it downtown, where I could then affix my notary stamp and send it back to them. What I did was I called the client and told them that I had to be in their neighbourhood anyways, and I would come and see them to sign the document. It was easier to explain the legal requirements about signing the documents when I was at their office. This also gave me the opportunity to meet them at their place of business, and they subsequently gave me a tour. I learned a lot more about my client's business, which led to a greater amount of work from them in the following years.

The above-noted example took a potential negative situation, which was going to inconvenience the client, and turned it into a positive experience for everyone, while at the same time educated the client about the reasons for the ethical and legal requirements. This client not only became a valuable client, but I remain close friends with them today.

Part of being properly prepared when presenting an offer is knowing at all times how to reach your client. Educate them in advance that offers may be signed back and forth during the day or night, and they must be available so that any changes can be properly reviewed. If this is properly explained ahead of time, the client will not be upset about meeting you to do any final initials; rather, they will appreciate and respect your professionalism. This confidence in your abilities is what leads to more referrals later. The client who is impressed with cutting corners is the kind of client that you should not be acting for in the first place. You do not need those kinds of referrals either, as they will ruin your reputation in the long run.

In a world where we can communicate almost instantaneously with our clients, there is no reason why we cannot obtain appropriate written instructions and authorizations when needed. Always use your contact information to keep the client informed, especially by e-mail, as virtually all clients now have an e-mail address.

I am not a big fan of clients who expect a salesperson to cut commissions in order to get the deal done. Some people feel that salespeople are overpaid and do hardly any work and thus should not be upset if they are asked to cut their commissions. But this request should not arise if you have done an appropriate job of demonstrating your professionalism at the time you obtain the listing or the buyer representation agreement and if throughout the process you listen to your clients and satisfy their needs.

You need to develop a policy of what you will do if this request does arise, and that policy should be to just say no. Cut your commission once and the word will get around, and you will always be asked to cut your commission. It may be better to let one deal go by refusing to comply with such a request than to create this kind of reputation.

However, if you do agree to rebate the commission, for any reason, then you must follow through on your commitment. In the discipline case of Szewczyk, decided October 3, 2003, the salesperson offered to rebate 1% commission to the buyer in order to make the deal happen. But he did not follow through on his promise, trying to explain himself to the client by saying he was having financial difficulties brought on him due to the actions of third parties. The penalty in this case was severe, $12,000, with costs in the amount of $1,750. The salesperson did not pay the penalty and subsequently lost his membership and registration.

The discipline proceeding of Sheppard, dated April 10, 2002, is instructive. This salesperson tried to seal a deal by making personal guarantees to the seller that if the buyer defaulted on the deal, he would back it up. In this way he convinced the seller to give the buyer additional extensions to complete the transaction. The facts of this case were complicated, but it became clear that as neither the buyer nor the salesperson was able to satisfy the purchase commitment, it led to one misleading event after another, until the lawyers came running.

The salesperson was deemed to have violated Obligation 37, Inaccurate Representations, above all by giving a guarantee without the financial ability to satisfy it. This resulted in a penalty of $12,000 and costs of $1,800 against the salesperson.

In another discipline case, one involving Ebrahim, dated January 9, 2002, the salesperson tried to put her own money into the deal to help secure extensions. She hoped these extensions would permit the buyer to come up with the money to complete the transaction, or enable her to find another buyer to complete the transaction. Although the salesperson meant well, she would have better served her seller client right from the start by letting them know the buyer was having difficulties and then letting the seller make the decision as to what to do. The result not only cost the salesperson the money she had put into the transaction, which was forfeited, but also a penalty of $2,000 and costs of $1,100.

In the discipline case of Lee, dated August 3, 2001, it was alleged that the salesperson, who left one brokerage for another, had attempted to have her former listing sellers cancel their listings with her former employer so that she could sign them up with her new employer. Not only was it found that she had interfered with her former broker's contractual relationships with these sellers, she had also put these same sellers at risk by having them sign new agreements with her current employer before they had been properly released from their earlier agreements. The fine in this case was $5,000 plus costs of $1,300. In deciding the penalty, the panel took into account the fact that the salesperson admitted that what she did was wrong and felt regret for her actions.

Claiming that you made a mistake, especially if it was a careless one, is not an answer to an allegation that you have violated this Obligation on ethical behaviour. The Obligation makes clear that you must be always up to date on current standards. In the discipline case of Ferri, decided March 19, 2002, the salesperson was careless in not checking the status of a basement apartment prior to renting it out for an owner. Had it been checked, the salesperson would have learned that the apartment was not permitted under the city bylaws. It was not a defence by the salesperson that "most salespeople did not know about this bylaw." Although there was no intent to deceive anyone, this careless act of the salesperson resulted in a violation not only of the Obligations regarding advertising, but also of this Obligation on ethical behaviour. The penalty imposed was $500, with costs of $1,650.

Part of ethical behaviour includes not taking shortcuts. An example would be where you decide to reduce a sale price on a listing without obtaining confirmation in writing from your seller. Many salespeople just do this based on verbal instructions. In the case of Thomson, decided March 1, 2001, the salesperson changed the listing price without written confirmation because it was "inconvenient to do so." As you can imagine, the seller later complained that they did not remember having authorized this change, and there was confusion as to the prices that should have been listed. The penalty imposed was $1,000. All of the confusion as well as the subsequent proceeding could have been avoided if a little more time was taken to obtain the change in writing directly from the client.

Another example is following through on what you say you will do. In a case dated November 21, 2002, the salesperson represented to the seller that they would take out advertising in a particular publication called the *Real Estate News and*

Buyers Guide. Advertising was done in another medium instead. The salesperson argued that he did provide the seller with equivalent advertising. Although the parties verbally discussed potential alternatives, nothing was reduced to writing. It was found that the salesperson was in breach of Obligation 11, Contents of Written Agreements, in not following an express term of the listing agreement. If there was to be an alteration, it had to be done in writing. The penalty in this case was $1,000 and $900 in costs.

Obligation 3, Fairness, Honesty, states that "A registrant shall treat every person the registrant deals with in the course of a trade in real estate fairly, honestly and with integrity." I could not have summarized this duty any better myself. This is also the cornerstone of providing loyalty to your own clients. If you want your clients to be loyal to you, you must also demonstrate this kind of loyalty to them. Follow this advice and you will avoid violating virtually all of the Obligations in any Code of Ethics.

Weisleder's Wisdom on . . . ETHICAL BEHAVIOUR

1. Your reputation or brand image is a valuable asset; protect it at all costs, even if it means losing a commission.
2. Do not disparage the name of another salesperson; instead, show how you are different.
3. Never try to save a transaction by providing a guarantee or contributing any financing.
4. Do not take any shortcuts, whether in taking instructions or preparing documents. Confirm all instructions in writing.
5. Always follow through on all of your written commitments, especially what you have agreed to on your listing agreement.
6. Demonstrate and explain your professionalism at all times.
7. Always ask yourself, "Is this worth losing my licence, or

being involved in a discipline or legal proceeding?"

8. Do not attempt to take a client away from an existing relationship with another salesperson. If people know you are good, they will find you the next time.

9. Be loyal to your clients in everything that you do, and they will be loyal to you in the long term.

UNPROFESSIONAL CONDUCT

Unprofessional conduct

39. A registrant shall not, in the course of trading in real estate, engage in any act or omission, that, having regard to all of the circumstances, would reasonably be regarded as disgraceful, dishonourable, unprofessional or unbecoming a registrant.

Abuse and harassment

40. A registrant shall not abuse or harass any person in the course of trading in real estate.

Unprofessional conduct is another Obligation that is so foundational it invariably is violated together with many of the other Obligations. Although most principles of this Obligation are straightforward and sound like common sense, it's amazing how quickly they can be ignored in the pursuit of the next commission.

Situations arise in which, as a result of your participation in a transaction, you may be paid commissions or incentives from various parties, or you may decide to invest in part of the transaction yourself. There is nothing inherently wrong with making this profit, as long as there is complete disclosure to everyone for whom you are acting and who is paying you anything. The safest course is to obtain the consent of all parties involved.

There was a case where a salesperson used information that he learned to acquire an interest in a property, without disclosing this information to his seller. The seller subsequently refused to pay the salesperson commission, which amounted to $10,000. The salesperson sued for the commission. The seller counterclaimed for the profit that the salesperson earned on the transaction personally. The judge awarded the salesperson his $10,000 commission. The judge also awarded the seller $325,000 in the counterclaim. And of course the lawyers took their full fees from both sides. I have already given my opinion about starting litigation to recover your commissions. This was a great example where the salesperson was very misguided in starting these proceedings. All of it could probably have been avoided if the salesperson had just disclosed his interest in the first place. The seller would have most likely consented to the salesperson making a profit, and the matter could easily have been resolved without litigation.

Do not bad-mouth another salesperson in order to obtain a listing. I have heard of numerous situations in which salespeople have attempted to discredit another salesperson in front of that salesperson's clients in order to embarrass the salesperson and demonstrate their own special skills. All the salesperson accomplishes is to demonstrate how truly unprofessional he is, usually leaving an impression to all concerned of rude, arrogant behaviour. It is so important, in a business that is so dependent on word of mouth, that you do not damage your own brand image in this manner.

This also applies to how you treat people in your office. We all learn very early in our professional careers how dependent we become on the administrative staff in an organization. You need their assistance and support, especially when you get busy. Treating them with respect and courtesy at all times ensures that you will have their continued support, which will ultimately benefit your customers. This is called living your brand image or reputation in everything you do, every day.

When you are angry, the worst thing you can do is confront a person. You are most likely to say something that you will later regret. This is especially true of messages that you may leave on someone's voice mail when the person is not reachable. This voice mail can be used as evidence against you in a discipline or court proceeding. It reminds me of a kidnapping case in the mid-1980s when the kidnappers called from a motel that had caller ID, before many members of the public were aware what that technology was about. It took the police about five seconds to see where the call originated and apprehend the criminals.

In the discipline case of Imough, decided April 19, 2002, it was alleged that the salesperson had left messages with the buyers attempting to dissuade them from concluding their Agreement of Purchase and Sale. The salesperson's defence was that it was a neighbour calling, who had wanted to disclose that the house being considered by the buyer had a leaky basement. As a result of these calls, the buyer withdrew from the property. The calls were traced back to the salesperson's office, through the applicable telephone records.

A RECO discipline proceeding is not a criminal trial, and therefore proof on a "balance of probabilities" is all that is needed. A tape of the telephone calls was played at the salesperson's hearing, and a number of people involved stated that they recognized the voice as that of the salesperson. This behaviour was found to be "unjustified, unfair, and unprofessional." As a result of the seriousness of this violation, the salesperson had her licence suspended for three months and had to pay costs of $1,980.

One can assume that the cost to this salesperson was much more than three months' worth of commissions. It also involved a negative effect on her reputation, her relationship with other members of her real estate firm, and her relationship with other members of the profession.

A similar error is disparaging another salesperson in your written material or communications. In the discipline case of Hope, decided July 4, 2002, the salesperson issued a newsletter indicating that he was proud of being able to obtain the highest prices for properties in his area. He proceeded to disparage another salesperson in the newsletter, implying that the other salesperson only cared about closing the deal and not about doing the best service for his clients, including obtaining the highest price.

Although the other salesperson was not mentioned by name, it could easily be found based on the properties identified in the newsletter. It was held that Mr. Hope acted unprofessionally by disseminating negative and derogatory information about a fellow member. It was noted that as this happened in a relatively small community, the act of disparagement was very serious. The penalty in this case was $2,000 with costs of an additional $1,550.

In the discipline case of Slavin, decided August 14, 2001, one salesperson attempted to take a listing from another salesperson, relying on the fact that the listing showed up for one day as having been cancelled on the MLS system. However, the mistake was corrected within 24 hours and could easily have been verified. Instead, the salesperson attempted to sign the seller to another listing agreement, exposing the seller to being bound by two separate agreements with two salespeople at the same time. It was irrelevant that the seller may have been unhappy with the first salesperson and wanted the listing to be cancelled. This was not sufficient justification for the second salesperson to try to take the listing.

The salesperson, on hearing that a complaint had been made by the first listing salesperson, left the following voice mail:

> I just got a call from the Real Estate Board saying that you've, ah, filed a complaint with them and RECO. Um, I think it is a shame that

you did that, but, ah, at the end of the day, um, over the next 12, 24, or 36 months, you will end up paying for this more than I will, and, ah, I will make sure, that, ah, I keep an eye on everything you do from now on and in the future, and I hope you don't break any rules and that you won't have any hassles from me. Always nice talking to you, take care, bye.

The salesperson was clearly upset after hearing about the complaint. It is only natural to become angry and want to yell at someone. Even if it was not intended to be threatening, the language used by the salesperson seemed to the committee to imply threatening behaviour. This entire tirade was viewed as unprofessional conduct as well as a violation of Obligation 40, Abuse and Harassment. The fine levied was $3,000.

The worst thing you can do when a complaint is made against you is to say anything during this initial period that will only get you into more trouble later. The best thing is to cool down and discuss the situation with your own broker or legal advisers to determine the appropriate next step. It is well documented that what you do right after a complaint has been made can go a long way in determining the kind of remedy that will be sought by the Office of the Registrar. It does you no good whatsoever to attempt to throw your weight around. All this does is further confirm to anyone investigating the complaint that you commonly engage in unprofessional conduct.

Weisleder's Wisdom on . . . UNPROFESSIONAL CONDUCT

1. Never make disparaging remarks about other salespeople, whether in verbal conversations, voice mails, e-mails, documents, or newsletters.
2. Treat every salesperson, client, and administrative staff with courtesy and respect at all times.

3. If a complaint is made against you, resist the temptation to become angry at the person who made the complaint. Do not contact them when you are in this agitated state.

DEALINGS WITH OTHER REGISTRANTS

Dealings with other registrants

7. (1) A registrant who knows or ought to know that a person is a client of another registrant shall communicate information to the person for the purpose of a trade in real estate only through the other registrant, unless the other registrant has consented in writing.

(2) If a broker or salesperson knows or ought to know that a buyer or seller is a party to an agreement in connection with a trade in real estate with a brokerage other than the brokerage that employs the broker or salesperson, the broker or salesperson shall not induce the buyer or seller to break the agreement.

Don't deal with another salesperson's clients or do anything that attempts to affect the relationship between a salesperson and their existing clients. It may be tempting at times to deal with another salesperson's clients, especially when they approach you themselves wanting your services. Typically, this involves buyers who feel that they can save a few dollars by cutting out their own salesperson, hoping that you will reduce your listing commission if it appears that you will also be double ending the deal.

If you are acting as a listing salesperson, be sure to ask a buyer if they are already being represented by someone else. Buyers will be very tempted to say no if they think this will result in a lower price to be paid for a property that they may find on their own.

The discipline case of Middleton, decided January 25, 2002,

illustrates this concept. The salesperson was deemed to have violated Obligation 7, Dealing with Other Registrants, by not informing the buyer salesperson what was going on when the buyers tried to complete the transaction directly with the listing salesperson without informing the buyer salesperson. The listing salesperson took the position that the buyers were not happy with the buyer broker service and that he was only trying to satisfy the customers' wishes.

The committee ruled, however, that once the salesperson knew that a buyer broker was involved, he had to satisfy himself that the buyer broker was made aware of the situation so that the matter could be resolved with all appropriate parties involved. The penalties were $3,000 each against both the listing salesperson and the listing broker, with costs of $1,950 against each party as well.

In the discipline proceeding involving Davis, decided April 17, 2001, the buyer salesperson acknowledged dealing directly with the seller's solicitor on a transaction, thereby avoiding the listing broker entirely. The salesperson was attempting to salvage the transaction, which had developed problems prior to closing as a result of concerns with the septic system on the property. The fine payable was $800 together with costs in the amount of $1,000.

In the case of Luzak, decided January 22, 2001, the salesperson advertised properties for sale even though the properties were under exclusive listing agreements with other brokers. This unauthorized advertising constituted unprofessional conduct, as well as a violation of the Obligations regarding advertising. The salesperson's position was that he was only advertising the properties as a potential buyer salesperson and that he could see nothing wrong with what he was doing. He further implied that these matters are not explained fully to most sellers who sign exclusive listings, and if sellers did understand, they would never have agreed to them.

On receiving complaints about these activities, the salesperson attempted to contact some of the sellers directly, to try to convince them that they had not truly understood what was meant by providing the listing salesperson with the sole authority to advertise that the property was for sale. This behaviour was further proof that the salesperson was attempting to interfere with the relationship between a listing salesperson and his client. The penalty in this case amounted to $6,000, with costs of $1,100.

In the discipline case of Woelk, decided February 4, 2002, the clients had a buyer representation agreement with a salesperson. During the currency of this agreement, the buyers then contacted the salesperson about other properties. Woelk did not inquire whether there was another firm involved, nor did he try to contact the other realty firm, going on to sign the buyers to a different buyer salesperson agreement. The buyers subsequently purchased a property through his efforts. It was held that his action constituted unprofessional conduct in that he did not make any attempt to verify the existence of a second buyer representation relationship with the buyers, and failed to advise the buyers that they were potentially making themselves liable to pay two commissions on the same purchase, to each of the buyer salespeople noted in their two separate agreements. The penalty in this case was $750 and $250 in costs.

Weisleder's Wisdom on . . . DEALING WITH OTHER REGISTRANTS

1. Always verify whether your client is under an agreement with another salesperson. Get this confirmation in writing.

2. Never try to contact a client of another salesperson directly.

BROKER RESPONSIBILITY

Brokers and salespersons

2. (1) A broker or salesperson shall not do or omit to do anything that causes the brokerage that employs the broker or salesperson to contravene this Regulation.

(2) Subsection (1) does not apply to a contravention by the brokerage of sections 32, 33, or 41.

Duty to ensure compliance

41. (1) A brokerage shall ensure that every salesperson and broker that the brokerage employs is carrying out their duties in compliance with this Regulation.

(2) A broker of record shall ensure that the brokerage complies with this Regulation.

In the decision of Madsen, decided April 30, 2002, the salesperson was reported as having advertised the following: "Don't be misled. We pay 2.5% commissions to every selling broker." There were several listings where 2.5% was not paid by this broker. Section 37, False Advertising, under REBBA had thus been violated. The salesperson paid a penalty of $1,200, and the broker paid $750 plus costs in the amount of $1,700.

The subject of misleading advertising is discussed in greater detail later in this chapter. The decision above was interesting in terms of the panel's views on broker responsibility for advertisements that bear the broker's name. The panel noted the following:

> Since transactions are carried out in the broker's name and the Real Estate and Business Brokers Act mandates that any advertisement by a salesperson clearly identify the broker with whom the

salesperson is registered, brokers should be scrupulous in ensuring that advertisements which are published are accurate and not misleading to the general public or to other RECO Members. Inaccurate, misleading advertisements do not only adversely affect the reputations of individual salespersons and brokers; they can also erode public confidence in the integrity of the real estate profession as a whole.

As you can see, the broker, for the general protection of the public, is held to an almost absolute liability standard when it comes to certain offences committed by the salespeople who work for them. For this reason, brokers must have proper guidelines in place as to how all advertising will be conducted. For example, they should ensure that the name of the broker is always prominently displayed in any advertising by any salesperson or broker from that brokerage. Also, each real estate office should develop a process by which written approval must be obtained for all advertising that is intended for the public, whether it is to appear in newspapers, on radio or television, or even just in newsletters and flyers.

In the case of Ebrahim, decided January 9, 2002, already discussed in detail under Obligation 3, Fairness, Honesty, the broker was also found to have been responsible for this salesperson's actions. In their defence, the broker indicated that they had no knowledge of any matters related to the transaction in question. No one had brought any concerns to the broker's attention, including the listing salesperson and all other parties in the transaction. The broker also brought in evidence that they held seminars for their salespersons regarding updates in the profession and had repeatedly advised each salesperson not to make any personal promises in a transaction, which was one of the key findings against the salesperson. The panel found that the broker did not provide adequate supervision and therefore was in breach of Obligation 41. The panel concluded that, given the mandatory language of Obligation 41, given that the activities of the salesperson in the circumstances were being carried out in the name of the corporate broker, and given the evidence that the salesperson's conduct was unprofessional, liability for the broker arises under Obligation 41. There is no stated requirement in Obligation 41 that the broker with whom a salesperson is registered must have had knowledge or ought to have known of unprofessional conduct on the part of a salesperson before responsibility under this Obligation 41 will arise.

Again we see that there is a standard of absolute liability that will be imposed in virtually all cases where a salesperson is found to have violated one of the Obligations. Not having knowledge of the behaviour is not accepted as an excuse. Many organizations have initial training programs for their new hires, beyond what is educationally required by the local real estate boards for membership. This includes ongoing supervision by senior salespeople in the office, especially in the first year of the junior salesperson's employment.

There are a number of positive benefits from taking this course of action. A broker that deploys its salespeople to act as mentors to other salespeople empowers its employees. The interest that they take in guiding less experienced salespeople will equally serve to reinforce these important principles in the entire brokerage. Such a broker is also creating loyal employees, and loyal employees are less likely to leave. It has long been demonstrated that those companies that have more loyal employees also have more loyal, and thus more profitable, customers. Engaging senior salespeople with junior ones reduces the risk of errors created by inexperienced salespeople that could result in liability under Obligation 41. It also provides the added benefit of creating long-term loyal employees for your company that will no doubt lead to long-term loyal relationships with your clients.

Weisleder's Wisdom on . . . BROKER RESPONSIBILITY

1. Remember that real estate brokers will be held to a very strict standard of liability for all actions of their employee salespeople.
2. Be vigilant in all advertising conducted by members of your company. Ensure that proper guidelines and approval processes are set.
3. Have a proper orientation for new employees, including all policies, procedures, duties, and systems that they will be expected to learn.
4. Set up a proper supervision and mentoring program for new salespeople, to ensure that the work is performed to an appropriate standard.
5. Creating long-term loyal employees will lead to long-term loyal clients.

COMPETENCE

Conscientious and competent service, etc.
5. A registrant shall provide conscientious service to the registrant's clients and customers and shall demonstrate reasonable knowledge, skill, judgment and competence in providing those services.

Providing opinions, etc.
6. (1) A registrant shall demonstrate reasonable knowledge, skill, judgment and competence in providing opinions, advice or information to any person in respect of a trade in real estate.

(2) Without limiting the generality of subsection (1) or section 5,

(a) a brokerage shall not provide an opinion or advice about the

value of real estate to any person unless the opinion or advice is provided on behalf of the brokerage by a broker or salesperson who has education or experience related to the valuation of real estate; and

(b) a broker or salesperson shall not provide an opinion or advice about the value of real estate to any person unless the broker or salesperson has education or experience related to the valuation of real estate.

Services from others

8. (1) A registrant shall advise a client or customer to obtain services from another person if the registrant is not able to provide the services with reasonable knowledge, skill, judgment and competence or is not authorized by law to provide the services.

(2) A registrant shall not discourage a client or customer from seeking a particular kind of service if the registrant is not able to provide the services with reasonable knowledge, skill, judgment and competence or is not authorized by law to provide the service.

I remember when I first graduated as a lawyer and was called to the bar in Ontario. Under the terms of my membership with the Law Society of Upper Canada, I was immediately deemed to know every law and every statute and procedure that affected any potential client in Canada. This meant that the minute I decided to represent someone in any matter, whether it was a real estate transaction, a civil proceeding, or drafting a will, I was expected to immediately know everything that someone would know who had practised in a specific area for 10 years. Talk about high — and unreasonable — expectations! I could never be expected to know everything — besides, everything wasn't covered in my textbooks at law school.

The fact is, most of what you do daily in the real estate profession is not available in a textbook. You can only learn by practising. At the beginning of my career, every file that I worked on was supervised by a senior lawyer at my firm. I was also given precedent files so I could review all the forms that were involved in a typical transaction and read up on related issues that affected the transaction as well.

Most who are involved in the day-to-day real estate law practice will tell you that even after 20 years of being expert in one area of the law, they are still learning new things. It is generally recognized that you must continuously update yourself with education programs as the law is always changing and the way we practise continues to change. Who would have thought 10 years ago that title transfers could be done with the push of a button from a computer in your office, in less than a minute, as compared with day-long lineups at the registry office?

Yet this is what the competency Obligation is all about. You are expected to know everything that a senior practitioner with experience would know when representing a client. It is never an excuse that you could not know something because you were not in the business long enough. That is why, if you are unsure about anything, or are dealing with a new situation, always ask for assistance, or refer the client to someone else who can provide the necessary assistance.

Even after I had developed an expertise in real estate transactions, I was still uncomfortable about handling a cottage property transaction, because I was not familiar with local issues. I remember doing a transaction and sending a letter to the Department of Health asking about the condition of the septic system at a cottage property. I received a letter in response telling me that I should contact the Ministry of Environment. So I sent a letter to that ministry and received a letter stating that I should be calling the Department of Health. Back to square one. I had no idea how to check the legality of the system. It was only through contact with local lawyers that I learned that in this particular town this fell under the jurisdiction of the local Building Department and that I should speak to a local inspector who was very knowledgeable about these issues.

Similar principles apply to real estate agreements. If you are not sure about something, ask for assistance. When you are relatively new in the business, never prepare an offer unless you have had it approved by a senior salesperson or the broker in your office who is acting in a supervisory role to you.

In the same way, do not assume that knowing how to do a certain type of transaction, such as a resale residential home in an urban area, automatically qualifies you to give advice on a cottage property purchase, a commercial property, or a condominium. Each area requires a certain expertise that only comes with experience. Recognize when you need assistance and do not be afraid to ask for help. It may take longer to get a transaction completed, or you may even be forced to give up a potential client, but in the end you will succeed in serving the clients you do take on in the most professional manner possible. This is what Obligation 8, Services from Others, is all about. Do not be afraid to rely on assistance, at any time, if it will benefit your client.

When we examine the errors that salespeople make under this Obligation, in many instances it is based on careless errors and is also often combined with Obligation 21, failing to discover the material facts in a transaction. When you don't check out all the proper facts, by not listening to your client's needs, you will be in violation of your duty of competence. Your client has the right to expect that when they tell you their needs and concerns, you not only will listen to them, but, more importantly, you will also find out anything that relates to their concerns and then protect them when drafting the written agreement.

The bar is raised as well when you are acting for a buyer,

both in recommending the appropriate conditions to protect them and then writing those conditions correctly when completing the agreement. In Chapter 1, in the discussion of conditions and the case of Marshall, we saw just how important it was to accurately state all appropriate language in a condition, especially when representing a buyer.

The discipline case of Sawan, decided September 24, 2002, involved a number of instances where the standards displayed by the salesperson did not satisfy the duty of competence. There was a residential tenant on the property being sold. It was understood by all that there would have to be vacant possession granted on closing. The salesperson took it upon himself to prepare the notice to the tenant, in accordance with the applicable tenant protection legislation. The notice was given on September 15, 2001, which meant that the tenant did not have to vacate until November 15, 2001. Yet the salesperson said to the buyer that it would be no problem to move the closing up from October 31 to October 18, 2001.

Anyone who practises in the area of residential tenancies knows that there is virtually no guarantee that you can ever give concerning when a tenant will actually vacate a property, regardless of when a notice is given. A seller is much better off obtaining an agreement from the tenant in advance to vacate the property, rather than rely on any notice to terminate. In order to obtain the voluntary agreement of the tenant to vacate, you will probably have to provide some compensation to the tenant. However, this is far more preferable to going through the landlord and tenant tribunal process. Most people do not realize that any notice to vacate given to a residential tenant states right on it that the tenant does not have to vacate the property on the date specified. The tenant has the right to dispute the reason for the notice, after which the landlord will have to commence proceedings to evict the tenant.

Tenants can be very clever in delaying these proceedings. Even if everything goes well, you still have to go through all the steps of serving the correct papers, obtaining a trial date (which usually takes three to four weeks), attending a trial, obtaining and then entering the order, and possibly, in the end, even resorting to calling in the sheriff to forcibly evict the tenant. You can also expect counterarguments from the tenants in these proceedings alleging all kinds of human rights abuses, failure to provide essential services, and of course, harassment — sometimes even sexual harassment.

There are also "professional tenants," experts in all areas of landlord and tenant law who know how to delay the process for up to six months. Even if all goes well, you are still looking at another 60 days from the date set out in your notice until the date you obtain vacant possession. Furthermore, if you have an uncooperative tenant, it will be difficult for you to conduct showings or open houses to even sell the property in the first place.

It is far more preferable, therefore, to obtain the voluntary agreement of the tenant in advance to vacate. This will lead to a more cooperative tenant when you show the property and provide no headaches when it comes time to deliver vacant possession on closing. Yes, it may cost the seller some money, maybe even two months' rent. But remember, the worst settlement is still much better than the best lawsuit. A typical landlord and tenant proceeding will take two to six months. You will waste at least one to two days at the tribunal hearing and incur legal fees on top of that which will be nearly impossible to recover.

Had Mr. Sawan practised in this area of real estate, he would have realized not only that the tenant did not have to move out until November 15, 2001, but that there was a possibility that he could still be on the property until well into 2002 if the notice was disputed. Fortunately for him, he was able to obtain the agreement of the tenant to vacate prior to the October 31, 2001, closing date.

It would not be a valid defence to state that you are not an expert in tenancy law. If you take it on yourself to obtain vacant possession of a property, you will be deemed to know all the consequences.

As part of the preparation process, whether with buyers or sellers, the issue of residential tenancies may arise. Whenever a seller has the property rented to tenants, you must immediately review with the owner the obstacles that they may face if they want to give vacant possession of the property on closing. Do not wait until an offer is signed to deal with what may be an uncooperative tenant. Do this right away, before a lot of time and money is invested in marketing the property for sale.

From a buyer standpoint, most first-time home buyers are currently renting an apartment. As the salesperson, you must therefore make inquiries as to what obligations they have under any lease commitment. Even if their lease is month to month, they will still have to provide the landlord with 60 days' notice prior to vacating their unit. You will want to ensure that you fix a closing date with this in mind, so that your clients are not paying additional rental costs on their current apartment after their purchase transaction has been completed.

We discussed in Chapter 1 how conditions should be worded. In the Sawan case, the salesperson inserted a condition for the benefit of the buyers as follows:

> This offer is conditional upon the buyer's solicitor reviewing the following condominium corporations documentation: Status Certificate, the last annual financial statements and finding all of the foregoing satisfactory to the buyer's solicitor's sole and unfettered discretion.

The clause was partially satisfactory but failed to contain the consequences clause: that is, what happens if the solicitor is not satisfied? Can the buyer get out of the deal? As we saw in the Marshall case, judges view the actual language in a condition very strictly. It is easy to see how mistakes such as these can be made. How many salespeople make it a practice to just copy the clause or simply cut and paste clauses from their office precedents into agreements? Not taking the proper care in preparing your documents is how errors happen.

The failure of the salesperson to include this consequences language was found to be a violation of his duty of competence by the discipline committee. The salesperson also told the buyer and the seller that it would be "no problem" moving the closing date of the transaction from October 31 to October 18, but nothing was obtained in writing. It is clear that any important change to the agreement, such as a change in the closing date, must be made with a written amendment signed by both parties. The salesperson's actions were deemed to be a violation of Obligation 3 and Obligation 4, Best Interests of Client.

Finally, there was a problem with the central vacuum system on the property. This system was not in operating condition on closing. The discipline committee found that the agreement should have contained language that at least stated that the chattels to be conveyed would be in good working order on closing.

Most sellers will not give warranties that survive closing. That is why they permit buyers to conduct home inspections, to satisfy themselves of the condition of the property and any chattels to be assumed on closing. However, most sellers will probably not object to a clause that states that these same chattels will be in good working order on the date of closing. The Sawan case indicates that this will be a minimum standard required of salespeople who act for buyers. If the clause is inserted and then removed by the seller, it can then be discussed with the buyer as to the consequences of its removal.

Then the decision is the buyer's to make. However, by not inserting the clause in the first place, there is no proof that the issue was ever even discussed with the buyer. The penalty given for all violations in the Sawan case was $2,500 and $1,900 for costs.

The discipline case of Porteous, decided May 15, 2001, is a good example of what happens when you act for someone buying a property in an area where you are not familiar with many of the local issues. In this case, the salesperson acted as a buyer representative. He showed the buyers a property in an area where he had not practised before, based on a newspaper advertisement that the buyers had discovered themselves.

The salesperson told the buyers that in his opinion, home inspections were generally of no benefit because inspectors needed to give favourable reports. He would have recommended a contractor instead, he said. The point is that no home inspection was conducted prior to the offer being signed.

The agreement did provide that the seller would supply a well driller's certificate confirming that the flow of water on the property was at least three gallons per minute, and a certificate from the Ministry of Health confirming that the water was suitable for human consumption. The health certificate was obtained. Only one water test was conducted.

It turned out after closing that there was a problem with the drinking water. It was normal in this area to conduct at least three such tests on any well prior to closing any transactions, and it was common knowledge for practitioners in the area. Proper tests were conducted by the buyer after closing, and it was found that the water was, in fact, unsafe for drinking.

It was also discovered after closing that nothing was filled in on the seller property information statement in the area asking, "Are you aware of any problem re quantity or quality of the well water?" This lack of disclosure was not conveyed by the salesperson to the buyer. In addition, there were many structural and mechanical problems with the house on the property that probably would have been discovered if an appropriate home inspection had been conducted.

Besides finding that Obligation 3, Honesty, Fairness, and Obligation 21, Material Facts, were violated, the panel deemed that there was a lack of competence. The salesperson should have investigated more thoroughly the suitability of this property to the buyer. A proper home inspection should have been conducted, and more care should have been taken with the testing of the water. This is especially necessary since the Walkerton tragedy in Southern Ontario in the year 2000. I know many people in other parts of the country who refuse to drink municipal tap water to this day, even though there is nothing indicating any problems in most municipal water systems. The penalty for the salesperson was $5,000 plus costs of $1,600.

The competence Obligation also makes clear that salespeople should only assign tasks to unregistered staff that are appropriate for unregistered persons to perform. Some of the duties that should not be delegated include attendance at open houses, as well as preparation and/or presentation of offers and negotiations about offers. In the case of Carmen, decided January 11, 2001, the salesperson brought an unregistered assistant on an offer presentation. The salesperson indicated that the reason she brought the assistant was because she was concerned about security since she was visiting several properties that day. While the committee acknowledged that security was a valid reason, the unregistered salesperson should still not have been permitted to attend the offer presentation and to make comments during the negotiations. The fine in the case was $1,000.

Other activities that cross the line in this context include having an unlicensed employee do door-to-door or telephone solicitations, or show properties. It also includes giving them access to lock boxes that enable other registered salespeople to show a property when the listing salesperson is not available. In the case of Amyotte, decided September 15, 2003, the salesperson used an unlicensed third party described as "part of the Amyotte team" to conduct a signback with the seller. This was also held to be a violation of Obligation 5.

Weisleder's Wisdom on . . . COMPETENCE

1. You will always be held to the standard of an experienced salesperson or broker who practises in the field you are working in.

2. This standard encompasses not only areas of law that relate to your business, but local issues that may only be known by local salespeople. Therefore, do not practise alone out of your own territory.

3. Do not permit unregistered salespeople to participate in any offer preparation, presentation, or negotiation.

4. If you are not sure about something, ask for assistance.

5. Do not give advice outside your area of expertise, such as landlord-tenant rights or whether a home inspection should be conducted.

6. Always listen to your client's instructions and follow through on any commitments you have made.

FALSE ADVERTISING

Advertising
36. (1) A registrant shall clearly and prominently disclose the name in which the registrant is registered in all the registrant's advertisements.

(2) A brokerage that identifies a broker or salesperson by name in an advertisement shall use the name in which the broker or salesperson is registered.

(3) A broker or salesperson shall not advertise in any manner unless the advertisement clearly and prominently identifies the brokerage that employs the broker or salesperson, using the name in which the brokerage is registered.

(4) A registrant who advertises shall,
(a) use the term "brokerage", "real estate brokerage", "maison de courtage" or "maison de courtage immobilier" to describe any brokerage that is referred to in the advertisement;
(b) use the term "broker of record", "real estate broker of record", "maison de courtage responsable" or "maison de courtage immobilier responsable" to describe any broker of record that is referred to in the advertisement;
(c) use the term "broker", "real estate broker", "courtier" or "courtier immobilier" to describe any broker of record that is referred to in the advertisement;
(d) use the term "salesperson", "real estate salesperson", "sales representative", "real estate sales representative", "agent immobilier", "representant commercial" or "representant immobilier" to describe any salesperson who is referred to in the advertisement.

(5) Despite clause (4)(c), a registrant who advertises may, before April 1, 2008, use the term "associate broker", "associate real estate broker", "courtier associe" or " courtier immobilier associe" to describe any broker who is referred to in the advertisement.

(6) A registrant who advertises shall not use a term to

describe any registrant that is referred to in the advertisement if the term could reasonably be confused with a term that is required or authorized by subsection (4) or (5).

(7) A registrant shall not include anything in an advertisement that could reasonably be used to identify a party to the acquisition or disposition of an interest in real estate unless the party has consented in writing.

(8) A registrant shall not include anything in an advertisement that could reasonably be used to identify specific real estate unless the owner of the real estate has consented in writing.

(9) A registrant shall not include anything in an advertisement that could reasonably be used to determine any of the contents of an agreement that deals with the conveyance of an interest in real estate including any provision of the agreement relating to the price, unless the parties to the agreement have consented in writing.

Inaccurate representations
37. *(1) A registrant shall not knowingly make an inaccurate representation in respect of a trade in real estate.*

(2) A registrant shall not knowingly make an inaccurate representation about services provided by the registrant.

Real Estate and Business Brokers Act

False advertising. Section 37
37. *No registrant shall make false, misleading or deceptive statements in any advertisement, circular, pamphlet or material published by any means relating to trading in real estate.*

Order of Registrar Re: False Advertising. Section 38

38. (1) If the registrar believes on reasonable grounds that a registrant is making a false, misleading or deceptive statement in any advertisement, circular, pamphlet or material published by any means, the registrar may,

> *(a) order the cessation of the use of such material;*
>
> *(b) order the registrant to retract the statement or publish a correction of equal prominence to the original publication; or*
>
> *(c) order both a cessation described in clause (a) and a retraction or correction described in clause (b).*

When we examine the Wheel of Misfortune for complaints made to RECO against real estate salespeople, the number one category is false advertising. In order to understand why salespeople are violating the false advertising provision under REBBA and Obligations 36 and 37, we need to understand what these provisions mean.

The law of false or misleading advertising in the private sector in Canada is governed by the federal Competition Act, yet the principles under RECO are very similar to the ones that flow from this federal legislation. The test used in any RECO hearing is the test that most judges use in any commercial dispute, asking, "How would a reasonable person in this situation interpret the advertising?" In the private sector, if the wording is written in a manner that is likely to deceive, substantial fines and penalties under the Competition Act may be invoked to serve as a deterrent and as a protection for the general public interest. The fact that these offences under the Competition Act carry significant civil fines and even criminal liability shows just how important this issue is to the federal government.

The test as to whether an advertisement in the real estate sector is misleading is not the meaning taken by the skilled and knowledgeable members of the public, but by the uninitiated and inexperienced who are exposed to it. In other words, what general impression does the advertisement leave? Let's look at some cases in which salespeople have faced difficulty under this obligation.

In the case of Siu, decided August 7, 2003, a complaint was made against the salesperson by another salesperson. At issue were the salesperson's advertising activities. The particulars were as follows.

• The salesperson claimed in his advertisements that "We sell 1 house every 3 days."

• The broker's name was considerably smaller than the salesperson's name.

• The salesperson advertised properties sold by him without obtaining the written consent of the buyers.

When the committee looked at the facts surrounding the salesperson's sales records, it was clear that he did not sell one house every three days, in the literal meaning of the words. For this reason, he had violated Obligation 37.

When a salesperson commits a violation of this Obligation, there is usually a violation of Obligation 3, Fairness, Honesty; Obligation 21, Material Facts; Obligation 38, Error, Misrepresentation; and Obligation 39, Unprofessional Conduct. (Unprofessional conduct can be looked at as a catch-all Obligation for any act that harms the interest of the public.)

The salesperson had to pay an administrative penalty of $3,000 as a result of this matter. His broker had to pay a $2,000 penalty as well, under Obligation 41, in which the broker is held responsible for the professional actions of members registered with it. The broker was deemed to have permitted the salesperson to place the advertisements that were false and misleading, that displayed the salesperson's name in larger type than the broker's name, and that did not disclose the salesperson's correct status as a salesperson.

Showing a salesperson's name much more prominently than the broker's name in an advertisement is a common violation of Obligation 36. It is worth noting the rather amusing situation involving Fulford, in a decision dated July 10, 2001. Mr. Fulford, an enterprising salesperson, rented a billboard in cottage country that displayed his name the same size as the broker's name. However, at night, the neon lights on the billboard displayed only the name of the salesperson, not the name of the broker.

In this case, the salesperson was required to repair the sign. A penalty was not awarded. I imagine the committee may have been slightly amused by his ingenuity. The salesperson had also been in constant contact with the RECO committee and had given his written undertaking to make the necessary changes to the sign shortly after being contacted about the problem.

In the case of Bird, decided April 15, 2003, the broker advertised that he was personally involved with 186 real estate transactions in 2001, or alternatively, that he "completed 222 transactions in 2001." It was later found that this was inaccurate because it also included sales by other salespersons who worked for the brokerage. Furthermore, this broker counted a sale twice if he acted for both the buyer and the seller. There was no qualifying language in the advertisements. The ad was found to be clearly misleading to the general public, in accordance with the general impression tests and principles noted above.

The issue of qualifying language brings up the discussion of typical disclaimers that are found on many advertisements, usually with an asterisk placed somewhere and then qualified in the fine print at the bottom. There are common-sense principles associated with how we can use qualifying language. For example, the fine print cannot be used to distort the main meaning of the advertisement. It should not contradict the more prominent aspects of the advertisement and should be clearly visible. Consider an ad in which the words "Safe Beach" were asterisked to a note in the fine print that said, "Don't go in the water." Hey, don't laugh — it happens.

In the case of Mr. Siu noted above, it was found that he did not clearly set out his registration status as a salesperson in the advertisement. It was noted that "inconspicuous at the bottom left-hand corner (of the advertisement), in extremely fine print, were the words 'Harry Siu, Sales Representative.'" It is clear, then, that RECO does not consider inserting this kind of information into an advertisement by means of an asterisk as having complied with the Code of Ethics. Mr. Siu was found in violation of Obligation 37 as a result of this action. The broker was found in violation of Obligation 41, Duty to Ensure Compliance, in permitting Mr. Siu to advertise in this way.

One of the ways the Bird case was resolved, besides the levying of an administrative penalty of $2,500, which Mr. Bird paid, was by receiving his agreement to use appropriate qualifying language in all his future advertisements. This language was to be "in a typeface and in a sufficiently prominent position, as appropriate to the advertising medium, so that they are clearly legible."

But he had also advertised that his clients saved "hundreds of thousands of dollars by using his firm." This was based on the fact that when his company acted on both sides of a transaction, they only charged 3.5% commission, while the assumption is that most sellers pay 6% for a similar listing commission with other realtors. The 6% was deemed misleading because this was not the uniform rate charged by most firms in this trading area at the time. Furthermore, the advertisements were deemed not to disclose sufficient information so that the reader could truly understand the basis of the claim being made.

As part of the final decision, Mr. Bird also agreed that in any future advertisement of this kind, he would clearly add in accompanying language that "the claim is based on the difference between the actual commission rate clients were charged and a hypothetical rate, as well as disclosure of the circumstances in which the actual rate was charged" (that it was in a situation where they acted for both the buyer and the seller). The statement also had to indicate that the hypothetical rate used was not a universal rate charged by all brokers and that commission rates are completely negotiable.

In addition, Mr. Bird agreed not to advertise any future property being sold without the consent of the owner, following up on the principle from the Siu decision as well (and as discussed in Chapter 4 on privacy legislation).

The reason for qualifying language is clear: to make sure that the public understands the real basis of any claim that you make and is not misled in any way.

I realize that in some of the advertisements I see in the newspaper, the disclaimer language is so small that it is barely readable or understandable. However, it usually will pass any challenge under the federal Competition Act. It seems clear from RECO's interpretation about the false advertising and misleading statement obligations under both REBBA and the Code of Ethics that there may be a higher standard expected of real estate salespeople in this area, to ensure that the public interest is protected.

Many principles have been developed regarding comparison advertising, such as when a company attempts to claim that its products are better than its competitor's products. Due to the high-profile nature of this type of advertising, and the negative effect it can have on the competitor's products, companies must be very careful to have the appropriate backup to prove what they say.

Suppose someone advertised the following:

I am the no. 1 agent in Canada*

* In XYZ realty.

As you can see, the fine print drastically modifies the statement. If someone did not read the small print, they would adopt a much different impression.

This was so in the case of Katirai, decided November 12, 2002. Ms. Katirai had signs similar to the above advertised on a property that was for sale. Someone driving by would not have seen the modifying language on the sign, which identified the brokerage in small print.

The discipline committee thus concluded that the advertising was in fact misleading, in violation of Obligation 37. The salesperson was fined $5,000. The broker was also found responsible for the salesperson's actions under Obligation 41 and was fined $2,500. Furthermore, the salesperson was charged $1,400 for the costs of the proceedings, while the broker had to pay $700 toward costs.

In the discipline decision of Siu, dated October 24, 2001, the salesperson claimed in flyers that were distributed that he was the number one salesperson in total units and dollar value sold in North Scarborough during the past 10 years. The committee looked at information obtained, which clearly indicated that another person was in fact the number one salesperson in total units and dollars sold in the area claimed by Mr. Siu in his advertising.

As the foregoing case illustrates, in order to make the claim that you are the number one salesperson, you must have the backup that proves the claim to the committee if challenged. For example, have you sold more homes than anyone else? Is the dollar value of all sales that you have done higher than anyone else? Did you earn the most real estate commissions in your area?

In the case of Boutette, decided October 30, 2003, the salesperson wrote the following on bench advertising: "Guelph's #1 Specialist." There was no qualifying language. The salesperson's name was also more prominent than the broker's and did not disclose the salesperson's status as a salesperson. Moreover, there was no evidence that the salesperson was a specialist. Besides violating Obligation 37, Advertisement, the case was found to be a violation of Obligation 38, Error, Misrepresentation, and Obligation 39, Unprofessional Conduct. The fine was $1,000 to the principal of the brokerage and $3,000 to the brokerage itself, with costs of $1,000.

Consider this advertisement:

> **I have sold 10 homes within 5 days of listing, all at full price or more.**

This claim came under scrutiny in the Clarke case, decided June 20, 2002. On further examination, it was learned that some of the properties sold below full price, and the number of days until some of the properties sold had been understated as well. The penalty for the false advertising claim was $3,000 together with costs in the amount of $1,700.

Or take a look at this advertisement that came up in the case of Wallis-Simpson, decided July 31, 2002:

> ### Guaranteed Sale Program.
>
> ### Move up to one of our homes and we will buy yours for cash.

There were no other qualifiers in the ad. Not even the words "Terms and conditions apply," which are sometimes found in similar situations. The broker had printed a brochure about this guaranteed sales program. An examination of all the conditions applicable to this promotion made it clear that few buyers would in fact qualify for the program. None of these terms was referred to in the advertisement itself.

It's easy to give a guarantee. It is a lot harder to stand behind it. If you are going to advertise an unconditional guarantee, you had better be able to stand behind it, or you will be the subject of a discipline or legal proceeding.

In the Wallis-Simpson example, the broker was found to be in violation of Obligation 37 and was required to pay a penalty of $3,500 and $1,700 in costs.

In a case involving Wilson and Flat Fee Realty Inc., decided August 16, 2001, the following ad appeared:

> ### WOW! Why Pay? 6% 5% 4% 3%
> ### Full Service for Less with
> ### Flat Fee Realty Inc.

The allegation in the case was that the advertising was misleading since it gave the impression that all fees would be less than 3% when in fact some fees were greater than 3% — and even greater than 6% under certain circumstances. The panel found that, while the phrase "Full Service for Less" was not in itself misleading, it was so when combined with the declining commission percentages. The penalty was $500 against Wilson, $1,000 against Flat Fee Inc., and costs in the amount of $900.

Here's another claim to consider:

> **Top three Companies,**
> **MLS Production Per Agent**
> **MLS Statistics from January 1, 2000**
> **till October 31, 2000**

This advertisement was not placed in the newspaper but was used by the broker as a recruiting tool to attract new sales-people to their office. This broker did in fact have supporting evidence to make the claim, and as a result, there was found to be no violation of the obligation. The following statement from the decision is also interesting:

> There is always "boasting" by firms in advertising, whether it be real estate or otherwise. In this case, as there was no clear false statement, we cannot find Broker A in violation. However, RECO does take a dim view of any member that purposely produces advertising that misleads or confuses either the public or other parties and reminds members that they must be vigilant in ensuring the accuracy of their advertising.

This can probably be distinguished from the tongue-in-cheek, humorous advertising we are all familiar with. I have seen an ad by a salesperson who purports to have sold the Canadian Parliament buildings in Ottawa. Perhaps many members of the public wish it could be that easy to get rid of the government. It is doubtful that anyone would bring an action for false advertising against this salesperson. Most members would take the ad in the spirit in which it was written. Similarly, I have seen a salesperson with a sold sign outside Casa Loma, one of Toronto's noted landmarks. Due to the fact that most people would not take this ad seriously, we can also say there was no attempt to deceive the public.

We will later review, under Obligation 21, the results of failing to discover the correct facts, and how this alone can get salespeople acquainted with the Wheel of Misfortune. Sometimes factual situations under Obligation 21 also catch Obligation 37, when you enter information onto the local MLS system. For example, if you do not do your homework in finding out the actual dimensions of a property or the building located on it, or any features describing the property, you will invariably contravene Obligation 37 when you try to advertise the property for sale, since you will be putting false advertising out to the public.

In the case of Swartz, decided June 14, 2002, the salesperson erred in collecting facts about the seller's property and advertised a building with 7,000 square feet when it only had 6,300 square feet. The facts, which were agreed to by both parties, were deemed to violate both Obligation 21 and Obligation 37. The fine for the salesperson was $2,000, as well as costs of $1,500.

In a similar situation, involving Boyko, decided June 12, 2002, advertising contained information that the property was comprised of 2.75 acres, when in fact it was only 2.02 acres. Even though there was no intent to deceive anyone, the salesperson was found to have been careless in not verifying the information. The salesman made the argument that they should not be held responsible when they were relying on information told to them by the seller. However, we can see from the decision that responsibility is placed on a salesperson to try to find out important information, such as lot size, from other sources if the seller does not have sufficient information, before making any advertising claims. The penalty in this case was $4,000, and costs amounted to $1,700.

To assign liability under Obligation 37, RECO does not have to prove that the salesperson or broker intended to deceive anyone. Even if the misleading statement is created inadvertently, the salesperson will still be held liable. In the case of Long, decided July 17, 2002, it was held that through inadvertence, the listing omitted information about an excluded third-party offer. Even though there was a finding of fact that this was not intended by the salesperson, the salesperson still had to pay a relatively small fine, $250, but also had to pay the full costs of $1,700.

A similar situation can be found in the decision of Kurtz, decided October 28, 2003. In this estate sale, the salesperson viewed the property personally to obtain the information for the MLS listing. He made an innocent error in describing that the house had aluminum siding when it really was wood. Although the panel found that this was the kind of error that could have been made by a salesperson of the "highest standards," it was still deemed to be a violation of Obligation 37. If the salesperson was not 100% sure, then he should not have included this detail on a listing. Even though the error was not deemed malicious, it also unfortunately violated Obligation 38, Error, Misrepresentation, about misrepresenting anything, as well as Obligation 39, Unprofessional Conduct. In the circumstances, there was no penalty awarded, but the salesperson was required to pay costs in the amount of $1,750.

Many will view this decision as being overly critical of the salesperson. Yet it does continue to illustrate the important principle of taking the time when you are gathering information from the seller to ensure that every fact contained in the MLS listing that will be viewed by the public is accurate and reliable. This will not remove any obligation of a buyer's salesperson to always be recommending a home inspection, but it does serve to protect the public interest by holding all salespeople to a higher standard when making this information available to the public.

Many real estate boards are now considering the practice of limiting situations in which brokers can insert the words "contact listing broker" in the remarks section of the listing. The intent is that all pertinent material information must be shown on the listing itself. All this reinforces your obligation to do what you can to get things right in the first place, when you are in the process of gathering information from your seller.

In Ontario, RECO has published a set of advertising standards guidelines to ensure that all issues surrounding advertising have been complied with by the brokerage. These include guidelines about the form of the advertisement and which terms can be used, such as when you can use the word "team." They also provide guidelines as to what verification you must have before you can make any performance claims. Finally, they refer to consents that you must have from buyers and sellers before advertising their personal information, in accordance with the privacy laws outlined in Chapter 4. By following these guidelines, you should have no difficulty with RECO, other salespeople, and more importantly, the public.

Regardless what your provincial Code of Ethics may say about advertising, these principles will remain the same. Since advertising by its nature is very public, and violations can have a negative effect on consumer perceptions toward the real estate profession in general, it's a small wonder that so many cases involving violations of the Codes of Ethics have to do with violations of this Obligation on advertising. By following the principles set out in this chapter, you stand a great chance of never running afoul of the Wheel of Misfortune.

Weisleder's Wisdom on . . . FALSE ADVERTISING

1. Always have your advertising reviewed by your broker or another salesperson in the office.

2. Ask yourself, "What impression am I creating with this advertisement? Is it likely to mislead anyone?" If you are not sure, get another opinion.

3. Make sure that the brokerage's name is at least as prominent as the salesperson's name.

4. Always specify your registration status in any advertisement, in a size that can be clearly recognized in the ad itself. Make sure your business cards also show the brokerage's name equally as prominent.

5. If you make any performance claim, make sure that you have the data to back it up.

6. Make no guarantees.

7. Make sure all your facts about a property are correct before you make any advertisements about the property.

8. If there is any qualifying language or disclaimer, make sure that it is large enough for anyone to see in the ordinary review of the advertisement, whether in a newspaper or flyer or on a billboard.

9. Print a copy of any RECO guidelines on advertising as a reference for all advertising produced in your office.

10. Make sure you have the proper consents of buyers and sellers before advertising anything about their properties, in accordance with the obligations under the federal Privacy Act.

11. Assume that every advertisement may be reviewed by your provincial real estate council.

12. If the advertisement seems a little on the edge, ask yourself, "Is this worth a proceeding for the next eight months

of my life, possible penalties, and a starring role on the RECO website?" Then read the ad again.

USING YOUR NAME CORRECTLY

Obligation 36 under advertising contains the requirement to use only the correct brokerage name that is registered with RECO. It is very important that all brokerages follow these guidelines, especially now that we have seen some of the consequences of on-line advertising and issues regarding the registration of domain names.

In the case of Tatomir, decided January 20, 2003, Mr. Tatomir registered website addresses containing his competitors' names, with pointers on the website. As a result of the pointers, if a consumer attempted to find the competitor's website, they were automatically routed to Mr. Tatomir's own website. Mr. Tatomir claimed that he did nothing wrong by purchasing these other website addresses as they were available and not being used at the time.

The panel found that this behaviour constituted a violation of Obligation 36 in that Mr. Tatomir was not conducting business under his registered name. It was also found to be a violation of Obligation 3, Fairness, Honesty, which protects the public from fraud, misrepresentation, or unethical practice in connection with real estate transactions. This was further found to be a violation of Obligation 39 because "most people would view this conduct as dishonourable and unprofessional."

The law is currently being written regarding website names and trademark violations in other commercial areas. None of those decisions was referred to in Mr. Tatomir's case. In the meantime, a very common-sense rule of thumb is being used: Is it likely that this practice could deceive the general public? In this case the answer was yes, and the penalty against Mr. Tatomir was $5,000.

In the similar case of Kewley, decided October 30, 2003, the salesperson registered domain names that were similar to other brokers in the area such that if someone typed in the name of the other brokers, they would be led to Mr. Kewley's website. The penalty in this case was $4,000 and $1,350 in costs.

As stated in the section about Obligation 3 on ethical behaviour, your reputation is your brand image that you build during the course of your career. It is what leads to successful referrals as well as loyal clients who return to use your services in the future. As these cases demonstrate, you must do everything you can to make sure that no one else tries to trade or encroach onto the brand name that you or your company creates in your community. This happens when salespeople open companies with similar sounding names, or use any website manoeuvring to try to show connections to your own company. Be vigilant.

In the case of Dodds, decided April 3, 2002, the salesperson was found to have violated Obligation 36 for carelessly carrying on business under the name of Jack Dodds when he was registered with RECO under the name of John Dodds. Although this seems a minor or technical violation, it serves to point out the importance of consistently using the name that you have filed with RECO, with no alterations.

RECO takes name registration very seriously. That is why they always take the position that the name that you use in identifying yourself to the public should be identical to the name that you have been registered under RECO. Do not use any nicknames or any other name that may confuse anyone.

Weisleder's Wisdom on . . . USING YOUR NAME CORRECTLY

1. Be vigilant in how your name is used in all correspondence, advertising, and signage; it must be

consistent with the name that you are registered under.

2. Make sure that no one else is trying to use your name or any part of it in any manner that would create confusion in the public.

3. Do not attempt to use anyone else's registered name improperly, either through Internet links or other advertising.

4. If you discover a situation in which someone is trying to use all or part of your name, act immediately with written correspondence, followed by legal action, if necessary, to protect your rights.

MATERIAL FACTS

Material facts

21. (1) A broker or salesperson who has a client in respect of the acquisition or disposition of a particular interest in real estate shall take reasonable steps to determine the material facts relating to the acquisition or disposition and, at the earliest practicable opportunity, shall disclose the material facts to the client.

(2) A broker or salesperson who has a customer in respect of the acquisition or disposition of a particular interest in real estate shall at the earliest practicable opportunity, disclose to the customer the material facts relating to the acquisition or disposition that are known by or ought to be known by the broker or salesperson.

In the decision of Polson and Bell, decided January 28, 2003, the seller told the listing salesperson that the property taxes were $5,300, and this amount was shown on the listing information. The sellers were not able to provide written confirmation. The listing salesperson did nothing further to verify the taxes. It turned out that they were in fact $6,248. The buyer salesperson also did not attempt to verify them, even after being advised that the taxes were approximate. It was found by the panel that both salespeople were thus in violation of Obligation 21 in failing to discover pertinent facts relating to a property. The fines were $1,800 for each salesperson and the broker and $1,000 in costs for each party.

These kinds of errors are not made intentionally. There is no intent to deceive anyone. It is a case of simple carelessness in not verifying all important facts about a property.

In a similar decision regarding Sidofsky and Tsang, decided May 10, 2001, the parties recorded the taxes as $1,680.96 in the listing information when in fact this amount was only the interim tax bill. The actual taxes were $3,361.95. Not only were the salespeople found to have violated Obligation 21, they were also deemed to have violated Obligation 37 relating to false advertising. The penalties in this case were $200 each. All this could have been avoided if they were just a little more careful.

As often happens, a violation of Obligation 21 also brings about a violation of Obligation 5, Competence, as well as Obligation 4, Best Interests of Client. In the decision of Bruno, decided February 13, 2003, the salesperson acted in multiple representation without obtaining a buyer representation agreement from the buyer. Although the buyer had expressed concerns about the water quality and recovery rate, no further actions were taken by the salesperson to verify these concerns or include a condition in the agreement to protect the buyer in this regard. The buyer later found out that the quality of the water was unsafe and that the recovery rate was inadequate.

Ms. Bruno was thus found to have breached Obligation 21 about discovery of material facts, Obligation 5, Competence, and Obligation 4, Best Interests of Client. As there was no buyer representation agreement entered into, this was also deemed to be a violation of Obligation 11, Written Representation

Agreements. The penalty was $2,000, with costs of $1,750.

In the case of Verbakel, decided July 17, 2001, the salesperson erred in advertising that the house contained hardwood floors throughout. In fact, many rooms were unfinished. Most of the floors were under carpeting or area rugs. The salesperson stated that he relied on the Seller Property Information Statement filled in by the seller. However, the form was not clearly explained to the seller, and the salesperson took no action to verify any of the statements made. This was deemed to violate Obligation 21, Material Facts, as well as Obligation 4, Best Interests of Client. This also resulted in a violation of Obligation 37 against misleading advertising. The penalty was $750 and costs in the amount of $350.

The salesperson in the case of Karson, decided April 20, 2001, who was acting for both the seller and the buyer, indicated to the buyer that the property was a fully serviced lot. She relied solely on representations made by the seller, without doing any independent verification. The panel found this to be a violation of Obligation 21 as well as Obligation 4. The penalty was $500, with costs of $500.

In the section on competence (Obligation 5) earlier in this chapter, I stressed that if you are not sure about a new geographic area, you should beware of acting in it alone, because you will be held to the same standard as someone who has practised in that region for years. It makes no difference that you were doing your best and were not trying to deceive anyone. In the case of Richie and Grime, decided November 30, 2001, the buyer salesperson, Ms. Grime, was not familiar with the region where the property was being purchased. Had she been from the community, she would have known that an adverse land designation had been passed affecting the property, which would probably have a detrimental financial effect on the property in the long term. The buyers indicated that they would never have signed the agreement in the first place had they known of this designation.

The panel found that Ms. Grime was honest, straightforward, and dedicated to her clients. Save for this lack of knowledge, she was also found to have otherwise acted as a good and prudent representative for her clients. Nevertheless, the panel found that she should have known about this designation, and it was no excuse that she hadn't known about the land designation since she did not live there.

The listing salesperson, Mr. Richie, did know about the adverse designation and did not disclose this, and was thus found in violation of Obligation 3 on dealing fairly, honestly, and with integrity with the public, other members, and third parties. The penalty for Ms. Grime was $1,000 and $300 in costs. The penalty for Mr. Richie was $3,000 and $900 in costs.

In a similar case of Woodley, Irwin, and Rolph, decided October 23, 2003, the seller had completed a Seller Property Information Statement, which indicated that the lands were zoned as "hazard land," meaning that there were limits as to what could be built on the property. This fact was left out of the listing information. The SPIS form was not requested by the buyer salesperson. The buyer salesperson was deemed to have violated Obligation 21 for not checking the seller's property information statement as well as not knowing about the hazard lands situation that affected many properties in this area. In failing to disclose this on the listing information sheet, the listing salesperson was also deemed to have violated Obligation 38 on Misrepresentation as well as Obligation 39 on Unprofessional Conduct. The fines were $5,500 for the listing and buyer salespeople and $1,500 in costs.

As I have indicated, when you violate the principles of the Code of Ethics, you may also put yourself in a position where legal proceedings are brought against you. Most legal cases are framed in negligence, whereby the salesperson has fallen short of the standard expected of him, either through commission of an act or omission. Besides violating the concept of full disclosure, which is usually one of the significant factors in any legal claim, the three Code of Ethics rules that are commonly associated with a legal claim based in negligence are Competence (Obligation 5), Material Facts (Obligation 21), and Misrepresentation (Obligation 38). When a salesperson fails in following these Obligations, he will also leave himself open to a potential legal claim for negligence.

In the legal decision of Winsham, decided April 20, 2001, a listing salesperson had described a property as having 46,600 square feet. The marketing package that accompanied the document attempted to include a disclaimer that the salesperson could not guarantee the accuracy of the document itself. The buyer expressed some concerns about the square footage but was advised by the buyer salesperson that the buyer could be protected with a clause in the agreement. No clause was included as the buyer relied on representations by both the buyer salesperson and the listing salesperson. It turned out that the property contained only 44,697 square feet.

In this case the listing salesperson was careless in that the documents in the seller's possession also indicated the discrepancy in the square footage. The buyer salesperson did not do enough to protect the buyer with a clause in the agreement and/or suggest to the buyer that he retain a surveyor or other expert to assist in the determination of the square footage if it was important to him.

The judge ruled that both the listing and the selling salespeople were partially responsible and had to contribute to the damage award. The buyer was also held to be partially responsible as he was deemed to be somewhat of an expert in these kinds of purchases and could have taken steps on his own to protect himself.

While the seller salesperson was simply not careful in

reviewing the documents that he had in his possession, the buyer salesperson did not listen to his client's concerns. If he had, he would have known that the square footage was important to the buyer and could have protected the buyer either with an appropriate condition or by obtaining an up-to-date survey of the property. Had both salespeople just taken the time to make certain that the facts about the square footage were carefully discovered, this entire legal proceeding could have been avoided.

Weisleder's Wisdom on . . . MATERIAL FACTS

1. Be very careful when checking all facts relating to a transaction.

2. Verify anything told to you by your client with written information or by proper visual inspection, where possible.

3. If information cannot be verified, disclose this as early as possible to your client so that they can make any required informed decision.

4. If a Seller Property Information Statement is available to a buyer salesperson, make sure you review it carefully with your client.

5. After determining your buyer client's needs, be careful in following up all facts necessary to satisfy your client's requirements.

ERROR, MISREPRESENTATION, FRAUD

Error, misrepresentation, fraud, etc.
38. A registrant shall use the registrant's best efforts to prevent error, misrepresentation, fraud or any unethical practice in respect of a trade in real estate.

When a salesperson is in violation of Obligation 38, you can bet that there are legal proceedings taking place at the same time. Any violation of this Obligation virtually also guarantees that the salesperson has violated Obligation 3, Ethical Behaviour, as well as Obligation 39, Unprofessional Conduct. When I look at the cases that have dealt with this issue, I can only wonder, "What were these salespeople thinking?" However, it is easy to criticize someone after the fact, with the benefit of hindsight, without understanding the individual or business pressures that the salesperson may have been under at the time, whether in their personal lives, from their broker who expects them to deliver transactions, or from clients who want to get the deal done.

The moral of many of these cases is that it is never worth it, regardless of the pressure that you may be under. When you falsify a document, or conceal a material fact that will affect a transaction, you are just asking for your membership and registration to be suspended or terminated. You are also leaving yourself open to legal proceedings. As indicated under the discussion about insurance in Chapter 2, there is an exclusion under the errors and omissions policy for fraudulent behaviour. Accordingly, not only may this type of behaviour lead to legal proceedings being brought against you, but the financial costs may be prohibitive to you or your broker if the insurer denies coverage in the circumstances.

In the discipline case involving Sharma, decided May 4, 2001, the salesperson had advertised that buyers could purchase a property with as little as 5% down and that there was a possibility that they could also get 3% of the deposit refunded as well. A buyer who responded to the ad was advised by the salesperson to see if they could initially qualify for a mortgage. As the buyer was only a temporary employee, Sharma advised them that they would not qualify for a mortgage.

Sharma offered to prepare a false employment letter to

assist the buyer and asked for a $300 fee to obtain this letter. The letter that was prepared showed an annual full-time salary of $40,000 and indicated that the buyer was a "valuable asset of the company." The buyer subsequently entered into an Agreement of Purchase and Sale and was able to obtain 90% financing on the basis of the letter. You guessed it: The buyer could not come up with the additional 10%, and the transaction was aborted, with the buyer losing their $3,000 deposit. At the hearing, Sharma filed an undertaking to provide restitution to the buyer.

Given the serious nature of the matter, Sharma was fined $12,000 plus costs of $900, ordered to attend a RECO Code of Ethics course, and placed on probation for the maximum two years.

In the discipline case of Ebrahim, decided March 14, 2003, the salesperson prepared a gift letter to attempt to deceive a financial institution into thinking that the buyers had the sufficient down payment out of their own resources to complete the transaction. The gift letter appeared to be on a standard form document prepared by the salesperson, implying that this tactic may also have been used by the salesperson in the past in other similar transactions. A false employment letter was prepared, showing a false company and a false annual income of $72,500, though there was no direct evidence that this letter was prepared by the salesperson. The transaction was ultimately aborted for a list of related reasons, given that the buyers did not have the resources to complete the transaction.

The salesperson did not attend the hearing. The preparation of the false gift letter was deemed an obvious violation of Obligation 38. There was also deemed to be a serious violation of Obligation 39, Unprofessional Conduct, and Obligation 3, Ethical Behaviour, in not protecting the public from fraud, misrepresentation, or unethical practice. Given that there was also a prior serious conviction against this same salesperson, the penalty granted was probably the most extreme possible, a $25,000 fine, $1,750 in costs, plus the matter was referred to the Registrar for removal of the salesperson's registration.

In the discipline case of Mugford, decided October 22, 2001, an offer was prepared with a Schedule A that provided a rebate to the buyer of $2,500, purportedly for "legal fees and other closing costs." In fact, this was done to artificially raise the purchase price due to the fact that the buyers were in financial difficulty. The financial institutions were never provided with Schedule A. The salesperson also tried to get the buyers to falsify the dates on a waiver related to the home-inspection condition. Furthermore, the salesperson gave money to the buyer in order to artificially show a higher bank balance, as proof of their financial stability. The penalty levied was $7,500 with costs of $1,500, a three-month suspension, and a two-year probation.

In the case of Edgecombe, Mainella, Vass, and Azan, dated April 12, 2001, an initial Agreement of Purchase and Sale was prepared between the seller and buyer for the sum of $178,000. A second agreement was then prepared between the same parties for the sum of $186,000, but the offer also contained an amendment that showed a credit of $8,000 to the buyer as a result of the fridge, stove, and broadloom not being included in the transaction. It appeared to the discipline committee that the entire second offer was created to enable the buyer to obtain higher ratio financing.

What was interesting in this decision is that it was the bank, which had turned down the application for financing, that complained to RECO about this matter. The decision was also interesting in that it showed what can occur when inexperienced salespeople work on a transaction without proper supervision. All of the defendants had to pay penalties ranging from $2,500 to $5,000 and were placed on probation, demonstrating the seriousness of these events.

In the discipline decision of Lesky, decided October 17, 2001, a property listed by Mr. Lesky attracted no offers when it was listed at $99,000. For no apparent reason, the listing price was raised to $115,900 and accepted by buyers introduced to the property by a buyer salesperson. There was also a direction that was separate from the offer in which the seller agreed to pay back certain funds to the buyer.

The transaction was conditional on the buyers obtaining 85% financing. Lesky forged a waiver signed by the buyers, waiving the financing condition. This was done to assist the seller in arranging for mortgage financing for a new property that they wanted to purchase. Lesky stated that he did this under pressure from the seller, who needed this to obtain the desired financing. The seller denied everything.

The panel found that Lesky did not act alone in falsifying the waiver and was duped by an unscrupulous client. This client also agreed to pay the buyers back the sum of $18,000, which effectively reduced the actual purchase price to $95,000. The bank became suspicious of the transaction, and the end result was that the buyers became tenants of the property.

Mr. Lesky attended the hearing and expressed remorse for his actions. The penalty against him was $5,000, with costs of $1,250, and his licence was suspended for a period of six months. It is not difficult to see that there were other unscrupulous parties in this transaction, including both the seller and the buyers, who were participating in transactions to artificially inflate the purchase price to obtain sufficient mortgage monies. But this is not a defence for any salesperson who willingly gets involved.

If you do your homework, it should not take long for you to see the true colours of a particular seller, right at the listing presentation. Find out the financial situation of the property immediately to see if the seller is overmortgaged and in need of an immediate sale. Have the SPIS form filled out, so you can determine whether the seller has any issues with disclosure of important matters related to the property. Above all, the minute your client asks you to do anything that causes ethical bells to ring, get out of the relationship.

Unscrupulous clients know all the tricks. They are like professional shoppers. These people feel that, if they can bother a salesman five times and take up hours of their time, the salesman will give them a better deal because they have already invested so much time with the buyer. Unscrupulous clients will try the same tactics. They will have you spend a tremendous amount of time with them before they start with the unethical suggestions, hoping that you will feel the same way — that you have invested too much time with them to walk away.

When you are faced with unscrupulous clients in your practice, think about the salespeople in these examples and the tragic results of their actions. Think about your licence to practise flying out the window. Think about the emotional and financial distress associated with RECO and possible legal proceedings. Then just say no.

In the discipline case involving Kiriakopoulos, decided May 1, 2001, the salesperson forged the signature of a seller to transfer a listing from the former broker's office where the salesperson worked to the new broker's office that employed the salesperson. The new broker terminated the salesperson's employment when he learned of the forgery. Not only was this behaviour deemed a violation of Obligation 38, Error, Misrepresentation, Fraud, it was also deemed to violate Obligation 39, Unprofessional Conduct, as well as Obligation 3, Ethical Behaviour. The penalty was $15,000, with costs of $1,300, and the salesperson was placed on probation for two years.

In the case of Barrow, decided October 2, 2001, the salesperson was a listing salesperson. The offer contained representations about the water well system and the septic system, two hot spots when dealing with these types of properties. In the course of dealings on this transaction, the parties agreed to retain a company to pump out the septic system, which was done. The invoice prepared by the company, which was given to the seller's salesperson, contained a recommendation that the system needed "baffle repair and bed treatment." The salesperson removed this recommendation from the invoice, and the buyer only found out about this after the deal had closed.

The salesperson's position was that since repairs might be needed in the future, this was not pertinent information relating to the property. The panel disagreed, finding that this action by Barrow amounted to a violation of Obligation 38, Error, Misrepresentation, Fraud, as well as Obligation 39, Unprofessional Conduct. During the course of the hearing, there were other allegations made against the salesperson about further duties owed to the buyers regarding the well and the septic system that were not proven. Accordingly, the penalty given was a reprimand, with costs of $600.

Weisleder's Wisdom on . . . ERROR, MISREPRESENTATION, FRAUD

1. Do not participate in any way with any forged or altered document or in any scheme to artificially inflate the value of a property.
2. Do not agree to witness any signature if you are not present at the time.
3. Be wary of any document prepared outside the scope of the written offer to purchase that changes the purchase price or any other material term of the agreement.
4. Do not let yourself be used or tricked by an unscrupulous client, even if it means walking away from a possible commission.

WRITTEN REPRESENTATION AGREEMENTS

Contents of written agreements

11. *(1) A brokerage shall not enter into a written agreement with a buyer or seller for the purpose of trading in real estate unless the agreement clearly, comprehensibly and prominently,*
- *(a) specifies the date on which the agreement takes effect and the date on which it expires;*
- *(b) specifies or describes the method for determining,*
  - *(i) the amount of any commission or other remuneration payable to the brokerage, and*
  - *(ii) in the case of an agreement with a seller, the amount of any commission or other remuneration payable to any other brokerage;*
- *(c) describes how any commission or other remuneration payable to the brokerage will be paid; and*
- *(d) sets out the services that the brokerage will provide under the agreement.*

(2) A brokerage shall not, for the purpose of trading in real estate, enter into a written agreement with a buyer or seller that provides that the date on which the agreement expires is more than six months after the date on which the agreement takes effect unless,
- *(a) the date on which the agreement expires is prominently displayed on the first page of the agreement; and*
- *(b) the buyer or seller has initialed the agreement next to the date referred to in clause (a).*

(3) A brokerage shall ensure that a written agreement that is entered into between the brokerage and a buyer or seller for the purpose of trading in real estate contains only one date on which the agreement expires.

Copies of written agreements

12. If a brokerage and one or more other persons enter into a written agreement in connection with a trade in real estate, the brokerage shall ensure that each of the other persons is immediately given a copy of the agreement.

Seller representation agreements

13. If a brokerage enters into a seller representation agreement with a seller and the agreement is not in writing, the brokerage shall, at the earliest practicable opportunity and before any buyer makes an offer, reduce the agreement to writing, have it signed on behalf of the brokerage and submit it to the seller for signature.

Buyer representation agreements

14. If a brokerage enters into a buyer representation agreement with a seller and the agreement is not in writing, the brokerage shall, before any buyer makes an offer, reduce the agreement to writing, have it signed on behalf of the brokerage and submit it to the buyer for signature.

Agreements with customers

15. If a brokerage enters into an agreement with a customer and the agreement is not in writing, the brokerage shall, at the earliest practicable opportunity and before any buyer makes an offer, reduce the agreement to writing, have it signed on behalf of the brokerage and submit it to the customer for signature.

In the discipline decision of Wong, decided October 21, 2003, the salesperson was representing an estate. As the listing price was not generating any offers, the salesperson reduced the listing price on the MLS. The salesperson claimed that he received verbal instructions from the seller, although the seller denied this. In any event, the panel found that under Obligation 13, any change to the listing agreement had to have been completed in writing. This was also deemed to be a violation of Ethical Behaviour (Obligation 3), Best Interests of Client (Obligation 4), and Unprofessional Conduct (Obligation 39). The penalty awarded was $2,750, with costs of $1,350.

In the discipline decision of Othmeier, decided November 1, 2002, the salesperson was purporting to do a favour for a friend. Because she did not intend to charge for her services, she did not prepare the usual representation agreements. The seller and buyer were introduced to each other by the salesperson, but the salesperson signed no representation agreement with either the seller or the buyer. She did assist in preparing the offer, with both the buyer and the seller attending at her office, and proceeded to explain the terms of the offer to the buyer.

The agreement contained clauses that were deemed to be unclear and ambiguous, causing concerns in their interpretation. The panel found that her actions constituted a violation of Obligations 13 and 14, in failing to document the agency relationships with both the seller and the buyer. She was also found in violation of Obligation 5, Competence, as she failed to add appropriate terms, conditions, and obligations into the agreement itself. The penalty was $1,500, with costs of $2,200.

The panel was quite clear in its findings that it made no difference that the salesperson was not receiving any compensation. The proper course of conduct would have been to refer the clients to other salespeople and to refer them to a lawyer to draft any agreement. The lesson here is obvious. Even if you are acting for free on a transaction, you will be held to the same standards as if you were being paid in full. You can see that you are in fact doing yourself no favours when you act in this way for clients.

Doing favours may be the best way, in fact, to lose your friends. The same can be said when you act for relatives for no pay. It is probably the best way to upset your friends or develop unnecessary animosity from your relatives. You may think it is a favour, but they will still expect your best, so if you are not prepared to give your best, do not get involved.

Weisleder's Wisdom on . . . WRITTEN REPRESENTATION AGREEMENTS

1. Avoid doing favours such as working for no remuneration. It inevitably leads to your not taking the same care in fulfilling your obligations.

2. If you are doing a favour, with no remuneration, remember that your standard of care must be exactly the same as if you were being paid in full.

WRITTEN TRANSACTION AGREEMENTS

Written and legible agreements

27. *(1) A registrant who represents a client in respect of a trade in real estate shall use the registrant's best efforts to ensure that,*

(a) any agreement that deals with the conveyance of an interest in real estate is in writing; and

(b) any written agreement that deals with the conveyance of an interest in real estate is legible.

(2) Subsection (1) applies, with necessary modifications, if a brokerage and a customer have an agreement that provides for the brokerage to provide services to the customer in respect of any agreement that deals with the conveyance of an interest in real estate.

Copies of agreements

28. *(1) If a registrant represents a client who enters into a written agreement that deals with the conveyance of an interest in* *real estate, the registrant shall use the registrant's best efforts to ensure that all parties to the agreement receive a copy of the agreement at the earliest practicable opportunity.*

(2) Subsection (1) applies, with necessary modifications, if a brokerage and a customer have an agreement that provides for the brokerage to provide services to the customer in respect of any agreement that deals with the conveyance of an interest in real estate.

Best interests
4. A registrant shall promote and protect the best interests of the registrant's clients.

In the case of Demosani and Paget, decided April 26, 2001, there was confusion in the offer preparation regarding whether the appliances were to be included in the purchase price. The seller wanted them excluded, and the buyer wanted them included. The evidence of both salespeople was that in the final agreement, the appliances were to be included, but the salesperson did not include this in the agreement through error. The seller did not agree to leave the appliances.

The panel found that this error constituted a violation of Obligation 27 in the failure to include this agreed upon term in the final written agreement. It was also held to be a violation of Obligation 4, Best Interests of Client; Obligation 39, Unprofessional Conduct; and Obligation 3, Ethical Behaviour. The buyer salesperson was given a penalty of $1,000 and the listing salesperson a penalty of $500. Both paid costs of $600.

In the case of Amyotte, decided September 15, 2003, the salesperson permitted the seller to accept an Agreement of Purchase and Sale even though the seller disagreed that the pool and the dishwasher should be included in the purchase price. The salesperson said it was no problem and that she would obtain the agreement of the buyers to delete the items in an amendment. The buyers never agreed to the amendment. This was found to be a violation of Obligation 27 as well as Obligation 4, Best Interests of Client. The penalty was $4,000, with costs of $1,000.

In the case of Carnell, dated January 28, 2004, the Agreement of Purchase and Sale had been faxed so many times during the offer and acceptance process that it was virtually illegible, yet the salesperson permitted it to be signed by the parties. This was found to be a violation of Obligation 27, and the fine was $3,000, with costs of $750.

When people ask me what qualities an organization looks for in new employees, I mention the obvious ones, such as being hard working, dedicated, loyal, innovative, and friendly. But another big one, in my opinion, is being careful in everything you do. If you take care in filling out the minor points, the larger issues will take care of themselves. Once you develop good habits of being careful in everything that you do, you will find yourself better organized and less stressed, and will be working with a large number of very satisfied clients.

Weisleder's Wisdom on . . . WRITTEN TRANSACTION AGREEMENTS

1. Make sure that everything you do is put into writing as soon as possible.

2. All changes to written documents should also be reduced to writing.

3. Be very meticulous when completing all chattels and fixtures.

4. Do not use offers after they have been faxed too many times and are for the most part illegible.

5. Take great care in filling out all sections of the Agreement

of Purchase and Sale, including all areas in the printed
provisions and any schedules.

DISCLOSURE OF INTEREST

Disclosure of interest

18. *(1) A registrant shall, at the earliest practicable opportunity
and before any offer is made in respect of the acquisition or disposition of an interest in real estate, disclose in writing the
following matters to every client represented by the registrant in
respect of the acquisition or disposition:*

> 1. *Any property interest that the registrant has in the real
>   estate.*
> 2. *Any property interest that a person related to the
>   registrant has in the real estate, if the registrant knows or
>   ought to know of the interest.*

*(2) A brokerage shall, at the earliest practicable opportunity and
before any offer is made in respect of the acquisition or disposition of an interest in real estate, disclose in writing the matters
referred to in paragraphs 1 and 2 of subsection (1) to every customer with whom the brokerage has entered into an agreement
in respect of the acquisition or disposition.*

*(3) A broker shall, at the earliest practicable opportunity and
before any offer is made in respect of the acquisition or disposition of an interest in real estate, disclose in writing the matters
referred to in paragraphs 1 and 2 of subsection (1) to every customer of the broker or salesperson with whom the brokerage
that employs the broker or salesperson has entered into an
agreement in respect of the acquisition or disposition.*

(4) A registrant shall disclose in writing to a client, at the earliest

practicable opportunity, any direct or indirect financial benefit that the registrant or a person related to the registrant may receive from another person in connection with services provided by the registrant to the client, including any commission or other remuneration that may be received from another person.

(5) A brokerage that has entered into an agreement with a buyer or seller that requires the buyer or seller to pay the brokerage a commission or other remuneration in respect of a trade in real estate shall not charge or collect any commission or other remuneration under another agreement entered into with another person in respect of the same trade unless,

> *(a) the brokerage discloses at the earliest practicable opportunity to the other person, in writing, the terms of the agreement with the buyer or seller that require the payment of a commission or other remuneration; and*
> *(b) the brokerage discloses at the earliest practicable opportunity to the buyer or seller, in writing, the terms of the agreement with the other person that require the payment of a commission or other remuneration.*

Throughout this book I have advised on the principle of full disclosure in everything that you do. This is what Obligation 18 is all about. Disclose everything, especially any personal interest that you may have in any transaction, or if you are in fact purchasing a property yourself from either a seller who is not your client or a seller who is your client.

When a salesperson represents a client or customer in any transaction, they can provide many types of services besides the common listing and buyer representation services. The salesperson may assist the buyer in obtaining financing, or having an appraisal done on the property. They may assist the buyer in obtaining insurance for the property. These other services could result in the salesperson's receiving a fee from a third party, which we could refer to as an additional profit that the salesperson is making for providing the services to a seller or buyer. There is nothing wrong in principle with making this kind of profit, provided that you disclose everything in advance and obtain the approval of your client.

In the case of Norm Macdonald and James Macdonald, decided December 18, 2001, representations were made to the buyers that Norm was the owner of a property. Norm and James were brothers and were also registered brokers working together on this transaction. Although the seller was shown as A Inc., the buyers were led to believe that Norm was the owner of this company. The buyers then began dealing directly with the party who was the actual builder of the new home on the property, as though he was the owner. The buyers gave the seller an additional $20,000 to complete the property, and the money was taken and not accounted for. They had also paid over $15,000 in deposits. Many construction liens started piling up on the property, as the trades were also not paid by A Inc.

In fact, Norm was one of the owners of the property itself and had planned to transfer the property to the buyers directly, after the new home was built. Although A Inc. would build the house, and would be paid by the buyers, the title would transfer directly to the buyers from Norm.

It was found by the panel that Norm did not go far enough to explain his financial interest in the property itself. The buyers were under the mistaken impression that Norm did have an interest in the company owned by the builder, and this was a factor in the buyers deciding to advance the extra funds directly to the builder in order to finish the house. Accordingly, Norm and James were found to have violated this Obligation on financial disclosure, and the penalty was $1,000, with costs of $300. They were also held to violate Obligation 27, Written Agreements, as well as Obligation 39, Unprofessional Conduct.

For the protection of the public interest, Obligation 18 makes it clear that a seller who is also a salesperson makes full disclosure of this fact to any buyer. What this Obligation and this case further clarify is that all details of any ownership, including any arrangements with third-party builders that may be permitted onto the property, must also be carefully documented and disclosed to any potential buyer.

Weisleder's Wisdom on . . . DISCLOSURE OF INTEREST

1. Always disclose, in a detailed manner, any interest that you may have in any property or in any aspect of a transaction.
2. Ensure that all financial disclosure is given in writing.

BEST INTERESTS OF CLIENT

Best interests
4. A registrant shall promote and protect the best interests of the registrant's clients.

Agreements with customers
15. If a brokerage enters into an agreement with a customer and the agreement is not in writing, the brokerage shall, at the earliest practicable opportunity and before any buyer makes an offer, reduce the agreement to writing, have it signed on behalf of the brokerage and submit it to the customer for signature.

Nature of relationship
17. If a registrant represents or provides services to more than one buyer or seller in respect of the same trade in real estate, the registrant shall, in writing, at the earliest practicable opportunity and before any offer is made, inform all buyers and sellers

involved in that trade of the nature of the registrant's relationship to each buyer and seller.

Properties that meet buyer's criteria
19. If a brokerage has entered into a representation agreement with a buyer, a broker or salesperson who acts on behalf of the buyer pursuant to the agreement shall inform the buyer of properties that meet the buyer's criteria without having any regard to the amount of commission or other remuneration, if any, to which the brokerage might be entitled.

Steps taken by registrant
23. A registrant shall inform a client of all significant steps that the registrant takes in the course of representing the client.

If someone asked me how to be sure that I was always complying with this Obligation, I would answer as follows: "Disclose everything every time."

In the discipline decision of Galiegue, dated November 27, 2003, the salesperson was also the actual seller of a property and also acted on behalf of the buyer. The salesperson completed an spis form in which he indicated that he was not aware of any problems with the quality or quantity of water supplied to the property. He even signed a representation to this effect in the agreement itself. It turned out that the well in question was not even hooked up to the property until just prior to closing and that the water was not fit for human consumption. As proof that the water quality was acceptable, the salesperson tried to deliver a water sample taken over a year earlier that was not even from the same well.

There was clear evidence available to the panel that the salesperson did know there was a problem with the water and did not disclose it. The salesperson was found to have violated Obligation 3, Ethical Behaviour; Obligation 4, Best Interests of Client; Obligation 27, Written Agreements; Obligation 37, False Advertising; and Obligation 39, Unprofessional Conduct. The fine against the salesperson and the broker, which was found liable under Obligation 41, Broker Responsibility, was $20,000 each and $1,000 each in costs. Neither the broker nor the salesperson paid the penalty, so their memberships and registrations were immediately terminated.

The buyer also commenced litigation proceedings against the broker as a result of the same facts, which will involve many more years of stress for the salesperson regarding this action over and above what was associated with the discipline proceeding. All of this could have been avoided had he been open and honest, the cornerstone of this rule, in completing the SPIS statement.

As I have stated in Chapter 1, filling out an SPIS form should not get you into any trouble unless you deliberately complete it falsely. So long as you disclose everything that is material, you will not get into trouble if you do deliver the statement.

In the case of Batson, dated November 20, 2006, the buyer salesperson was preparing an offer on a property that had been listed for over 90 days at $449,000 with no offers received. Prior to submitting the offer, Batson, the listing salesperson, conveyed information to the buyer salesperson's assistant to the effect that there was a strong possibility that a second offer was coming in from another brokerage office. The buyer salesperson then requested whether they could still bring in their own offer later that evening and was told by Batson that he would wait for the buyer salesperson's offer before presenting all offers to the seller.

The buyer salesperson then discussed all facts with their buyers and the buyers changed their offer from the low four hundred thousands to a full price offer of $450,000, with no conditions. At the time the offer was presented, Batson knew that the buyer salesperson was under the mistaken belief that another offer was coming in, but said nothing to dispel that belief.

The panel held that acting in the best interests of your client in trying to obtain the highest price for them does not relieve the salesperson of dealing with all other members in a transaction fairly, honestly and with integrity, which is the corner stone of Obligation 3, Ethical Behaviour.

This was also held to be a violation of Obligation 38, Misrepresentation, as Batson knew that the buyer offer was presented under a false understanding of the situation by the buyer. Finally, this was deemed to be a violation of Obligation 39, Unprofessional Conduct.

The penalty imposed was $10,000. This decision was confirmed on appeal, dated July 10, 2007.

Another important lesson to be learned from this decision relates to multiple offers. Situations may change between the time you express an interest in a property and the time that an offer is presented. Some buyers may change their minds before an offer is presented. It is thus very important for buyer salespeople to confirm again at the time they submit an offer in a multiple offer process as to how many offers have actually been received or are still expected, so that buyers can make as fully informed a decision as possible.

In the discipline decision of Yeung, decided July 19, 2001, the listing salesperson did not submit an offer from a buyer salesperson when he stood to benefit personally from a second offer where he could double end the commission. Besides being violations of Obligation 3, Ethical Behaviour; Obligation 39, Unprofessional Conduct; and Obligation 24, Conveying Offers, it was deemed to be a violation of Obligation 4, Best Interests of the Client. The penalty was $9,000, with $1,500 in costs.

In the case of Whittal, decided October 17, 2002, the listing salesperson did not present to his seller an offer for $75,000 that was received, and instead stated to the buyer salesperson that the seller would not look at an offer unless it was at least $120,000. No other offers were received, and the seller ended up selling the property for $57,000. Besides violating Obligation 24 in not presenting all offers to the client, the salesperson was deemed to have violated Obligation 4 to protect the client's best interests. The penalty was $4,000, with costs in the amount of $1,750.

The salesperson in Kow's case, decided September 15, 2003, signed a listing agreement with the seller, and was also the salesperson for the buyer in an offer that was presented. The salesperson knew that there was a tenant on the property who had a right of first refusal to buy the property and that she would not be paid commission if the tenant exercised this right. The buyer that was Ms. Kow's client approached the tenant on his own to purchase the property together with the tenant. The buyer agreed to pay Ms. Kow the commission that she would lose if the seller accepted the tenant's offer. Ms. Kow did not bring this information to the attention of the seller. The transaction with the tenant was completed, and Ms. Kow received commission from the buyer.

It was found by the panel that in not disclosing the foregoing information, she had violated Obligation 4 to promote the best interests of the member's client. The penalty was $3,000, with costs of $1,000.

In the case of da Costa, decided December 19, 2001, the salesperson was found to have been careless in permitting sensitive personal information about a client to remain lying around on a cluttered desk, accessible to others, such that a third party was able to use that confidential information to fraudulently obtain a mortgage loan. This was found to be a violation of Obligation 4, Best Interests of the Client, as well as a violation of Obligation 39, Unprofessional Conduct. As we will see in Chapter 4 on privacy, all brokers and salespeople must be extra vigilant in protecting any sensitive or confidential personal information that they may have in their possession about their clients and customers. The salesperson had to pay a penalty of $5,000, with costs of $1,000.

In the case of Burt, decided September 15, 2003, Mr. Burt, the listing salesperson, disclosed to a potential buyer that the seller may have overpaid for the property initially, and that was the reason they were firm on the asking price. The salesperson thought that the buyers might submit an offer through him and was surprised when the buyers used another salesperson to actually submit the offer. The penalty was $2,500, with costs of $1,000.

Weisleder's Wisdom on . . . BEST INTERESTS OF CLIENT

1. Always treat the client as though they are your best friend: disclose everything.
2. Present all pertinent information, including all offers and counteroffers, to your clients.
3. This Obligation is still subject to you always treating everyone else in a transaction fairly, honestly and with integrity.
4. Ensure that all obligations, conditions, and waivers provided for in any offer are followed through in a timely manner.
5. Keep everything you hear from a client confidential.
6. Make sure that your clients are aware that this is in fact your policy regarding anything confidential.
7. Do not leave any confidential information unsecured where it can be accessed by third parties.

INFORMATION BEFORE AGREEMENTS

Information before agreements
10. *(1) Before entering into an agreement with a buyer or seller*

in respect of trading in real estate, a brokerage shall, at the earliest practicable opportunity, inform the buyer or seller of the following:

1. The types of service alternatives that are available in the circumstances, including a representation agreement or another type of agreement.

2. The services that the brokerage would provide under the agreement.

3. The fact that circumstances could arise in which the brokerage could represent more than one client in respect of the same trade in real estate, but that the brokerage could not do this unless all of the clients represented by the brokerage in respect of that trade consented in writing.

4. The nature of the services that the brokerage would provide to each client if the brokerage represents more than one customer in respect of the same trade in real estate.

5. The fact that circumstances could arise in which the brokerage could provide services to more than one customer in respect of the same trade in real estate.

6. The fact that circumstances could arise in which the brokerage could, in respect of the same trade in real estate, both represent clients and provide services to customers.

7. The restricted nature of the services that the brokerage would provide to a customer in respect of a trade in real estate if the brokerage also represents a client in respect of that trade.

(2) The brokerage shall, at the earliest practicable opportunity

and before an offer is made, use the brokerage's best efforts to obtain from the buyer or seller a written acknowledgement that the buyer or seller received all the information referred to in sub-section (1).

Disclosure before multiple representation

16. A brokerage shall not represent more than one client in respect of a trade in real estate unless it has disclosed the following matters to the clients or prospective clients at the earliest practicable opportunity:

1. The fact that the brokerage proposes to represent more than one client in respect of the same trade.

2. The differences between the obligations the brokerage would have if it represented only one client in respect of the trade and the obligations the brokerage would have if it represented more than one client in respect of the trade, including any differences relating to the disclosure of information or the services that the brokerage would provide.

Nature of relationship

17. If a registrant represents or provides services to more than one buyer or seller in respect of the same trade in real estate, the registrant shall, in writing, at the earliest practicable opportunity and before any offer is made, inform all buyers and sellers involved in that trade of the nature of the registrant's relationship to each buyer and seller.

The main purpose of the Obligation sounds simple enough: That salespeople will explain to their clients as soon as possible the nature of the role and the services that they will be supplying in the transaction. When salespeople get into trouble with this Obligation, it is almost always in the very murky area of multiple representation, or dual agency.

Multiple representation is very confusing to clients. It can be very lucrative to salespeople. If you alone are acting as a dual salesperson, you will be double-ending the deal — receiving the commission payable to both the selling and buying salesperson. Multiple representation can also arise if two salespeople from the same brokerage company represent the buyer and the seller. But how does one fairly represent both the buyer and the seller? The process begins by reviewing the multiple representation provisions of the listing and buyer representation agreements as soon as possible with your seller and buyer.

We are told to disclose everything material in a transaction to our clients. In the context of multiple representation, we are disclosing the material terms that we will not be disclosing to our clients. For example, when you act only for the seller and the buyer salesperson confides in you how high they think their client might go, you are obligated to tell this information to your seller, while at the same time telling the seller that you cannot guarantee the information, it is only what you have heard. However, in a multiple representation situation, you cannot give this same information to the seller. It is very important that these provisions be reviewed carefully with both your buyer and seller clients so that they understand the consequences and provide their informed consent to your acting for both the buyer and the seller.

Many sellers believe it's a good thing when you act in multiple representation. They think it will be easier to ask you to reduce your commission, since you are double-ending. They fail to understand that there is also the restricted disclosure that will also take place. With respect to reducing your commission, I encourage you to think twice before agreeing to do this. You should not be punished for the fact that you have the connections or client base to be able to bring a buyer and seller together. Unless this was agreed to at the time the listing agreement was negotiated, you should refrain from cutting your commission, even if it means losing a transaction. Remember your own reputation or brand image. As discussed earlier, once you cut your commission one time, the word will get out, and you will be pressured to always cut it.

Although there are certain restrictions on disclosure, this does not reduce a salesperson's obligations to both buyers and sellers for each of the other Obligations of the Code of Ethics. In fact, you can argue that there is an even greater obligation to protect both of your clients' interests in this situation, even if it means referring either or both of them to their respective lawyers for advice before they sign the agreement. For example, you should ensure that the Seller Property Information Statement has been accurately completed, delivered, and reviewed with the buyer before any agreement is signed.

In the discipline decision of Lowes, decided July 29, 2003, the salesperson acted in multiple representation without explaining his role in the transaction or obtaining the acknowledgement from the buyer as to his role. He failed to have the seller sign the spis form and also did not disclose to the buyers the fact that the driveway on the property belonged to the Ministry of Transportation. He also failed to suggest that the buyer obtain independent advice in reviewing the survey for the property in the event that he was not capable of doing so himself. The salesperson paid a penalty of $3,000 with costs of $1,350 for violating Obligation 10, Information before Agreements.

There is always a potential for conflicts of interest when you represent both a buyer and a seller. In the case of Scocchia, decided January 9, 2003, the salesperson acted for the buyer and the seller on the sale of a property for the sum of $120,000. However, before the offer was even signed, the salesperson was also acting for the buyer on a potential resale of the same property to a third party for almost three times the value, without disclosing any of this information to the seller.

Both transactions eventually closed on the same day, within minutes of each other, which was the point when the seller found out about the resale for the first time.

The discipline panel found it was clear that the salesperson was representing both the seller and the buyer. But it was incumbent on the salesperson to explain to both parties the nature of the services that he would be providing to each, including whether there would be any resale activity. He had even put the buyer at risk by permitting the buyer to sign the resale offer before he had actually completed the signing of the initial agreement with the seller. As soon as the salesperson heard of the third-party higher offer, he was in an immediate conflict of interest. He then proceeded to favour the interest of the buyer over the interest of the seller. The panel therefore found the salesperson to be in violation of Obligations 3, Ethical Behaviour; 4, Best Interests of Client; 38, Error, Misrepresentation; and 21, Material Facts. The penalty was $20,000, with costs of $2,000, and the salesperson was put on immediate suspension for four months and on probation for two years.

In many cases, it is possible the salesperson does not think that they are representing the buyers, while the buyers mistakenly believe that the salesperson is acting for them. It's precisely for this reason that it is so important for salespeople to outline their roles and the services that they will provide as soon as possible upon meeting a client.

In the case of de Giacomo, decided December 16, 2002, the salesperson's name was posted on the sign at a sales office for new lots in a project. The buyers called the salesperson and expressed an interest in the property. Although the salesperson did not sign anything with the buyers, it was found by the panel that he was in fact representing the buyers in the transaction as well as the seller. He further permitted the buyers to write the deposit cheque payable directly to the seller when he knew that the seller was having financial difficulties with the project. The seller eventually went bankrupt, and the buyers' deposit was lost. The penalty imposed was $15,000, with costs in the amount of $1,750.

The case of Dodge, dated March 31, 2004, was another situation involving a salesperson working for a builder. A buyer showed interest in a property, and the salesperson then prepared the offer and reviewed some of the provisions with the buyer, without explaining her role in the transaction. The buyer was told to review the offer with her lawyer, and a condition was inserted that the offer was conditional on the approval of the buyer's lawyer as well as on financing.

Although neither condition was satisfied, the salesperson was not cooperative in enabling the buyer to be released from the transaction. The committee found that there was an obligation on the part of the salesperson, even in this situation when the salesperson was obviously working for a builder, to confirm the role with the customer as soon as possible in writing and to properly explain whom she was acting for in the transaction. The fine imposed on her was $4,000. This is a lesson to all salespeople who may act for builders. Make certain that all potential buyers are given written advice confirming that you will not be acting on their behalf, other than perhaps to complete the agreement itself, and that they are to obtain independent legal advice with respect to any matter contained in the offer.

In the case of McGinty, decided August 13, 2002, the salesperson acted in multiple representation without disclosing his role to the buyers. He further erred in describing the property as being 50 feet by 400 feet when it was only 50 feet by 308 feet. The panel noted that based on the evidence, the salesperson failed to properly explain his role in the transaction and took no measures to ensure that all documentation was provided to the buyers, and that he displayed little attention to details in completion and execution of documentation and failed to verify key facts relating to the property. The penalty imposed was $7,000, with costs of $2,450.

Weisleder's Wisdom on . . . INFORMATION BEFORE AGREEMENTS

1. Explain all services that you will provide to a client as soon as possible, including any multiple representation possibilities.
2. When you are acting in multiple representation, be aware that there is almost a greater responsibility for you to take more care in carrying out all of your duties and obligations under the Code of Ethics.
3. Consider advising either or both of your clients to seek independent legal advice before signing the offer, especially when you act for a builder of new homes.
4. Complete the SPIS form with your seller and review it with your buyers.
5. If any conflict of interest arises during the course of the transaction, immediately review the matter with your own broker and legal advisers to determine the most appropriate method to protect the interests of both of your clients.

CONVEYING OFFERS AND COMPETING OFFERS

Conveying offers
24. *(1) A registrant shall convey any written offer received by the registrant to the registrant's client at the earliest practicable opportunity.*

(2) A broker or salesperson shall establish a method of ensuring that,

(a) written offers are received by someone on behalf of the broker or salesperson, if the broker or salesperson is not available at the time an offer is submitted; and

(b) written offers are conveyed to the client of the broker or salesperson at the earliest practicable opportunity, even if the broker or salesperson is not available at the time an offer is submitted.

(3) Without limiting the generality of subsections (1) and (2), those subsections apply regardless of the identity of the person making the offer, the contents of the offer or the nature of any arrangements for commission or other remuneration.

(4) Subsections (1) and (3) are subject to any written directions given by a client.

(5) Subsections (1) to (4) also apply, with necessary modifications, to,

(a) written amendments to written offers and any other written document directly related to a written offer; and

(b) written assignments of agreements that relate to interests in real estate, written waivers of conditions in agreements that relate to interests in real estate, and any other written document directly related to a written agreement that relates to an interest in real estate.

(6) Subsections (1) to (5) apply, with necessary modifications, if a brokerage and a customer have an agreement that provides for the brokerage to receive written offers.

(7) Subsections (1) to (5) apply, with necessary modifications, to brokers and salespersons employed by a brokerage, if the brokerage and a customer have an agreement that provides for the brokerage to receive written offers.

Competing offers

26. *(1) If a brokerage that has a seller as a client receives a competing written offer, the brokerage shall disclose the number of competing written offers to every person who is making one of the competing offers, but shall not disclose the substance of the competing offers.*

(2) Subsection (1) applies, with necessary modifications, to a brokerage that has a seller as a customer, if the brokerage and the seller have an agreement that provides for the brokerage to receive written offers to buy.

Agreements relating to commission

27. *(1) If a brokerage has a seller as a client and an agreement between the brokerage and the seller contains terms that relate to a commission or other remuneration and that may affect whether an offer to buy is accepted, the brokerage shall disclose the existence of and the details of those terms to any person who makes a written offer to buy, at the earliest practicable opportunity and before any offer is accepted.*

Obligations 26 and 27 bring up the recent phenomenon of bidding wars that break out when a property is listed in an extremely hot market. It is very important that salespeople prepare both their seller and buyer clients in advance for this experience. Bidding wars are unusual and extremely stressful, and thus require that salespeople be extra careful that they are taking all normal precautions with their clients, even under these trying conditions.

Before anyone submits an offer, the salesperson should review all the standard printed provisions with the client, so that the only clauses that will have to be dealt with later are the conditions and the final sale or purchase price. The client will have to be educated that the seller does not necessarily have to deal with the highest offer, and in some cases may try to deal with more than one offer at the same time by making one a back-up offer, which would only take effect if another offer falls through.

The Obligations under the Code of Ethics assume that salespeople will be honest with one another. It is required that a salesperson disclose the exact number of multiple offers to all salespeople involved. This way their buyer clients can make the informed decision as to whether or not they wish to participate in this kind of free-for-all scenario. There is a duty for the listing salesperson to present all offers to the seller, and not attempt to only present offers where they may be double-ending the commission. The seller can ask that all offers be faxed instead of being presented in person, which can cause additional problems, especially when the listing broker is also presenting one of the offers. It is important that all this information be disclosed in advance to your buyer client, so that they can make an informed decision as to whether or not to participate in this bidding process.

The best advice you can give a buyer client in a multiple offer situation is that the process itself is essentially unfair to buyers in general. They do not have much in the way of leverage, and there is room for abuse by unscrupulous sellers. The chances of winning may be not greater than 20% in most cases. If you are successful in at least managing expectations right from the start, it is less likely that you will be blamed by your buyer client if their offer is rejected or not considered.

For sellers, a variety of strategies is emerging in order to create a larger "buzz" about a specific property. Typically, the property is listed with the proviso that, although it will be open for inspection for several days, no offers will be considered until three to four days later. This is done in order to create hype about the property and afford buyers the opportunity to conduct an inspection in advance so that they can submit a "clean" offer, with no conditions. Some sellers, as discussed earlier, arrange for a home inspection in advance and make it available to potential buyers during this three-to-four-day period.

If more than six offers arrive, I have seen situations where sellers have narrowed the offers to three and have told everyone else that they will only deal with these three offers. They then invite the three to improve their offers. The strategy here is to try to make each of these three buyers think that their chances of winning have now improved dramatically and to get them to consider going even higher.

A new phenomenon is captured by the phrase "bully offer," which occurs in the following situation. A selling salesperson discloses on MLS that the seller will be accepting offers in five days in order to permit inspections and to create hype about a property. A potential buyer comes in immediately through a buyer salesperson with an offer, indicating that it is open only for six hours, to try to obtain the property before anyone else can submit an offer.

The issue becomes complicated when this is a very good offer and the seller wants to deal with it. Under Obligation 24, Conveying Offers, the salesperson must convey this offer to the seller. What should the selling salesperson do? In my view, if the seller wants to consider this offer, the selling salesperson must do whatever they can to notify all other potential salespeople, either privately if they have expressed an interest or publicly through MLS, that the seller will be considering offers immediately due to the emergence of this new offer.

There is no obligation currently on sellers to provide any details about the contents of any offer, just the total number of competing offers. This is part of the problem, in that many buyers suspect that sellers and salespeople are providing false or misleading information about the total number of offers in order to pressure buyers to increase their offers. There is no current method that permits an unsuccessful or even successful buyer from verifying whether the seller was telling the truth after the fact. Nevertheless, as illustrated by the case of Batson discussed earlier in this chapter, there will be significant penalties if listing salespeople lead buyers into mistakenly believing that there are competing or "phantom" offers when none actually exist.

Some salespeople have been requesting the names of the other salespeople who are involved in the "bidding" process to at least know which offices they are up against, and sometimes sellers are in fact conveying this information, although there is no legal obligation on them to do so.

In some offices where multiple offers are occurring, and where one or more of the offers are in fact coming from the listing salesperson or other salespeople in the same brokerage office, a practice has developed that the process of presenting all offers to the seller is in fact handled by a senior manager of that office, as opposed to the listing salesperson, to ensure that the seller is given an unbiased look at all of the offers being submitted. I encourage this sort of action, as it adds more integrity to this entire process.

In my view, the profession needs to consider a new "fair offer process" that would provide more protection to potential buyers and provide more integrity to the system. For example, there should be an obligation to provide the names of every brokerage involved in the process during the process itself and perhaps an ability to confirm the price of the other offers afterward, through an independent third party, with the names of the buyers not being disclosed for confidentiality reasons. As I advocate throughout this book, full disclosure about all aspects of a transaction brings more integrity into the process.

Let's assume the offer is to be presented in person and you are told in advance that there will be multiple offers. What do you do if you arrive on the listing and there are no other offers present? It is possible that the seller's salesperson did not mislead you but that the buyers with the other offers changed their minds. In this circumstance, prior to your presenting the offer, you have a duty to advise your buyer client as to this new development and to then take instructions as to whether or not the offer is to be presented.

In many multiple offer situations, there will be pressure on buyers to submit a clean offer, with no conditions, because these will obviously be favoured by the seller. If you are considering doing this, you must be very careful to obtain written instructions from your buyer. You must also ensure that they are adequately protected, if possible. For example, by pre-qualifying the buyer for financing, it may be possible to shorten or eliminate the time period for the financing condition, such that the only condition would be for the financial institution to approve or qualify the property itself. It is still advisable to always conduct a home inspection. In this situation, advise the buyer to obtain a home inspection before they submit the offer, so that they can be satisfied with the condition of the property instead of taking it in an "as is" condition. The seller should be accommodating to this kind of request. If the buyer refuses your advice about obtaining the home inspection, document these instructions in writing, because the buyer is unlikely to remember this conversation the moment they discover defects in the property after closing.

I am often asked whether a salesperson should insert the home-inspection condition and have the buyer client expressly strike it out or simply rely on the printed provision where the buyer acknowledges having had the opportunity to include a condition for inspection but chose not to do so. In my view, the inspection condition should always be included ,and the buyer should strike it out and initial this. The reason is that at this very important Moment of Truth, buyers may be more concerned with whether they can afford the prices that are being bid on the property and may not fully appreciate the significance of the home inspection. They will very likely not even remember talking to you about this later, especially if they obtain the property and then discover defects later. By having them strike out the inspection condition, they cannot advance this argument later.

From an emotional standpoint, a multiple offer listing is almost like an auction process. Most of this is also happening around 11 p.m. in the evening, with time limits placing further pressure on the parties. In most cases, salespeople will deliberately list a property under market value in order to generate multiple offers. We have seen properties listed at $399,000 in Toronto that are sold subsequently for $475,000 a few days after the listing began. This can cause a tremendous emotional strain on buyers as well as sellers when the stakes become so high and multiple parties are involved. That is why it is so important that buyers are educated in advance as to what to expect in these kinds of situations, so that they will not be disappointed later if their offer is not accepted.

In the discipline decision of Ash, dated June 6, 2002, the buyer broker phoned Mr. Ash to inquire whether there were competing offers and was told that there was none. Mr. Ash did however insist that the offer remain open until October 5, 2001. On that day, at 7:30 p.m., the buyer salesperson was told that the seller had in fact accepted another offer — an offer from another client of Mr. Ash.

Although not technically a violation of Obligation 26, since all offers were in fact presented to the seller, this action was deemed a violation of Obligation 3, Ethical Behaviour; Obligation 4, Best Interests of Client; and Obligation 39, Unprofessional Conduct. The penalty was $3,500, with costs of $1,500 against the salesperson.

In the same vein, a listing salesperson must be careful to tell a client and potential buyers about every potential offer, and not to try showing only offers where the salesperson is receiving commissions from both the seller and the buyer. In the discipline case of Stephenson, dated October 12, 2001, the listing salesperson did not disclose to the buyers that there was another offer involved where the listing salesperson was also acting for the buyer. This would have considerably affected the price that the second buyer might have contemplated. Failure to disclose this information was held to be a violation of Obligation 26, Competing Offers, as the salesperson stood to profit from this non-disclosure, and it could also have compromised the ability of his own seller client to obtain the highest price for the property. The fine was $5,000, and costs were $1,000.

Weisleder's Wisdom on . . . CONVEYING OFFERS AND COMPETING OFFERS

1. Always present all offers as soon as they are received, regardless of whether they are from your own office or another broker's office.
2. Disclose the existence of multiple offers to all salespeople who are involved.
3. Prepare your clients for potential bidding wars, including the stress that is likely to occur. This will help keep them calm in what can be an intense process.
4. Protect your buyer clients by satisfying any conditions in advance, where possible.
5. Document instructions if you are told to waive or delete conditions that have not yet been satisfied.
6. Make sure that you insert the inspection condition into the offer and have the client strike it out themselves, if these are their instructions.
7. Before presenting, confirm again with your seller the exact number of competing offers that have actually been received or are still expected. Circumstances may have changed during

the day or night.

8. Ask for the names of the other salespeople involved in the multiple offer process.

9. If you are presented with a "bully offer" and your seller wants to consider it, immediately disclose this change of strategy to all other salespeople, through MLS as well as privately to anyone who has expressed an interest in the property.

10. If there is a competing offer or offers from the listing office, consider having a senior manager of the listing brokerage present all offers to the seller.

DEPOSITS

Delivery of deposits and documents
29. *Except as otherwise provided by law, if a registrant is representing a client or providing services to a customer in connection with a trade in real estate, and the client or customer has entered into an agreement in connection with the trade that requires the registrant to deliver a deposit or documents, the registrant shall deliver the deposit or documents in accordance with the agreement.*

Real Estate and Business Brokers Act
Deposit within five business days
17. *(1) If an amount of money comes into a brokerage's hands in trust for another person in connection with the brokerage's business, the brokerage shall deposit the amount in the trust account maintained under section 27 of the Act within five business days.*

(2) In subsection (1), "business day" means a day that is not,
   (a) Saturday, or

(b) a holiday within the meaning of subsection 29(1) of the Interpretation Act.

18. *If a brokerage receives a request for a disbursement from the trust account under section 27 of the Act and the disbursement is required by the terms of the applicable trust, the brokerage shall disburse the money as soon as practicable, subject to the terms of the applicable trust.*

The legal status and significance of the deposit have caused much confusion over the years in practice and with legal decisions concerning the deposit. Under the new REBBA and the Code of Ethics, greater detail is inserted governing how deposits are collected and disbursed. There have even been changes made to the Agreement of Purchase and Sale standard form so that everyone understands the specific time limits and guidelines.

Most offers stipulate that the deposit will be paid "forthwith upon acceptance." However, there was confusion over what this meant. Did it mean immediately upon acceptance, or within 24 or 48 hours, or even longer? Was extra time presumed if you were purchasing an out-of-town property? Furthermore, there was also confusion in determining what the actual date of acceptance was, given the many signbacks that often take place.

Under the new Agreement of Purchase and Sale form used in Ontario, a line has been added so that the parties clearly confirm the date and time of acceptance, so that there is no confusion. It also states in the deposit section that, unless the parties state otherwise, "forthwith upon acceptance" means that the buyer will deliver the deposit within 24 hours of acceptance. It also means that the deposit must be deposited into the selling brokerage's trust within five business days of this date, to avoid a violation of Obligation 29 of the Code of

Ethics and Section 17 of REBBA.

What if the buyer is late with the deposit? Can the seller get out of the deal? In the recent decision of *1473587 Ontario Inc. v. Jackson*, decided in 2005, an offer was prepared by the buyer to purchase property. The agreement provided that the deposit was due and payable within five days. It turned out that, due to an administrative error, the deposit was not delivered until seven days after the date stipulated in the agreement. The seller refused to accept the deposit and took the position that the agreement was over and sold the property to a new buyer. The buyer sued and lost. The judge focused on the standard form clause in the agreement that says that "Time shall be of the essence of this Agreement," meaning that time limits are significant and must be followed. The judge ruled that this constituted a fundamental breach of the contract, permitting the seller to take the position that the agreement was at an end.

How will this decision affect a situation today if a buyer is more than 24 hours late in paying their deposit? Could a seller take the position that the deal is over? In a very hot market, many sellers may be willing to take that position if they find out there is another buyer willing to pay more. Should you advise the seller to cancel a deal if a buyer is late in paying the deposit? As you know, I do not like litigation, and when you try to cancel a deal you run the risk of the buyer starting a lawsuit and tying up the property in court. The best you can do when advising a seller in this position is to immediately have him contact his lawyer for advice on how to proceed. The ideal solution is to quickly obtain the deposit.

However, when you act for a buyer, you can't predict how your seller is going to react. If your buyer tells you she needs two or three days to get the deposit together, then say so in the offer so that there is no confusion. Warn your buyer in advance that, if the offer is accepted, she must get the deposit to you within 24 hours so that there is no confusion and no risk of the deal being terminated by the seller.

What if a deposit cheque bounces? Will this cancel a deal? Based on the 1473587 decision, this could very well be grounds to permit a seller to cancel an agreement. However, I would caution anyone in giving that advice to a seller since there may be other reasons why a cheque bounces that are beyond the control of the buyer. What you should do first in this situation is contact your seller and inform them that the cheque has bounced. It may then be advisable to contact the seller's lawyer for instructions as to how to proceed next. You may decide to continue with the deal, provided that the buyer increases the amount of the deposit.

Be vigilant about who is writing the cheque for the deposit. As I will discuss in Chapter 5 on identity theft, a new practice has emerged where unscrupulous buyers steal a company cheque from an organization that writes many cheques and then change the "payee" name to the brokerage company involved. They then submit the deposit with an agreement, together with a short conditional period. They then cancel the deal, claiming they are not satisfied with the condition, and then ask for their money back. They receive the cheque from the innocent brokerage company before the other organization recognizes the deception. Be very vigilant in looking at where these deposit funds are coming from. It will impact your brand image if you are associated with this kind of activity in any way.

More and more brokerages are now insisting on certified cheques or bank drafts for all large deposits to avoid issues surrounding bounced or forged cheques. This is perfectly legal and should be considered if appropriate.

Clients should also be educated on the legal significance of the deposit and your trust account. A deposit cannot be disbursed from your trust account unless the transaction closes or there is a mutual release by the parties or court order. If there is a dispute and the matter goes to court, the money is either paid into court or stays in the trust account until the matter is decided by the court. If a buyer defaults under an agreement, the court will usually determine that the deposit will be forfeited to the seller, even if the seller subsequently sells the property for more money. This is due to the fact that, by paying the deposit, the buyer is not only paying part of the total purchase price but also showing good faith that they intend to complete the transaction. By not closing, they violate this good faith obligation and will thus forfeit the deposit.

The brokerage is not entitled to this deposit unless it had an express agreement with the seller providing that, in the event of default and in the event the seller obtained all or part of the deposit, it would be shared with the listing brokerage. This type of provision can sometimes be found in commercial listing agreements, but it is rarely provided for in residential listing agreements.

In the case of Richard B. Agent, decided June 12, 2001, the salesperson was careless in not following up on the deposit cheque from the buyer. The panel found that not taking active measures to obtain the deposit cheque from the buyer in a timely manner was a violation of not only Obligation 29 but also Obligation 4, Best Interests of the Client.

Weisleder's Wisdom on . . . DEPOSITS

1. Make sure that buyers and sellers understand the legal requirements and obligations regarding delivery of any deposit.

2. Warn your buyer in advance that deposits must be delivered within 24 hours of acceptance of any offer.

3. Ask questions if the deposit is not being paid by the actual

parties to the transaction.

4. Consider requiring certified cheques for all large deposits to avoid any fraud or bounced cheques.

This chapter's review of the RECO obligations, and examples in which they were not followed, should help you make your practices as a salesperson more professional and help you bulletproof yourself against disciplinary as well as potential legal proceedings. At the same time, by following these principles, you will end up with long-term, satisfied loyal clients. Now let's turn to new legislation on privacy that you should be aware of.

CHAPTER 4

Casting Light on the New Privacy Act

As of January 1, 2004, the new federal Privacy Act became applicable to most commercial activities in Canada. The act has created much concern in many industries, including real estate, regarding the consequences of not complying with the new privacy rules.

Real estate is a good example of an industry that uses personal information on a daily basis. Therefore, all real estate salespeople and brokers should understand their rights and obligations under the Privacy Act. There are two main reasons for you to do so:

- to ensure that you do not violate any of the act's provisions and invite an audit by the Privacy Commissioner's office in Ottawa (which I assure you is not kept private!), and
- to learn how to use these privacy principles as a marketing advantage in your practice.

Before looking at the implications of the act for you as a real estate salesperson or broker, let's consider the act itself and what gave rise to it.

A BIRD'S-EYE VIEW OF THE ACT

The legislation passed by the federal government is called the Personal Information Protection and Electronic Documents Act and is commonly referred to as PIPEDA. The act is divided into two parts. The first part deals with the protection of personal information. The second part promotes electronic commerce by providing for the use of electronic means to communicate or record information or transactions. Real estate professionals should focus on the former.

The main purpose of the first part of the act is stated in section 3:

> The purpose of this part is to establish, in an era in which technology increasingly facilitates the circulation and exchange of information, rules to govern the collection, use, and disclosure of personal information in a manner that recognizes the right of privacy of individuals with respect to their personal information and the need of organizations to collect, use, or disclose personal information for purposes that a reasonable person would consider appropriate in the circumstances.

The creation of the Internet was the driving force behind worldwide privacy legislation. Countries were not only concerned about how businesses shared consumer information with other businesses in the same country, but also about the implications when potential businesses had the ability to transmit this information to other companies all over the world.

The first action taken in this regard was by the European Union. Countries in Europe would not do business with each other unless the other particular countries passed specific laws related to privacy, similar to the principles of PIPEDA. When Canada sought to join this electronic commerce union, they were required to pass a similar privacy law, and this is why PIPEDA was passed in its current form. The law came into effect on January 1, 2001, but was only applicable to federally regulated businesses such as the telecom industry and the banking industry. The rest of the country's businesses became regulated effective January 1, 2004.

Under the Canadian Constitution, matters of personal information are typically under the jurisdiction of the provincial governments. In Ontario, for example, the government has passed the Consumer Reporting Act, which deals with how consumer reporting agencies, commonly known as credit bureaus, handle the personal and credit information of customers. Accordingly, there is an express provision in PIPEDA that it will no longer be effective in a province once that province passes its own privacy legislation. Quebec, Alberta, and British Columbia have already passed privacy legislation, and Ontario was expected to pass its own privacy law at the end of 2004. The Ontario government is now taking the position that it will wait a little longer to see how the federal legislation is interpreted in practice before introducing their own privacy legislation. In any event, the principles of all the privacy laws passed to date are alike.

Personal information is any information that can identify an individual, excluding their name, business address, and business phone number. In the real estate business, any facts about a person's home, including the property address and its sale price, are considered personal information because that information can be used to identify the owner of the property. It makes no difference that you can look up this information in other public databases, such as the local land registry office. You can only use personal information with the consent of the individual.

WHAT GAVE RISE TO THE ACT

Why was the act introduced in the first place? One of the main objectives of privacy legislation is to protect ordinary consumers from invasions of their privacy, including the sharing of personal information about them without their permission. Advances in electronic technology have made this an all-pervasive problem in many countries.

If I asked you to indicate what you felt was the most annoying invasion of your privacy on a daily basis, you would probably answer telemarketing calls at home, closely followed by spam e-mails, unwanted fax advertisements, and the direct mail and junk mail that cascade out of your mail box. How did these people and businesses obtain your telephone and fax numbers, your e-mail and home addresses? Initially, most telemarketers simply went through the phone book to obtain this information. However, after they were successful in selling their products or services to a list of customers, this list became very valuable information, which the telemarketers then sold to others. The Privacy Act prevents this type of selling of lists going forward, unless individuals have consented to this in advance.

I also receive many annoying recorded voice messages telling me to call a number to hear about a great product or marketing opportunity. I used to wonder why any telemarketer would think that anyone would ever bother to call this number, as I usually hang up the phone within two seconds of realizing I'm on the other end of a canned pitch. I later learned that telemarketers are more interested in when we pick up the phone than in how we respond to the pitch. When we pick up the phone is valuable information that they can share with other telemarketers. (I have also learned that you can abort this fact-gathering by pressing the # key six times before hanging up.)

Canada does not yet have a national "do not call" list. However, you can go to the website of the Canadian Marketing Association (CMA), www.the-cma.org, and register your phone and fax numbers and mailing address if you do not wish to receive any further invasions of your privacy. The list is updated every three months and then circulated to all of the members of the CMA. About 80% of all telemarketers in Canada are members of the CMA and follow this list. The penalty for not following the list is having your number disconnected by the local phone service provider. So while I cannot guarantee that you will not receive a fax from Nigeria telling you that you can have $75 million transferred into your trust account by paying a small $5,000 "transfer" fee, you will be able to cut down on most of these unwanted communications.

The U.S. experience with their own "do not call" list demonstrates just how annoyed the U.S. consumer is with these kinds of invasions. When the "do not call" list was introduced in the U.S., it was expected that two million consumers would sign up. As of March 31, 2007, over 80 million consumers in that country had signed up, and it is expected that eventually 100 million will add their names to the list. As a direct result of these lists, and the penalties associated with calling someone who is registered on the list, several U.S. call centres have closed, and companies are reducing their workforces in these areas.

Recent surveys have shown that 70% of Canadians would consider adding their names if a similar list was established in Canada. The Canadian Marketing Association expects the federal government to introduce do not call legislation either in late 2007 or 2008. As realtors engage in many forms of marketing their services, they will have to be very mindful of these realities in the marketplace.

THE PRIVACY ACT AND THE REAL ESTATE INDUSTRY

In the real estate industry, the question that you have to ask yourself is, "Are my actions going to bother someone or invade their privacy to such an extent that they will bring a complaint to the Privacy Commissioner in Ottawa or launch a court action for damages?" You can see on the Privacy Commissioner's website (www.privcom.gc.ca) that there have already been many investigations and decisions by the Privacy Commissioner's office as a result of complaints made by consumers claiming their privacy has been invaded.

The Real Estate Council of Ontario (RECO) publishes a similar list of decisions at its own website (www.reco.on.ca), regarding any discipline proceedings that have been brought against salespeople. As I have stated in previous chapters, one of the main reasons to follow the principles in this book is to avoid a claim being made against you that could lead to your being included on this Privacy Wheel of Misfortune. Obviously, you want to avoid the negative publicity, fines, and penalties that arise when you become the subject of a disciplinary proceeding under RECO. You also do not want to take a star turn on the Privacy Commissioner's website.

Any consumer is free to complain to the Privacy Commissioner's office about your actions. Once the commissioner decides to investigate or conduct a privacy audit, it will cause you the same anxiety, stress, and expense as an income tax audit. The fines and penalties can be as high as $100,000 for companies, $20,000 for individuals. Since this legislation is still in the early stages, the Privacy Commissioner's office is trying to mediate situations between complaining consumers and the allegedly offending organizations, and, more importantly, to ensure that the organizations in question have adequate privacy policies in place going forward so that similar complaints do not arise in the future.

Many salespeople say to me, "You make a big point that we should disclose everything that is material and relevant to my client, then you turn around and tell me that I can't disclose certain things because they are 'personal and confidential.' How can we reconcile these two principles?" In fact, privacy law is just an extension of common-sense principles that we already use on a daily basis in the business. Many salespeople act in multiple representation on a regular basis, representing both buyers and sellers. When you act in multiple representation, you are not permitted to tell a seller client how high the buyer may go, even if the buyer confides this information to you. Most sellers will tell you that this is the most material information they could think of, yet you do not have to disclose it. The reason? When you mention the multiple representation relationship to your clients in the first place, you explain very clearly that you will not be disclosing these facts. In other words, you are disclosing what you will not disclose. In this way, you are in fact fulfilling the obligations regarding full and complete disclosure. Privacy law is a further extension of these same principles, in that you are telling someone in advance what you will be using their information for.

Virtually 95% of all real estate buyers require a mortgage to complete their purchase. The first thing the bank will request is a credit check on the prospective buyer. For the bank to do a credit check, it must get a written consent from the buyer because the bank will be basing its decision on the customer's personal information. The main source of information for the bank is the customer's credit history.

Most people across Canada who have ever applied for a credit card or loan have their own unique credit history at the credit bureaus. How the credit bureaus use this information is governed by the Consumer Reporting Act in Ontario and similar legislation introduced by the other provinces. For example, this legislation says that when you ask a customer for permission to do a credit check, the font of the sentence must be bolded and of a certain height so as to come to the attention of the customer. (That is why the printed provision number 23, "Consumer Reports," in the Agreement of Purchase and Sale form in Ontario is bolded while most of the other printed provisions are not.) The legislation and this provision give sellers the opportunity to have a credit check done on buyers if they are worried whether the buyers have the ability to complete the proposed transaction.

Under the same credit protection legislation, consumers are able to access their own files by making an appointment with one of the credit reporting agencies. These agencies usually require photo identification before releasing this information, because it is very private and sensitive. An individual also has the right to have the information in their file changed if it is incorrect by submitting support material from the relevant bank, landlord, or business.

10 PRINCIPLES OF PRIVACY

The Privacy Act codifies 10 principles of privacy that were first introduced by the Canadian Standards Association in 1996. If you and your organization understand the applicability of these 10 principles, you should be able to deal successfully with any related privacy issue that you will face in the course of your business.

But first, consider these three overriding principles to understanding the 10 principles of privacy. If these three are understood, the rest will merely serve as further clarification.

• Appoint someone in your office to be responsible for all privacy issues, including handling any complaints from the public, educating all staff, and protecting any personal information in your or your office's possession.

• Disclose to your client, either before or at the time you obtain their personal information, what you will be using their personal information for.

• Obtain the consent of the client.

And now . . . the 10 principles of privacy, including examples of how these relate to the real estate industry.

Principle 1 — Accountability

An organization is responsible for personal information under its control and shall designate an individual or individuals who are accountable for the organization's compliance [with the principles of the act].

Every real estate office must have its own privacy officer, someone responsible for all issues related to privacy in that office. If that office's number comes up for an audit, the Privacy Commissioner's office will want to know who this officer is. There is no requirement that the privacy officer be a real estate broker. It can be a salesperson in the office or even an administrative worker. The key is whether this person has the authority to deal with any privacy issues that come up and is ensuring that everyone in the office is following the privacy policies set up by your office. (Many businesses give someone a new title when they do not want to give them a raise. This could guide you in giving someone the new title of privacy officer!)

Principle 2 — Identifying Purposes

The purposes for which personal information is collected shall be identified by the organization at or before the time the information is collected.

This is the main principle of all privacy legislation. You must tell someone what you plan to use their personal information for either before or at the time you collect the information. In a typical listing situation, you are collecting personal information about a seller — facts about the property being sold and the listing price to be offered. You must identify this to the seller at the time you obtain the listing, either verbally or in writing.

Accordingly, the listing agreements nationwide have been modified such that the seller is now providing consent to the salesperson to use and disclose all the personal information about the seller's property in order to sell his or her property. This consent gives the salesperson the right to let everyone know that the property is for sale, by any means necessary.

While this may seem obvious in a listing situation, it becomes less clear in other instances. An example would be the sign-in sheet that buyers are asked to sign when they visit an open house. The buyer is usually told that the reason for the request for the buyer's name and address is for "security reasons." The seller needs to know who was visiting the property. What usually happens a few days later is that the listing salesperson decides to contact the potential buyers by telephone to see if they are still interested in that property. He may also be looking to solicit these customers to purchase other properties that he may have listed. In either case, he did not identify the purpose for this call when the customer originally signed in at the open house. He has not been given permission to make this call, and is in fact now bothering the customer at home. Is he much different from the rest of the annoying telemarketers?

This situation can be easily avoided by stating on the sign-in sheet that the buyer also consents to being contacted by the salesperson after the visit to discuss the property or other properties. The salesperson has identified the purpose of the request for personal information, and no complaint can be made. No one will object to your calling them at home if they have given you permission in advance to do just that.

Can a salesperson market to a seller whose listing has

expired? This personal information is available on most MLS services. However, when the seller consented to list the property, she only gave permission to the salesperson to do anything necessary to sell the property "during the listing." She did not give permission for other salespeople to use this personal information to solicit her after the listing expired. Accordingly, as this purpose was not identified or agreed to at the time of the listing, contacting this seller is a violation of privacy law.

Many salespeople have asked whether it is okay to call the seller and ask for permission to send them information. What you must remember is that just telephoning the seller as a result of your use of the personal information is already a violation.

The conundrum of how to contact the seller reminds me of something that happened at a major brokerage house. The president of the company called the bond trader desk inquiring what the interest rate spread was that day. The trader replied in irritation, "Don't you realize how busy I am?" The president replied, "Have you any idea who you are talking to? I am the president of the bank." The trader gulped and said, "Do you have any idea who you are talking to?" The president replied, "No." "Good," the trader said and hung up.

You will have to make your own determination or risk assessment as to whether or not someone will complain as a result of this kind of action. Most sellers have a reasonable expectation that they will be contacted after their listing expires and thus are not too upset when it happens. However, some may in fact be very bothered and could complain.

There was a recent case before the Privacy Commissioner of Canada where a consumer did complain after being contacted once her listing had expired. No express consent was given by the consumer. As expected, the Privacy Commissioner's office did consider this to be a violation of this privacy principle.

It was interesting that the Privacy Commissioner recognized that this was an industry issue and suggested that the real estate boards across the country solve this problem by disclosing and obtaining consent of the consumer at the time the listing is originally obtained. Accordingly, the following language is now found in listing agreements in Ontario:

> In the event that this Agreement expires and the Property is not sold, the Seller Does _____ Does Not_____ consent to allow other real estate board members to contact the seller after expiration of this Agreement to discuss listing or otherwise marketing the Property.

Depending on what the consumer chooses, the board is then able to insert this information into the MLS listing so that it becomes clear to every board member whether they can contact a consumer after the listing expires. Other provinces have made similar changes to their listing processes to deal with this issue.

Many have asked whether salespeople are permitted, as a way of making contacts, to offer their services to owners who are trying to sell the property themselves, via the common "For Sale by Owner" (FSBO) signs. The answer is that you can contact these owners. Others question whether you can contact them if their sign states "No Salespeople." In my view, you can still contact them by saying something like, "I understand that you have advertised that you have no salesperson. Well don't worry, I am here." On a more serious note, you should keep track of how long an FSBO is on the market. Once it is over four weeks, there is an opportunity to approach the owner by saying something such as, "I am trying to be updated on all market activity in this area. Would you be offended if I took a quick look at your home?" Most owners will not complain with this approach.

Another difficult issue concerns a real estate appraisal. Typically, an appraisal consists of sold prices and listing prices of comparable properties. In most jurisdictions in Canada, when someone now lists a property on a multiple listing service, they are giving permission for the listing information and subsequent sale of the property to be used in any future comparative market analysis (CMA) or appraisal. That purpose has been identified in the listing agreement. However, for any sale that happened prior to 2004, the owner did not give permission for the sale price to be included in this appraisal or CMA report, nor was the purpose identified at the time of the listing. For any such property, appraisers and real estate salespeople are now being advised to quote only a range of prices without identifying the actual address with a specific price. This reasoning is difficult for most salespeople and appraisers to accept due to the following.

• The information about sale price of virtually any property is available at the local land registry office.
• The seller probably relied on a similar appraisal report when they purchased the property in the first place.
• The context of an appraisal or CMA report is typically confidential between a salesperson and a private customer or between an appraiser and their own client. It is not intended to be released to the general public.
• This use of personal information is not likely to bother any person identified by the information.

To be extra cautious, you should obtain from your clients a written statement that they will keep the contents of the CMA report confidential. It could be as simple as the one-line statement: "I agree to keep the contents of this CMA report confidential and not to disclose the contents to any third party." An example of confidentiality provisions can be found in Appendix D.

In my view, the combination of these powerful arguments and obtaining a confidentiality agreement would be looked at favourably should the issue ever go to the Privacy Commissioner for adjudication. The risk of someone complaining in this situation is very low, and it will become even lower as we move forward and more and more sales that are the subject of the CMA occur after January 1, 2004. For this reason, most appraisers have not changed their form of appraisal at all, continuing to use the same methods. What it comes down to is that most sellers would not be bothered if the sale price of a home that they sold some time ago is included in someone else's appraisal report, which is being used to determine the value of similar homes in the area.

We have now had the benefit of three years of potential complaints to the Privacy Commissioner over the CMA issue. To my knowledge, there have been no complaints raised. This does not surprise me as, for the most part, consumers are not bothered if this information is used only in situations involving the private disclosure of the information only to consumers who are looking to buy or sell similar properties in the area.

It is a very different situation, however, if a nosy neighbour calls your office the day after you have sold your seller's house and asks you what the house sold for. I believe that disclosing this information without the seller's permission could bother the seller. Being cavalier about this kind of personal information to virtual strangers makes you look unprofessional. You should instead consider using privacy in this situation as a positive marketing opportunity. Imagine saying the following to the nosy neighbour:

As you know, the sale price of the home is personal information of our client. We value this information and keep it private. If you are interested in listing your own home, we would be happy to share the same marketing expertise that we used to sell your neighbour's property to serve your own needs.

Instead of considering privacy as a barrier to your marketing and selling efforts, use it as a positive marketing opportunity wherever possible.

A favourite marketing tool of a salesperson after a successful sale of a property is to send out cards announcing that they have sold the property at, for example, 102% of the listing price. This value being advertised is in fact personal information. In a typical listing agreement, the salesperson's marketing purpose has not been identified to the seller, and therefore it is not permissible under privacy law. What is permissible is to state that you have sold a home in the area or to say that you have sold three homes in the area with an average price of, for example, $300,000. If the purpose had been identified and agreed to by the seller, then you would be able to send out the cards immediately after the sold sign is placed on the property. (I will demonstrate under Principle 8 a method in which you are able to obtain this consent of the seller very easily, again by using privacy as a marketing opportunity.)

Marketing your sales is further complicated by another issue: whether you also require the permission of the buyer to advertise the successful sale of a property by a listing seller. The listing salesperson only has a relationship with a seller, not a buyer (except in multiple representation circumstances). Yet the sale price of a property is also the personal information of a buyer. Dealing strictly with privacy law, you could make a strong argument that you only need the permission of the seller to do this kind of successful marketing. However, most organizations governing the real estate industry, such as the Real Estate Council of Ontario, take a different view as to what consents are required for proper advertising.

Looking at decisions issued by RECO, it appears that the sale price of a home is the personal information of the seller from the date the agreement is entered into until the date of closing or title transfer. After closing, this same personal information belongs to both the seller and the buyer. So here's the distinction. Once the sold sign goes in the ground, you require the permission only of the seller to send out listing cards. After closing, however, you require the permission of both the seller and the buyer. Remember, to even put the "Sold" sign in the ground once the agreement is signed, you must have the permission of the seller included in your listing agreement.

In the RECO discipline decision regarding Siu, reported December 29, 2003, Mr. Siu faced proceedings for having violated several RECO rules relating to improper advertising. The main violations were that he advertised that he "sold a house every three days," his name was larger than his broker's in several advertisements, and he did not obtain the permission of buyers to advertise that he had sold their properties, after closing.

The safest practice, therefore, would be to obtain the permission of both your seller and your buyer before you do any marketing of the successful sale of your property.

What about taking photographs of the chattels and fixtures of a property when conducting an inspection? Would this be permitted? Chattels and fixtures would be considered personal information as defined by the Privacy Act. People might wonder what harm taking pictures could do to anyone. It is interesting that in Ottawa recently a cabinet minister sold his home and was told by his salesperson that she had permitted the buyer salesperson to take pictures of the home. The cabinet minister was extremely upset since he feared that these pictures could find their way onto the Internet or into magazines in order to embarrass him. This would clearly be a violation of someone's privacy.

You must therefore make it clear that the sole purpose of taking these photos is to provide documented proof of what the buyer expects to receive from the seller after closing, so that there are no misunderstandings. Then obtain the consent of the seller to take the pictures, as noted in the next principle.

Principle 3 – Obtaining Consent

The knowledge and consent of a customer are required for the collection, use, or disclosure of personal information except where inappropriate.

This third rule is the easy answer to all privacy questions. If you obtain the prior consent of the client to whatever you are planning to do, you will not have any complaint later. The secret is to obtain this consent in a positive manner, using privacy not as a restriction on your business but as a marketing opportunity for your business.

We have seen that the most common form of consent in the real estate industry is now found in the listing agreement itself, whereby the client gives the listing salesperson consent to use whatever means possible to effect the sale of the property, including the ability to disclose personal information about the property to anyone who can assist in selling the property. A copy of the relevant listing language is disclosed below, found in section 11 of the Ontario Real Estate Association Listing Agreement, and has been adopted by most real estate boards in Canada:

> The seller consents to the collection, use, and disclosure of personal information by the Broker for the purpose of listing and marketing the Property including, but not limited to, listing and advertising the Property using any medium including the Internet; disclosing Property information to prospective buyers, brokers, salespersons, and others who may assist in the sale of the Property; such other use of the seller's personal information as is consistent with listing and marketing of the Property. The Seller consents, if this is an MLS listing, to placement of the listing information and sales information by the Broker into the database of the appropriate

MLS system(s) and acknowledges that the MLS database is the property of the board(s) and can be licensed, resold, or otherwise dealt with by the board(s). The Seller further acknowledges that the board(s) may: distribute the information to any persons authorized to use such service which may include other brokers, government departments, appraisers, municipal organizations, and others; market the Property, at its option, in any medium, including electronic media; compile, retain, and publish any statistics including historical MLS data which may be used by licensed board members to conduct comparative market analyses; and make such other use of the information as the board deems appropriate in connection with the listing, marketing, and selling of real estate.

The seller is thus agreeing to the salesperson's conveyance of personal information to any other salesperson or other person for the purpose of selling the property. If the property is listed on MLS, the seller authorizes the MLS service to disclose the information to any other party at its discretion, including other board members, government agencies, appraisers, and others. The seller further consents to subsequent sales data being retained by the board and compiled and used by any other member for a comparative market analysis, as discussed under Principle 2.

The seller now understands the identified purpose of the disclosure of personal information — to sell his property — and he has given his consent by signing the listing agreement.

If you want to use information associated with the sign-in sheet at an open house, you must obtain the customer's consent on the document itself. It should be informed consent: Consumers must understand what they are consenting to. While there has been much debate as to how to obtain this consent, two methods have been deemed acceptable by the Privacy Commission: opt-in consent and opt-out consent.

- In opt-in consent, consumers must check off a box indicating that they agree to have their personal information disclosed for a particular purpose. In the open house sign-in sheet example, the clause would read as follows:

   The undersigned consents to X using my personal information to contact me about this property and other similar properties.

The consumer would then check off a box beside the statement, agreeing to receive the information. This method is stronger proof that the person has consented.

- In an opt-out consent, unless the consumer checks off the box, he has agreed to accept the information. For example:

   You agree that X may use your personal information to send you information about this property or similar properties. If you do not wish to receive this information, please check the attached box.

In this case, customers who have not checked the box are deemed to have consented to your sending the information.

What about the mailing lists that we have assembled over the years? Can we continue marketing to these clients, if we are not sure whether we have obtained their consent in the first place? There is also the concept of implied consent. If you can demonstrate that there is implied consent within the client relationship for you to send information, you can continue to do so. Therefore, if you have been using your mailing list in the past to send your clients cards, calendars, and marketing information, you can continue to do so, without any further consent. This is the concept of "grandfathering" that the legislation recognizes. However, if you intend to change the use of this information (sell or give it to a third party), the consent of each of your clients would be required. You are advised, as you market to clients or customers in the present "privacy age," to include the following opt-out language in your marketing material:

We value your personal information. If you wish to be removed from our mailing list, or have any other questions about the use of personal information, please contact us at. . . .

I am not suggesting that you insert this kind of language on your Christmas cards. However, you should include it whenever you do a targeted mailing or e-mail marketing campaign. It would be difficult for any recipient to make a complaint when you have given them the means to stop receiving this kind of information.

As discussed under Principle 2, if you would like to send out cards advertising the fact that you have had a successful sale of a client's property, the easiest way to do this is to obtain the client's permission, using the opt-in or opt-out forms of consent. You should try to obtain this consent as soon as you get the listing agreement signed. It can be as simple as one sentence saying, "I agree that you may use my personal information to market the successful sale of my property." By getting this consent in advance, you avoid any possibility of bothering the client later when you do in fact advertise how successful you were in selling the property.

Principle 4 – Limiting Collection
Members shall limit the collection of personal information to that which is necessary for the purposes identified.

There is no reason to collect personal information beyond what is required to carry out your responsibilities. As we will see under Principle 7, there is a duty to protect and safeguard personal information that is in your possession. Therefore, because of the potential damage that could result from your improper or accidental disclosure of personal information, you should not obtain information that you don't absolutely require.

For example, there is no need to collect a customer's social insurance number unless you expect that the interest earned on a deposit will exceed $50, in which case you would have to issue a T5 slip to the customer. There is no other reason to keep this confidential information.

Principle 5 — Limiting Use, Disclosure, and Retention

Members shall use or disclose personal information only for the reason it was collected, except with the consent of the consumer or as required by law.

On the surface, this appears to be an easy concept to understand. Unless the information is required by law, you cannot disclose personal information unless you have received permission from your customer or client. We tend to associate "required by law" to mean if required pursuant to a legal warrant or subpoena or similar demand. But consider if the seller says the following sorts of things to you:

"This used to be a grow house operation, but I have cleaned it up, so no one has to know about it. It's personal information."

"A sexual predator lives in the basement apartment next door, but that's okay, that's personal information. Besides, he hasn't bothered anyone for the last six months."

"The prior owner committed suicide in the house, but that's a private family matter. It's no one else's business."

Under privacy, you could argue that if the seller is saying you do not have permission to disclose this information, you would probably have to follow his instructions. However, think about this for a minute. Is this material information that you would want to know if you were buying the property? If the answer is yes, then you know that you should be disclosing this information to a buyer. Remember the concept of full disclosure discussed in Chapter 1; no privacy rule can change a seller's obligation to disclose what should be disclosed.

There is much debate as to whether a stigma house should have that fact disclosed. If you disclose everything, you cannot be successfully sued by any buyer. You do not want to be a part of any lawsuit or discipline proceeding, so disclose everything, whether it is a suicide, accidental or natural death, group home in the neighbourhood, damage to the property itself, or anything related to it. If your seller is pressuring you not to disclose this information, your answer should be, "Please go and get yourself another salesperson." It is very likely that if something does go wrong, the seller will have disappeared, and you will be left with a lawsuit on your hands. Do not be fooled by a seller's attempt to use privacy as a cover-up for something illegal. Take no part in this scheme, and you will be rewarded with very few complaints in your career.

In order to both satisfy your obligations of disclosure of this type of sensitive personal information and to also protect the privacy of the person to whom it pertains, you should also obtain a confidentiality agreement from the buyer at the time that the information is disclosed. In this way, the buyer can only make use of this information for the purpose of considering whether they want to enter into this transaction for the purchase of the property and for no other purpose. The agreement can be as simple as one line, with the buyer agreeing to keep all personal information included in this disclosure confidential, and to only use it for the purpose of deciding whether to enter into and complete the transaction contemplated by the agreement of purchase and sale and for no other purpose.

Principle 6 — Accuracy

Members shall keep personal information as accurate, complete, current, and relevant as necessary of its identified purpose.

When you are relying on information to make a decision about a consumer, you must keep that information as accurate and current as possible. For example, anytime you apply for a mortgage loan or credit card, you must pass a credit check. The laws and regulations surrounding the credit reporting agencies in Ontario, or credit bureaus as they are commonly called, are governed by the Provincial Consumer Reporting Act, but the principles relate very closely to the new privacy legislation. The credit reporting agencies are constantly updating their credit files with current information, because they understand that companies are relying upon this information in order to make decisions about whether to grant credit to a particular consumer.

If you are acting as a property manager for a landlord, you also have this obligation. You must keep your tenant files as current as possible with relevant information, because the landlord will be relying on this information when making decisions affecting the ongoing relationship with a tenant — relocation of the tenant into a different unit, sharing of any capital improvements, and decisions whether to grant any extension of the lease upon renewals.

Principle 7 – Protecting Information
Members shall protect personal information with safeguards appropriate to the sensitivity of the information.

It is common sense that if we are entrusted with the personal information of clients, we should be doing our best to protect this information from being released to third parties. This is especially true given the recent phenomenon of identity theft and the fraudulent duplication of social insurance numbers, credit cards, and automatic banking cards to defraud consumers and financial institutions. We have read about hackers getting through an organization's firewall computer protection for the purpose of obtaining sensitive financial information on the company's customers in order to orchestrate this type of identity theft. It has caused companies to spend enormous sums of money ensuring that their computer systems are protected from outside threats. As an extra precaution, only a few people within the organization understand the systems that protect the company information. Any company that gathers personal information from consumers needs to protect this information. The nature of the protection that your organization will need will depend on the sensitivity of the information you are collecting.

If you are careless in how you safeguard and protect personal information, you may be held liable in a civil action. There is always the possibility that a consumer can take you to civil court to assert a claim for damages in relation to violation of their privacy rights. While it is debatable whether most violations under the privacy principles will give rise to a civil claim for damages, the careless release of sensitive personal information could lead directly to losses and damages suffered by the consumer. It would form a logical basis for a claim for damages against you in a civil court.

How should your organization protect the personal information that you collect? As with your entire privacy policy, you must make all employees in the organization aware of the importance of maintaining the confidentiality and security of personal information. Sensitive personal information should be accessible only to those who need to know it.

Many of these principles of protection are just common sense. You should conduct an inventory of your respective offices to see where sensitive information is stored. If it is in a cabinet, then the cabinet should be locked and accessible only to those who need the information contained in those files. Fax machines should never be in an open environment. They should be under the care and control of a specific person who can then distribute the faxes to the persons for whom the information is applicable.

I heard about a privacy officer in one real estate office who took her responsibility so seriously that she locked the fax machine in the closet after she left the office at 5:00 p.m. That's a bit extreme. We all understand that salespeople need access to their fax machines at all times, due to many deals that are signed and accepted at all hours of the night. Yet it would be a good idea to have another person appointed to be responsible for this information in the evening hours — it's that important.

The Privacy Commissioner's office rendered a decision recently that it is not sufficient that you throw sensitive personal information into the wastepaper basket. Personal information should in fact be shredded before being thrown out. This brings into question your company's relationship to the cleaning companies that enter your offices, often in the evenings when no one is there. It is quite possible that they may obtain access to sensitive personal information. Many companies are now requiring cleaning suppliers to sign confidentiality agreements. All salespeople and brokers should practise the proper disposal of personal information.

Principle 8 — Openness Concerning Policies and Practices

Members shall make readily available to consumers specific information about their policies and practices relating to the management of personal information.

This principle states that each organization needs to have a privacy policy that clearly sets out what your company does with personal information. Furthermore, this policy should be available in the event anyone asks you about it.

A copy of a standard privacy policy is found in Appendix C. It details the essential information you need in order to comply with privacy obligations. It's very important for every employee in your office to read and understand your privacy policy and to be able to explain it to any consumer who asks about it.

In my view, you should be doing much more with your privacy policy. It can be a great marketing opportunity for your company. Put your privacy policy into a brochure and show it to your sellers as early in the listing process as possible. Use the brochure to show potential clients how much you value their personal information and how it will only be used for the purpose of selling the property. Have your clients then sign the brochure, confirming that they agree with your privacy policy terms, as shown in Appendix E.

You could go even further. In your policies, include language that makes it clear that you will also be using this personal information to market the successful sale of the property after the agreement is signed. You may go still further and say that you will post this information on your own company website as a service to all your clients. Sellers should not object if you explain this in the following way:

> Our firm values and respects the personal information of our clients. We use it only to do everything we can to sell your property and then to let others know how successful we were in selling your property.

It should then not be difficult to have your seller consent to your privacy policy terms. Just like that you have obtained the permission of your seller client to send out listing cards announcing your successful sale of the property. You should consider this, too: Whenever buyer salespeople call to tell you that they will be bringing in an offer, fax them a copy of your privacy policy and ask them to have it signed by the buyer before the offer is submitted. If the buyer salesperson explains this properly, the buyers should not be caused much concern, especially since buyer salespeople should be explaining their own privacy policies to their own clients. In this way, you have now obtained the permission of buyers to market the success-ful sale of their property as well.

You may now have solved all the privacy issues relating to your ability to market the successful sale of a property. If all real estate offices make a coordinated effort to adopt this mar-keting practice, most salespeople will be able to market the subsequent successful sale of any property without any fur-ther permissions required and, more importantly, without violating any privacy principles.

A related issue is how long salespeople should retain files and personal information. Under regulation 579/05 under REBBA, all records that are required to be made, such as the trade record sheets, need to be retained for up to six years. Any financial information relating to transactions and commis-sions earned also needs to be retained for up to seven years for income tax purposes. With respect to your financial records, ask for advice from your company accountants. In addition, ask for guidance from your legal advisers and insurers as to how long you should retain information due to the possibility of legal actions being commenced against your firm based on a file that may have been closed years earlier.

With respect to computer information, my advice is that you print important e-mails and attachments and file this information instead of storing everything electronically and then having to worry about where the information is stored, whether it was properly backed up, or whether some new computer virus will destroy it in the future.

Principle 9 — Consumer Access

Upon request, members shall inform a customer of the existence, use, and disclosure of his or her personal information and shall give the individual access to that information.

This is another common-sense principle of privacy law: A consumer should be permitted access to whatever information of theirs that you have in your files. As we discussed in Principle 7, Protecting Information, this has long been the accepted practice with respect to your own credit information on file with the consumer reporting agencies or credit bureaus. All of us have the right to call a credit reporting agency and make an appointment to review our files. There may be incorrect information on file that is affecting our ability to receive credit. Sometimes there can be instances where minor systems problems may affect your credit ability without your knowledge. For example, when you apply for credit at any given organization, not only does the credit reporting agency provide a history for the requesting organization, it also tracks the number of times a credit check has been done on you. The higher the number of credit checks, the more difficult it becomes to obtain credit, as it appears that an individual is trying to pay one debt off by taking another debt on, or even worse, running up credit everywhere. Many times this can happen in error, such as when one company, through its own systems error, conducts multiple credit checks on the same consumer.

The principle of being able to apply to have a credit error corrected applies to any organization that holds your personal information. They must, upon request, make personal files available for review. Typically, organizations have 30 days to make the file available and this should be communicated to the consumer as soon as possible to avoid any complaint to the Privacy Commissioner's office.

In most cases, real estate offices do not keep in their files any personal information that is already available in the client's lawyer's file. As a result, you should not receive many requests from clients to review their personal information. However, in the unlikely event that you do receive such a request, you should do your best to make certain the request is satisfied on a timely basis.

Principle 10 – Challenging Compliance

A consumer shall be able to address a challenge concerning compliance with the above principles to the designated account-able person or persons in the member office.

Managing this principle may well be the most important duty of your office's privacy officer. Privacy officers must be empowered to address any questions or concerns raised by the public about your privacy policies, which will involve doing everything possible to address a consumer complaint.

Consumers are not required to approach an organization directly about a complaint before advising the Privacy Commissioner's office. Therefore, you should welcome any complaint that comes to you first as an opportunity to resolve the customer concern before it escalates to a formal review by the commissioner's office. By complaining, customers are giving you the chance not only to solve their complaints, but also to develop procedures in your office to ensure that other customers do not suffer the same treatment. In this way, you can use the complaint as a positive means to make your privacy policies that much better going forward. Many successful organizations do the same thing by proactively soliciting complaints from their existing customer base, in order to nip any problem in the bud before it spreads to the rest of their customer base.

Principles 7, 8, 9, and 10 apply directly to privacy officers.

These officers should be the ones to educate your staff about the importance of privacy and to educate your clients, too. The policy should always be available for review in your office and, for the reasons set out in our discussion of Principle 8, should be used as a marketing opportunity every time you meet with a potential client. The privacy officer should also make available personal information files for review by clients upon request and should be diligent in satisfying any customer complaint that comes into your organization about your privacy policies.

If you spend the proper amount of time training and educating your staff about your privacy obligations, you may actually see an increase in your business. More importantly, you should be able to avoid any potential complaints or legal challenges. Stay off any future Privacy Wheel of Misfortune.

ISSUES RELATING TO MORTGAGE BROKERS

The 10 principles of privacy are just as applicable to mortgage brokers as to salespeople. However, there are some points that apply specifically to the mortgage broker community.

Collection and Protection of Sensitive Personal Information
Mortgage brokers are in the business of collecting as much personal information as possible in order to qualify customers for the needed financing to complete their purchase and sale transactions. Because most of this information is sensitive, brokers should take even greater measures to protect it, including shredding any personal information that is to be destroyed.

Consent from Third Parties
Since most applicants are in fact consumers, issues may arise when they provide certain information, such as support pay-

ments from a spouse. It is thus arguable that since the applicant is authorized to submit this information to the mortgage broker, the broker is also authorized to submit this together with the rest of the applicant information even though it is personal information about a third-party spouse. Perhaps one could consider removing the name of the third-party spouse from the application, leaving only the notation that the applicant is in fact receiving this additional source of income. It would not be surprising if family law practitioners include a term in future separation or divorce proceedings such that spousal support is information that can be disclosed by the receiving spouse for the purpose of verifying income received by any third party, for the purpose of any loan or other application.

Passing Information on to Other Brokers or Lenders

Similar to Principle 2 regarding identifying purposes, so long as the purpose is identified to the consumer, then personal information can be passed on by the mortgage broker to other brokers or lenders. This purpose could easily be incorporated as part of the existing language whereby the broker obtains the consent of the applicant to conduct a credit check. Consent should be expanded to include the disclosure of any personal information to any other person required in order to successfully secure the financing requested by the applicant.

Soliciting Past Clients When Their Mortgage Renews

A practice has developed whereby some lenders check the mortgage details of consumers from the records at local land registry offices and then attempt to contact these consumers with marketing information as their mortgages are about to expire, in order to get them to transfer their mortgage. This method of contacting clients is very similar to the practice by some real estate salespeople of soliciting expired listings, which is a violation of the Privacy Act. Lenders will have to amend these practices going forward, or they will be subject to potential privacy claims.

However, if the mortgage broker is marketing for renewal purposes to his existing customers because their mortgages are about to expire, I would consider this to be normal follow-up to the initial mortgage agreement. It can even be argued that the customer gave implied consent to this when he first entered into the mortgage application. Nevertheless, it makes sense, going forward, to include this purpose either in your mortgage application in accordance with Principle 2, or in your Mortgage Broker Privacy Policy, as mentioned under Principle 8.

Obtaining a Confidentiality Agreement from Lenders

I think there is a difference between lending institutions and private lenders in terms of the privacy policies adopted at each. It is important, whenever you are dealing with private lenders who may be likely to contact a customer, that you obtain a confidentiality agreement that they will also protect any personal information you may disclose to them. Some people may even want to obtain such an agreement from an institutional investor, but we can assume that they already have measures in place to protect customer information.

Passing Information on to the Buyer Salesperson

In order for a buyer broker to waive any condition regarding financing put in place by a buyer, it is prudent for the salesperson to request information in writing that the buyer has in fact been approved for the financing. For this reason, this permission should also be included as part of your privacy policy or included in your mortgage application. However, when buyers are prequalified for a mortgage, they may be reluctant for their salesperson to know the upper limit of this approval so that the salesperson does not disclose this value in the course of negotiations with the salesperson for the seller. There is no reason to disclose this information to a buyer salesperson without the express permission of the mortgage applicant.

Weisleder's Wisdom on . . . THE PRIVACY ACT

1. Prepare a privacy policy for your office.

2. Appoint a privacy officer in your office and ensure that they are responsible to educate the rest of your staff on the importance of complying with all Privacy Act obligations.

3. Indicate in your privacy policy that you will market the successful sale of your client's property.

4. Use your privacy policy as a marketing tool as soon as possible when you sign a client to a listing or buyer representation agreement.

5. Use confidentiality agreements whenever possible.

6. Ensure that your open house sign-in sheets and company newsletters have proper privacy language.

7. Make it a practice to always ask permission before taking photographs of chattels and fixtures; ensure that everyone is aware of all steps you are taking to avoid any misunderstandings about what is included in the deal.

8. Do not let yourself be fooled by unscrupulous clients; you must still always disclose material information to the other parties in a transaction; this is not "private." Remember full disclosure principles.

9. Always deal with any complaint from the public as quickly and respectfully as possible, to avoid a claim to the Privacy Commissioner's office.

CHAPTER 5

The Internet Threat, Identity Theft, and Real Estate Fraud – It's All about Information

THE INTERNET – IS IT A THREAT OR AN OPPORTUNITY?

The Internet is an evolving miracle of information accessibility and is changing the way business operates every day. Those businesses that accept and embrace what the Internet has to offer invariably succeed in making their businesses even more profitable, while those that ignore the Internet usually pay the price by going out of business very quickly.

Consumers are doing more and more research on the Internet before they make any decision to buy. The companies that recognize this and make it easy for consumers to access their information and see what makes them superior also succeed in generating more sales. Companies can also learn about customers' behaviour by the way they navigate on a particular website, and they can then change and customize the Internet experience for those customers in the future, ensuring that information, products, and services that would be potentially appealing to them are the first ones viewed when they enter the site.

Yet one can also safely say that there is too much information on the Internet and that there is thus also a distinct advantage to anyone who is able to sift through all of the available information to deliver exactly what a consumer needs to make an informed decision. When there is too much information, the consumer does not know where to start. When the information is incomplete, consumers won't receive the best value for their money.

Is the Internet a threat to how the real estate salesperson commission model will evolve over time? We are now witnessing more and more forms of websites, each offering a different kind of experience, offering to assist consumers in either buying or selling their homes for a fraction of what they would pay a traditional brokerage. In reviewing these models, there are some questions that we need to answer.

- Is this any different from the "for sale by owner" (FSBO) methodology that has been around for years?
- What are the business models associated with these websites? Do they make any money?
- Are there any comparable lessons to be learned from the way that the Internet impacted the travel agent industry?
- How can salespeople and brokers use the Internet as an opportunity to grow their businesses?
- How can real estate boards and associations assist in this process?
- Will the government get involved?

The real estate salesperson community has long been the target of uneducated consumers who have failed to see the value of the services of the real estate professional. This view led originally to the FSBO industry, where consumers were enthralled by the "promise" that they could sell their properties themselves very easily for the same price as if they used a realtor and could thus save the average realtor commission, 5%–6% of the sale price.

Yet the lessons learned by almost everyone who has tried

the FSBO experience are exactly the opposite. They do not get the same exposure of their property to as many potential buyers, they do not have complete, accurate information about what their property should be selling for in the first place, they are not prepared for the number of disturbing phone calls, unqualified buyers, and stressful negotiations that will take place, and they are not aware of all the potential legal and other issues that could impact the closing of their property.

I have heard the comparison made to being a pilot. We could all be pilots if all there was to it was flipping a switch to "automatic pilot" and then letting the plane's computers do the rest. However, it takes years to learn how to properly take off and land a plane or handle an emergency. It's the same in the real estate experience.

The National Association of Realtors in the United States did a study in 2003 and found that the average FSBO sale price was 17% lower than the average local MLS sale price in the same markets during the same time period. So, while these owners claim that they may have saved up to 5%–6% in commissions, they still ended up with a net overall loss in actual money received for their properties. And this study didn't take into account all the disturbing phone calls and visits that they received from anxious buyers, many of whom were not even properly qualified to purchase a home in the first place due to a poor credit rating.

When you list a property with a salesperson, it's the salesperson who receives all the calls and ensures that only qualified buyers have the opportunity to see the property. It's also the salesperson who gathers all the feedback from potential buyers and gives it back to the seller to address any concerns coming out of the showings in an unbiased manner.

There are many websites today, such as privateexchange.ca, that offer a variety of services to consumers in an Internet FSBO model. The services can range from on-line advertising, time on a television cable channel, sign kits to display on the property, brochures or guides on how to sell your home, and referrals to related services such as how to prepare your home to market, lawyers, appraisers, and mortgage brokers. The fees can range anywhere from $250 to $1,000, depending on the services requested. In fact, most of these same brochures are available for little or no fees from most real estate board offices as well as most salespeople.

The main item working against the success of all these models is that they don't have access to the largest group of potential salespeople and buyers, those who are looking at and comparing the properties on the local MLS board listings.

Furthermore, any buyer who approaches an FSBO seller automatically expects to receive a 2.5%–3% reduction in the overall sale price as their "share" of the realtor savings. If the buyer is represented by a salesperson, the seller will usually agree to pay a 2.5%–3% fee anyway, especially after they see little or no activity on their property, while other similar properties in the neighbourhood are generating much more interest. Yet this salesperson is acting only in the best interests of their buyer client, so the FSBO seller will not benefit whatsoever from this experienced salesperson, even if they agree to pay the commission.

As I have stated many times in this book, there are many aspects of a property that need to be properly disclosed to buyers prior to their submitting an offer, especially things such as latent defects that are not readily observable upon inspection. Sellers who sell with no advice in this area are destined to be involved in unnecessary litigation with unsuspecting buyers that can drag on for years. When sellers are properly advised, deals close quickly and cleanly, without any aggravation afterward.

It's easy to see how these websites make money. They do not offer much in the way of added value, save for some signs, brochures, and on-line advertising that few people see in the first place.

THE TRAVEL AGENCY EXPERIENCE

An interesting parallel can be found with the travel agency industry and two men who changed the industry forever, Richard Barton and Lloyd Fink. Barton and Fink, two former Microsoft executives, convinced Bill Gates that consumers would benefit from a more transparent process of booking flights and hotels on-line, and with Gates' backing Expedia, the on-line travel booking company, was born.

Expedia had a dramatic impact on the travel industry as more and more people started booking their trips on-line. In many cases, small travel agencies closed up, and there was an industry consolidation. Yet many other travel agencies became even more successful, even after the launch of Expedia.

To learn some of the reasons why, I interviewed Ruby Silvertown, the president and CEO of The Travel Network Corporation, one of the leading private travel agencies operating in the Toronto area for the past 23 years. According to Ruby, it wasn't the Internet that had the dramatic impact on the industry; it was the decision of the airlines to unilaterally reduce the amount of commissions they would pay travel agents for conducting business. This is what ultimately forced so many companies to close; there wasn't enough profit margin available to stay in business.

In fact, business has never been better. As Ruby explains, think about your last experience booking a trip on-line. You always have to prepay your ticket or hotel reservation immediately, with no opportunity to "hold" a seat or room while you make up your mind. Any changes or cancellations will come with a large penalty. Most of the cheapest flights offered require you to make a connection, which is very time consuming and irritating, adding another layer of "possibility of things going wrong" to your flight experience. Expedia offers you only the seats that airlines want you to see. Therefore, you may not even see that you could get a direct flight to your destination for only $20 more, because Expedia doesn't have access to those seats.

What about the hotels you choose? You have no way of knowing whether the hotel has had a change in management, whether part of the hotel is undergoing renovations, and whether your room is in the most impacted area. Given that you are paying the lowest price, the hotel will be less likely to accommodate any change requests you may make when you arrive. In most cases, hotel staff just don't care, as they can always sell the cheap hotel rooms to willing Internet buyers.

This illustrates the main problem with booking anything on-line: The information you see on the Internet is incomplete for the most part. For many people, this may not matter, but for most serious travellers this is a critical factor.

The Travel Network is proud of the many partnerships it has developed with airlines, hotels, car rental agencies, and cruise lines to ensure that the entire customer experience is second to none, from the moment you leave your home until the moment you return, including every moment of truth. Nothing is left to chance.

For example, every cruise tour guide is interviewed in advance to ensure that they are the right person for the group. Research is done on all of the guests to ensure that they are travelling with like-minded individuals. For older people, care is provided to ensure that there is not too much walking on tours, if that would be uncomfortable, and simple details, such as not being close to any service elevator or other noisy area, are monitored.

For regular hotels, it's about knowing which hotel rooms have the best views, so you get absolutely the best value for your money. It's about making arrangements for complimentary drinks and fruit waiting for you in your room when you arrive, helping you feel that you are now officially "on vacation."

Good travel agents with connections are able to hold reservations for a specified time period, without requiring payment in advance. They can permit you to make changes sometimes to your reservation as a result of their relationships with many airlines. They may have access to seats using "airmiles" or other rewards programs unavailable on a regular basis to the general public.

Sometimes Ruby will offer to hold a reservation for a client and then permit the client to see whether they can find a better deal on their own. Invariably, the client calls to confirm the reservation being held.

Ruby's team uses the Internet to gather all useful information for their clients. For example, many clients are unaware about what their credit card will cover regarding car rental damage or health coverage should anything go wrong while they are out of the country. Most credit cards have detailed "exclusions" or "deductibles" if something happens to you. Ruby makes sure her clients are aware of this in advance and always checks to make sure they have proper coverage.

My own advice is that for $150 per year a family of four can obtain comprehensive out-of-country insurance with a reputable Canadian operator, such as Manulife Financial. This will cover almost any medical emergency while you are out of the country. I can speak from experience. My daughter had to have an emergency appendectomy in Miami during a family vacation five years ago. The total cost of the surgery and hospital care was $30,000 U.S. It took only one phone call to the insurer on a toll-free number when we checked into the hospital, and they took care of everything. Don't rely on your credit card coverage. The same is true with car rental insurance. Take the daily "bumper to bumper" coverage plan. It may add $25 per day to the cost of the rental, but you'll have worry-free driving no matter what may happen to the car itself while you are away.

The Travel Network Corporation has harnessed the power of the Internet to find the information that its clients need to enjoy a first-class trip, from the moment they leave home until the moment they return. This is why they remain loyal clients who also refer many new clients to the company. "Business has never been better," says Ruby, and it's easy to understand why.

It is interesting that the creators of Expedia, Richard Barton and Lloyd Fink, after selling Expedia, decided to create zillow.com, the website that touches the real estate community. Their goal was similar to that for Expedia — to provide more information to the average consumer looking to buy or sell their home by providing a valuation for almost every home in the United States. To date, they claim to have a valuation for over 70 million homes in the United States, and this database is constantly updated using information from local property assessment rolls, recent sales, and other valuations.

Zillow claims that it's not trying to replace realtors; it's just trying to provide more information to educate consumers. The consumer still requires the services of a salesperson to actually negotiate the Agreement of Purchase and Sale and assist with all other marketing and inspection efforts typically associated with buying or selling a home. Zillow claims that it will make its money on advertisements on the site itself, from realtors, lawyers, mortgage brokers, and others who are associated with the real estate industry and who see the possibility of many potential leads coming from these kinds of websites.

However, there is also a new verb in the United States — being "zillowed." This occurs when you check to see what your property is worth on zillow.com and it mistakenly says $300,000 instead of $400,000, the actual current value. This is what happens when information is not completely up to date.

There are other Internet companies, such as redfin.com,

that are taking this one step further. Redfin is an on-line realtor serving several West Coast U.S. cities such as Seattle, San Diego, and Los Angeles. It claims to provide on-line search capabilities equal to any property that you could find on the local MLS service. If you are successful in locating a property that interests you, then you can fill out an offer on-line and contact a local Redfin salesperson, who will take care of the negotiations, in person, if necessary. The company primarily works for buyers. The business model is based on Redfin obtaining the 3% typical buyer portion of the sales commission directly from the seller and then refunding 2%, or 66% of this buyer commission, directly back to the buyer. The Redfin salesperson is compensated by salary, based on how satisfied the buyer is with the services. Redfin therefore claims that its salespeople will work harder for their buyer clients because, if they don't, they won't get paid. The 1% commission that Redfin keeps is supposed to be refundable to the buyer if the buyer is not completely satisfied with the service. In theory, this concept does appear to overcome many of the difficulties inherent with the old FSBO websites in that buyers will have access to all the available listings on the local MLS service and can still use a local realtor to negotiate for them and get 2% of the commission refunded.

Redfin also claims that, based on its statistics, its buyers pay on average the same price as those who buy from traditional realtors in these cities, so in fact they end up with more money in their pockets. It's still much too early to determine whether this model will hold up over the long term. It's unclear whether the company has done enough sales to even make a profit using this business model; it would have to generate an extraordinary number of sales and/or advertising spots on its site to be able to fund the entire operation on just a 1% commission basis. It's also unclear just how many services are free or when the consumer has to start paying extra. For example, the local Redfin salesperson may provide free services to show only one or two properties, but if the buyer wants more then they have to pay extra for this.

Furthermore, there is a difference in working primarily out of an office, relying mostly on on-line information, as opposed to understanding all the local conditions that impact properties. Salespeople who are expert in a particular area know the equivalent of "which hotel rooms have the best view." They know, for example, where the best local grocery store is, where to do your dry cleaning, where to get your nails done, which schools have waiting lists. They know every business that is thinking about relocating into the area as this will impact the neighbourhood. This is just part of the "information" package that they bring to the table. Much of this type of information will never be available on the Internet in a timely manner. Yet so much of it will be vital to a family thinking about moving into a particular area.

With the explosion of available information, we may soon have "too much" information. Everything about area demographics, crime rates, et cetera will soon be just a click away. The successful salesperson will be the one who can look through all this available information and gather just what is necessary for a client to make an informed decision about buying or selling a home. It will be very similar to the travel agent experience described above.

Successful salespeople are already using the Internet to effectively market their properties. Some salespeople immediately register a new domain name for every property they list and then show the domain name right on the for sale sign on the lawn. It's easier for any potential buyer to remember this domain as they drive by, such as "1000ontariostreet.com." You can then upload your own virtual tour of the property onto this website so that buyers can have many of their questions answered on-line, before ever coming to see the property. You can also establish links to your other listed properties as well as other useful information already available, such as the demographics in the area, schools, and subway stations.

Real estate associations and boards can do their part by ensuring that the MLS website is world class, easy to navigate and easy to find relevant information. The Canadian Real Estate Association (CREA) is the owner of the MLS trademark across Canada. It has gone to great lengths to protect the integrity of this trademark by making sure that all information that appears on MLS is personally verified and that all board members are given the opportunity to cooperate with each other to ensure that the public is always provided with the most complete and accurate information possible. CREA should strive to ensure that all MLS websites are as complete as possible and then leave it to local salespeople and brokers to use this information in the best way possible to further the interests of their buyer and seller clients.

Will the government get involved? Most of the Internet discount providers are attempting to lobby the government that the real estate profession may be restricting competition by the rules and regulations governing the services provided by members of their local boards in using the MLS trademarks. The philosophy of the government in general is that nothing should be done that restricts competition in the markets.

In my view, the consumer is practical and understands that, as is the case with most businesses, you get what you pay for. I don't believe the profession should have any fear of any Internet on-line discount brokerage, regardless of the business model presented. The general public will be the final decision maker about whether they will have any success. As long as salespeople and brokers continue to provide a first-class end-to-end experience, they shouldn't be afraid of any kind of competition.

Weisleder's Wisdom on . . . THE INTERNET

1. The Internet is not a threat to the real estate business but an opportunity to grow your business even further, by using it to your advantage.

2. There are comparisons between the discount Internet websites and the FSBO lessons learned long ago.

3. The travel agent business has continued to thrive in spite of the on-line experience created through sites such as Expedia.

4. There will be too much information as well as incomplete information available on-line. The successful salesperson will know how to find the right information and use it to their client's advantage.

5. Real estate associations must do their part by ensuring that all appropriate property information is available in a format that is easily and practically accessible by the general public, while at the same time protecting the interests of buyers, sellers, and salespeople.

IDENTITY THEFT

The phenomenon of identity theft continues to grow. The dollar value of fraud continues to increase at an alarming rate and is now into the hundreds of millions of dollars per year in Canada. In the United States, this number is in the billions. Corporations are spending ever-increasing amounts on security to try to prevent this wherever possible. The federal government is now in the process of introducing legislation to make identity theft a distinct federal crime.

We live in an age when so much of our critical personal information can be stored in the black stripe on the back of your debit or credit card. If a thief is able to put your card through a false "reader" that can access your password, your bank or credit card funds can be accessed almost immediately and be withdrawn. Never let your credit card out of sight when paying for any item. You may not become aware of these charges until you receive your next bank statement. How many of you are careful in reviewing every item on your bank or credit card statement every month?

Many thieves go through the garbage outside people's homes to obtain copies of discarded credit card or bank statements or steal mail from your mailbox before you even have the chance to open it. Before doing something as simple as throwing out the garbage, consider buying a shredder to destroy any personal information that could compromise your finances. Do not even throw out your paper garbage until just before your garbage is picked up from the curb.

Other thieves try "phishing," an Internet attempt to obtain your information. In this scam, you receive an e-mail from a website that looks exactly like one of the chartered banks. It explains that there has been a security breach and that you need to change your password or update your account information to make sure you are protected. Invariably, you provide your old and new passwords, and the thieves then use this information to take the money from your real account.

Many people have home networks, permitting multiple computers in the home to access the Internet at the same time. However, unless you have proper firewalls installed, it's easy for someone outside the home in the immediate area to hack into this system and obtain your personal information.

Weisleder's Wisdom on . . . IDENTITY THEFT

1. Never share personal information, whether on the phone or through e-mail or the Internet, unless you have initiated the contact.

2. Ignore e-mails that seem to be from your financial institution asking for user names, passwords, or account numbers.

3. Use a firewall to protect your home network and family from potential hackers.

4. Avoid using passwords such as your birthday or your children's birthdays, your SIN, or your phone numbers. This is where thieves will start their search.

5. Never reveal personal information to anyone without verifying how it will be used and whether it will be shared with anyone else.

6. Try never to let your credit card out of sight when paying for any item.

7. Use a shredder to destroy all documentation before you throw it in the trash. Throw out all paper garbage just before it is actually picked up.

REAL ESTATE FRAUD

There are two kinds of real estate fraud that salespeople need to be aware of. The first is fraud by forgery, and the second is fraud by identity theft and impersonation.

In a forgery situation, fraudsters prepare a phony deed from the registered owner and then register it on title to the property. They also prepare a discharge document for any mortgage registered on title and register it as well. They may deliberately choose a property where the owner doesn't reside so as not to alert any appraiser or home inspector. These thieves then approach you as the legitimate seller of the property or may go directly to a bank to apply for a new mortgage on the property.

In this case, the fraudsters probably have valid ID to prove that they are the person or persons now registered on title. They either sell the property and receive the proceeds of sale or put a new mortgage on the property, take the funds, and disappear. The innocent third-party buyer and/or the new financial institution giving the mortgage is duped, along with the original owner and/or the bank that has had their own title and mortgage transferred or discharged.

In a related fraud, fraudsters register multiple transfers of the same property, artificially raising the price each time. They then use the last price as a basis to borrow a large amount of money — and then disappear.

In an identity theft situation, the fraudster impersonates the true owner with false ID and then arranges either a sale or a mortgage of the property and then runs away with the money. Again this is usually accomplished when the actual owner doesn't reside on the property.

How many of you ever check the deed to a property for a new listing to determine whether there has been a recent conveyance? How many pieces of ID do you ask to see, if any, when you attend a listing presentation for a new client? Be wary if someone only gives you a cell phone number. Check the land line number for the property by calling it or go to canada411.com to find it. Remember, if you are ever associated with a fraudulent transaction, even if you are completely innocent, it will have negative consequences on your personal brand image, and you may become part of lengthy legal proceedings.

In many instances in this book, I advise salespeople to always recommend that their buyer clients obtain title insurance. There are many benefits, such as to correct encroachment or other survey issues, zoning setback violations, tax arrears, or errors made by the municipality in answering inquiries. However, the most important protection is right here, protecting a buyer's title from any theft, whether through forgery or impersonation.

The cost to repair a title once a fraud has occurred, including all legal and other expenses, has averaged over $30,000.

This amount is not recoverable if you do not have a title insurance policy.

Recommend title insurance for all of your clients, whether they are existing homeowners or new buyers. All they have to do is contact their lawyer, who can make the arrangements quickly and at a reasonable cost. If you don't have title insurance on your own home, obtain a policy today and have peace of mind always.

Weisleder's Wisdom on . . . REAL ESTATE FRAUD

1. Be extra careful when dealing with a new client.

2. Create processes and procedures to help identify suspicious transactions.

3. Are you checking to see the date the seller acquired title to the property? Is it relatively recent? Was it on the MLS before?

4. Always ask for at least two pieces of government-issued ID.

5. Verify the client's land line phone number by calling it, or go on-line to www.canada411.com.

6. Look for the following suspicious circumstances.
   - Is the transaction being completed in a hurry?
   - Are sale proceeds being paid to an unknown third party?
   - Can the client only be reached via cellphone?

7. Educate your entire staff on these issues.

Risk Management

Many salespeople think, "It doesn't really matter if I make a mistake — that's why I carry insurance, to protect me. It is just the cost of doing business. And if my professional real estate council calls me onto the carpet for anything, I will just apologize and move on. They are a group of real estate professionals like me, so they will understand." Unfortunately, it is not that simple.

One of the main goals of this book is to help you avoid legal actions against you or involvement in a provincial real estate council discipline proceeding. In order to better illustrate the consequences, I want to take you through what occurs in a legal or discipline action involving real estate salespeople.

LEGAL PROCEEDINGS

I went bankrupt twice in my life. The first time when I lost a case. The second time when I won.

– Voltaire

Most people understand when they are contemplating bringing a civil proceeding against someone that the legal costs are going to end up being substantial. This alone is usually a sufficient deterrent to commencing legal proceedings. However, if you ask litigation lawyers what the subject matter is of most commercial litigation, they will tell you that a vast majority of cases involve real estate disputes. This is primarily due to the large sums of money involved in most of these transactions. Just consider that in the Toronto and Vancouver real estate markets, the sale of million dollar homes is a regular occurrence. Accordingly, if things go wrong, the amounts of money involved, unfortunately, justify legal proceedings.

The Legal Process

Here is a summary of what would probably take place if an action was brought against you as a result of something that went wrong in a real estate transaction, including the time frames involved and the fees incurred.

Upon receiving a claim, you will experience a combination of surprise, shock, and indignation that someone would institute proceedings against you. Defence counsel I've spoken to who defend negligence actions against professionals say that most salespeople are ill prepared for the consequences of a legal action, both professionally and emotionally.

Next, several negative effects kick in. Inevitably the broker is named as a party as well, meaning that this action will immediately affect your relationship with your broker. It will also affect your working relationship with other salespeople in your office. The real estate community is small, especially in smaller regions. Claimants speak to their neighbours, and soon your problems will become public knowledge, even before many of the legal papers have been filed. As the real estate brokerage business is largely a word-of-mouth referral business, this can have immediate repercussions on your ability to earn a living. (I have even heard of situations in which a legal action has torn apart an entire small-town church where both the complainant and the salesperson were members of the same congregation.)

It is one thing to be sued when someone slips on the ice outside your home. It is quite another when someone questions your livelihood, alleging that you are negligent in what you do for a living, or even worse, that you have committed some sort of fraudulent action. Even if your immediate reaction is that the allegations contain no merit whatsoever, you will still feel a great deal of emotional turmoil. Most people in this situation take these kinds of allegations personally and, as such, seriously.

As you can see, the action itself has barely started, and yet your entire world has been turned upside down.

I watched with interest when Martha Stewart was interviewed after being sentenced in her own criminal proceeding. Here was a woman who was the queen of advice on almost everything related to domestic life, from cooking to decorating to raising children. Yet she was quite frank in admitting that there were no books or magazines with advice that could have adequately prepared her for the stress and the complexities of the legal process.

According to most errors and omissions policies, the salesperson and broker must report the claim to the insurance company as soon as possible. There is information on the RECO website regarding obtaining the Notice of Claim and instructions regarding where to forward all relevant information about the claim that has been made. This information will be used by the insurance adjuster as well as the lawyer who is appointed by the insurance company to act on your defence.

In some cases, the situation will be reviewed by the insurance adjuster after conducting an interview with the claimant as well as the salesperson involved. In order to avoid costly legal proceedings, the adjuster may recommend a settlement to the insurance company if the claim has merit and the damages are easily ascertained. However, if the claim is of a nuisance nature, or it is not clear as to liability or damages, then defence counsel will be retained to act on your behalf.

The lawyer will want to meet with you to review the allegations made in the claim and will need you to produce any documents, e-mails, or notes that you may have in your possession that relate to the claim. This may include any notes that you keep in your daily planner as well as your diary. You will be asked detailed questions by the lawyer as to what every notation means. Besides the fact that you may not remember what all the notations refer to, some of the material may be very embarrassing to you personally.

Most salespeople will be certain that they did not do or say anything wrong but will have little in the way of documentation to support their claims, due to the fact that they are generally working on many transactions at once and do not have the time to document everything. Most defence counsel who practise in this area relate that with virtually every claim made, there is a point in the process at which the defendant salesperson says, "Had I known this would happen, I would have written everything down," or "I wish I had taken notes about that."

The first interview as well as subsequent reviews of the statement of defence and any changes to it will probably take up to five working days of your time in preparation. This does not include any motions that may be brought to strike out some offensive paragraphs in the statement of claim that may not be relevant. In support of any motion, it is usual for the salesperson to have to file a supporting affidavit. It will take extra time to review the material before it is filed.

The claimant or plaintiff lawyer is also given time to cross-examine you on the subject matter of any affidavit that is filed. This will involve more preparation and then personal attendance for the actual cross-examination. The cross-examination is recorded and can be used later in any upcoming motion and at trial. For any motion, add another three days of time that you will lose in preparation for and attendance of the cross-examination.

Did I mention the lack of sleep that you will have on the night before the examination, thinking about the questions that the lawyer is going to ask you? We are not even close to the actual court hearing, yet you have probably already lost two full weeks of time that could have been used productively in other ways.

The next main document that has to be prepared is the affidavit of documents, where both sides must provide a list of all the written documents that are to be produced at trial in support of their positions. For this document, you will be required to dig up everything you can find, including any e-mails that relate to the matter, any phone records that relate to conversations that may have been held on a specific date, and your own personal diaries.

Once the affidavit of documents is completed, then the lawyers for both sides have the opportunity to examine each party on what is called a discovery, in order to learn what the facts and legal positions are that each party will be relying on at trial and what documents will be brought in support of the position, so that there will be no surprises at trial.

Besides using this process to review everything that may be written in your own diary, the lawyer for the complainant will ask many detailed questions about all the training you have undergone and all the update courses, conferences, and seminars you have taken or attended. They are searching for a way to discredit your ability. Thankfully, most jurisdictions have continuing education requirements in order for salespeople to retain their licence and registration. Taking the proper training as well as ongoing training not only will equip you to deal with this ever-changing business, it also will provide you with a useful tool to defend any attack on your ability to do your job. In addition, the lawyer will ask for examples of your other transactions. They are looking for a negligent pattern that they can point to, for example, that you never document anything so there is a strong likelihood that you are confused or that you have been careless in previous transactions.

The discovery proceedings are also recorded, and the information obtained can be introduced at the trial as well. In many cases, defence counsel will also request that the salesperson attend while the plaintiff (complainant) is being questioned, in the event that the salesperson defendant can assist counsel with any of the questions to be asked as a result of the responses given by the plaintiff. This process usually takes another full week.

Other motions can be brought between the discovery stage and the trial, which could result in further attendances by the parties to answer questions and sign affidavits in support.

The trial itself usually takes one to two weeks, depending on the complexity of the facts and the number of witnesses. The preparation for trial will usually take at least another week, as you will have to reread your examination for discovery to familiarize yourself with all that has taken place. The trial is often held three to four years after the initial claim has been filed, and the salesperson is expected to be at the trial at all times. The hours spent in court are often very exhausting. You should not expect to get any work done while a trial is in progress. By then you will be totally consumed by it.

Most salespeople involved in the process are amazed by the amount of paper that is generated in the case file. Even something as small as a "slope in the kitchen" (as we soon will see) could result in detailed structural engineering reports being prepared by experts who will also have to appear at trial to give evidence.

The total time you might spend on this matter, and over the course of a three-to-six year trial, is at least two full months, to say nothing of the stress of having this action hanging over your head for the entire three-to-four-year period. Can anyone really quantify the true amount that is lost by the salesperson as a result of this process, both from the money that could have been earned during those lost two months, and the loss of health as a result of the stress related to the lawsuit itself? For many years medical researchers and doctors have stated that stress directly and indirectly contributes to health problems, including heart disease and cancer.

There is also the possibility that the results of the action will become public knowledge, as all legal proceedings are public information. The case results could be discussed in a newspaper article, or the case may appear on the Internet, resulting in negative publicity about you or your broker that will have a definite impact on future business. So much of our business is based on reputation and word-of-mouth referrals. Nothing could be worse for business than having a reputation of being involved in nasty court battles. It never matters to third parties who was right — just being involved carries a stigma.

The following is an actual case summary of proceedings against a salesperson, from the time the claim was issued until the matter was finally decided. The case was *Wood v. Lautenbach*, and the action commenced in 1998. The trial took place in the spring of 2004, six years later, and lasted four weeks.

The matter began simply enough. The property was listed by a seller who had lived in the property for several years. Some minor renovations had been done on the property. The buyer noticed the property after seeing a for sale sign while driving by. They immediately contacted their salesperson because they wanted to see it.

The property had a slope in the kitchen that some witnesses said was visible when inspecting the house while others said it was not. In this case, the buyers and their salesperson did not notice the slope in the floor. Another buyer who had put in an offer at the same time did in fact notice the slope on their own. The slope was stated to be 11 inches from one end of the house to the other.

The buyer admitted that there was some discussion about having a home inspection but that they had finally determined not to do so. The buyer salesperson did not make a strong argument that a home inspection should be done.

The transaction closed. Sometime after closing, the property began to deteriorate. It turned out that the slope in the floor was the symptom of a problem with the foundation. Ultimately, some years after the transaction had closed, the house had to be demolished. The buyer claimed damages from the sellers, the listing and selling salespeople, and the town.

The issues at trial were whether the listing salesperson was aware of the defect, and thus had a duty to disclose it, and whether the buyer broker should have inspected the property more carefully to the point where they should have strongly recommended a home inspection.

The case began with a statement of claim being served in 1998. The trial was completed in the spring of 2004. The end result was that the buyer salesperson was held responsible for not recommending that the buyer conduct a home inspection, which would have uncovered the defect. The township was also held partially responsible for not ensuring that the house complied with the Ontario Building Code and for failing to conduct proper inspections during construction. Due to complicated expert engineering evidence required, the trial took 16 days. It is safe to say the legal fees exceeded the total value of this property. These six years of stress and costs could have been avoided if the parties had only taken the time to examine their respective duties to disclose and protect their respective clients.

In summary, here are the steps involved for the salesperson in the legal process.

• The salesperson must provide the insurer's lawyer with an initial report – a written synopsis of events that occurred – as well as all file documentation.

• The salesperson then has to meet or have a telephone conference with the lawyer regarding the facts that are in the synopsis, and may have to obtain further information.

• The salesperson has to review the defence prepared by the lawyer and provide any comments.

• The salesperson has to provide all documentation to be included in the affidavit of documents to be delivered to the plaintiff and will also have to attend personally to execute this affidavit of documents.

• Examinations for discovery require the salesperson's attendance for the purpose of giving evidence under oath while being questioned by lawyers adverse in interest, including the plaintiff's lawyer. The salesperson has to meet with the insurer's lawyer prior to the examination for discovery to prepare for it.

• Mediation is now generally compulsory and requires that the lawyers and the parties attend in an effort to resolve the matter out of court. Mediations are generally a minimum half day and may take a full day. Prior to the mediation, the lawyer will provide the salesperson with a copy of the mediation brief for review and comment.

• The rules of civil procedure in legal actions also generally require that the parties attend a pre-trial settlement conference. This is similar to mediation but takes place before a judge. Again, there is an exchange of a pre-trial memorandum for review and comment by the salesperson prior to the session. Pre-trials are generally one hour in length and require the salesperson's attendance and participation.

• Preparation for trial could involve substantial time on the part of the salesperson in terms of gathering information for the lawyer and meeting with the lawyer, assisting in discussions with respect to retention of experts and review of their report, and, of course, giving evidence at trial. Trial requires attendance of the salesperson for the purposes of giving evidence, which includes cross-examination by lawyers adverse in interest in open court. Salespeople are also asked in many instances to remain in court to listen to other evidence that is material to the case, to provide any comments or other input.

Insurance Issues

RECO's errors and omissions insurance policy is meant to protect salespeople and brokers should they make a mistake in the course of a transaction. However, these policies should be examined to determine what in fact they do cover since all policies contain some exclusions.

For example, if a salesperson commits fraud in the course of a transaction, and it is proven, there will be no coverage. If fraud is alleged, the insurer will defend the action, but if the allegation of fraud is proven later at trial, then the costs will have to be paid by the salesperson and/or broker.

Furthermore, if the salesperson is involved in the transaction with a financial interest, either as a buyer or as a seller, then again there will be no coverage. That means the salesperson and/or the brokerage will have to pay the full legal costs to defend the action as well as the full amount of any judgment that is awarded, which can be prohibitive.

Many policies do not cover the salesperson for property damage. Consider a case in which a salesperson has not properly qualified a proposed tenant and this same tenant turns the property into a grow house, cultivating illicit marijuana for sale, with significant damages done to the property. An action may be brought against the salesperson for damages because the salesperson did not properly qualify the client. The salesperson's errors and omissions policy will not cover this type of damage. The practice of most insurance companies is to decline to cover damages caused by illegal acts. Both brokers and salespeople should acquaint themselves well with the gaps and exclusions in their insurance policies so that, if necessary, they are able to purchase supplemental coverage.

Following receipt of an initial notice that a claim may be made or is being made, many salespeople would like to see the matter just go away as soon as possible. Some make the mistake of trying to call the person making the claim in an attempt to settle the matter before informing the insurance company. Doing this could have disastrous consequences. If you say anything in the course of your discussions that the insurer deems to have materially affected their ability to defend you, the insurer may deny coverage immediately, and you will have to deal with the entire matter on your own.

Most salespeople indicate that they do not want to proceed to trial. The insurer, however, will not agree to resolve a matter if they are of the opinion that there is no liability. If the insured salesperson continues to insist on resolving the matter, it will be at their own expense.

Sometimes, the insurer may recommend that the matter be settled, but the salesperson insured does not agree to settle, particularly when they feel that their own reputation will be detrimentally affected. In such a case, the insurer will end their involvement with the case, and the salesperson will have to pay all costs from that date going forward. This includes the risk of paying the full damages if the matter does in fact proceed to court and the salesperson is unsuccessful.

There are other potential pitfalls with your insurance policy. One standard clause requires the giving of notice to the insurer as soon as a claim arises or circumstances arise that could result in a claim. A potential claim arises where the salesperson could "reasonably foresee" that his or her actions could give rise to a claim. If there is a problem with a closing of the transaction or if a complaint is made by someone about the salesperson's actions either before or after closing, this is the moment that the insurer will likely say that notice of the claim should have been provided to the insurer.

Salespeople, therefore, must understand the necessity of notifying their insurer of such potential claims immediately. The notice allows the insurer to make an investigation at an early stage when memories are the best and it can obtain the best factual account of what has occurred. It is also possible that the insurer may be able to repair the situation and keep expenses at a minimum.

Unfortunately, too many salespeople make the determination that they are not liable even when it is apparent that there is a problem. They just do not feel that they are the source of the problem and believe that it must arise out of someone else's actions. This type of person often goes into denial mode and fails to report the matter. Sometimes these salespeople try to assist their own clients by providing statements or affidavits to the client's lawyers. Salespeople should be very wary of this practice. They should refrain from providing statements or taking any steps to assist parties to a dispute without first consulting their insurer. Ultimately, any such statements may contain admissions of liability of the salesperson that may result in the insurer denying coverage to the salesperson later.

All insurance policies contain a cooperation clause, requiring the insured salesperson to attend all hearings, mediations, arbitrations, trials, and examinations, and to give evidence and assist in obtaining the attendance of other witnesses helpful to the case. While the salesperson may have insurance that will pay for the cost of the defence and any damages that are found by a court or in a settlement, the defence of such matters requires the salesperson's active participation as if the salesperson himself or herself was the party responsible for making the payments.

If the salesperson declines to participate and assist, the insurer may withdraw coverage, in which case the salesperson will have to take personal responsibility for the payment of the defence of the action and any damages.

Financial Involvement

Even when it is determined that you are covered by insurance, your financial involvement is far from over. To begin with, there is a $2,500 deductible, meaning that you will be required to pay the first $2,500 of any actual damage or indemnity paid by the insurer on your behalf. If it was as simple as a payment of $2,500, many salespeople might continue to be cavalier about the matter. But it becomes much more than that, even if you win and do not have to pay anything further; there are the costs of lost business, of sick days caused by stress, of loss of confidence in doing your job, and, in some cases, the loss of one's profession if the salesperson is banned from practising real estate.

Settle!

If, unfortunately, you do become involved in a legal proceeding, try to reach a settlement, and the earlier the better. As already mentioned, the very worst settlement is still preferable to the best legal position. Once a matter is settled, it is over, and since the terms are usually confidential, there is no negative publicity associated with it either. I have heard too many times the phrase, "It's not the money, it's the principle." Forget it. It's always about the money. And if you just factor in what it really costs you, in terms of time and stress, you are actually in a better financial position, in almost every situation, by settling.

However, because most court cases against salespeople will be defended by the salesperson's errors and omissions insurers, it may not be a simple matter to just settle the action. The insurer does not want to establish precedents that it is easy to just bring a claim against a salesperson and collect a quick settlement from the insurance company. The insurer may also feel that the claim has no merit and should thus be defended, all the while having regard to the legal fees that have to be paid to defend the case. It will likely not be the salesperson's decision alone whether to settle the matter. But, if you are in this position and have an opportunity to do so, urge that a settlement be made, so you can put the matter behind you.

RECO PROCEEDINGS

Many salespeople do not understand the role of RECO in the real estate profession. Accordingly, I would like to discuss briefly RECO's structure and mandate. (Much of what I say applies to the other provinces' real estate councils as well.)

The government of Ontario, by virtue of the Real Estate and Business Brokers Act, the Safety and Consumers Statutes Administration Act, and regulations under those acts along with an agreement between the Ministry of Government Services and RECO, has established a set of guidelines giving powers to the real estate profession so that it has become, in many respects, self-managing.

This power is not exercised in a cavalier manner. RECO takes its responsibilities to the profession, the public, and the government very seriously. There is no desire by the real estate salesperson profession as a whole to be completely regulated by government officials who do not understand the business. In order to earn the trust of the profession, the government, and the public, great care must be taken to ensure that salespeople continue to receive proper and updated training so that the public interest is properly served. Furthermore, RECO must ensure that improper behaviour by salespeople or brokers is disciplined appropriately in order to deter other salespeople from this kind of behaviour and, more importantly, to continue to maintain the public trust. (A similar process and mandate are found in the Law Societies across

Canada, which self-regulate the legal profession, both in edu-cational and practical requirements as well as their own discipline proceedings.)

A person applying to become a broker or salesperson must first apply to the Registrar for registration. Terms of registra-tion require continuing professional education and continued membership in RECO.

Contrary to a belief held by some salespeople and the public, RECO is not a collection agency that consumers can go to in order to collect amounts that they feel are owing to them by a salesperson or broker. If that is what a consumer wants, they can go through the legal proceedings noted above.

The new REBBA establishes the Code of Ethics as an integral part of REBBA itself. This was one of the major changes in the new REBBA legislation. It forms the basis to ensure that sales-people are dealing with each other as well as with members of the public in good faith at all times. To ensure and enforce compliance, the Code of Ethics also sets out the procedure for discipline of any salesperson who has had a complaint regis-tered against them, including how people are appointed to the discipline and appeal committees that oversee these proceed-ings. There is a full procedural scheme that goes into effect once a complaint has been made. There are various possible outcomes once a complaint is made, at the discretion of the Registrar.

RECO may provide the registrant salesperson or broker who is the subject of the complaint with a written copy of the com-plaint or RECO's understanding of the nature of the complaint. RECO will also provide a description of the Registrar's Complaints and Inquiries process and require the salesperson or broker to submit a written response to the complaint. Some of the possible outcomes of the complaint could be that the Registrar takes no action or requires that the salesperson or broker attend a meeting, mediation, or take additional education courses. When the matters involve more serious violations of the Code of Ethics or REBBA, the matters could be referred to the RECO Discipline Committee, they could be prosecuted under the Provincial Offences Act, or the Registrar could make a proposal to suspend or revoke a salesperson or broker's registration with RECO. For the Registrar's office, the protection of the public interest is the guiding factor in deciding which recommendation to make.

Many salespeople assume that every complaint goes to a discipline hearing. This is not the case at all. In fact, only a small percentage of the total number of complaints received actually goes through the process of a formal hearing. In the latest statistics obtained from RECO, for the fiscal year of 2006–07, out of 906 complaints that were received, only 37 discipline hearings were conducted.

Most of the matters were resolved in other ways, such as outright dismissal of the complaint, a written caution to the salesperson, or requiring the salesperson to attend education courses. In determining the appropriate response, the Registrar will consider the seriousness of the allegations as well as the remedies that are available.

If the response is very detailed and explains the circumstances, and if the salesperson is cooperative with the person investigating the matter, then the case may well be settled quickly by the salesperson agreeing to take additional educational courses and/or signing undertakings not to engage in the kind of activity complained of again. The matter may also be referred to alternative dispute resolution (ADR), in which the parties attempt to resolve the matter through mediation.

If a mediated solution is reached, then an agreed upon statement of facts or summary is presented to the RECO discipline committee for approval. The recommendations are generally approved in most cases. The results of these hearings, including the names of all salespeople and brokers, are posted on the RECO website for at least a five-year period. Any member of the public can take a look at these decisions by clicking on the website. This is also generally the same in all provinces of Canada, where similar councils operate and manage the real estate salesperson community.

Some would argue that because the information posted is personal information about a salesperson, RECO should not be permitted to publish the name of the salesperson who is involved in a legal proceeding due to privacy laws. However, RECO is not engaged in a commercial activity, as defined under the privacy legislation, and has declared by a member-approved bylaw that these decisions can be made public. When salespeople become members of RECO, they agree to be bound by its bylaws, and RECO (and other provincial councils like it) is thereby in a position to publish the results of any discipline proceedings.

In a RECO proceeding, it doesn't matter whether the original complaint is made by a fellow salesperson or a member of the public — the "plaintiff" in the action is RECO. RECO brings the action and retains lawyers to act on its behalf. Any fine or penalty that is levied against a salesperson goes to RECO, to be used to support their costs and programs. None of this money is given to any complaining salesperson or consumer. If the matter is serious, it will usually proceed to a hearing. The process is faster than a typical legal action, but will still take approximately eight to twelve months from the time a complaint is received until the actual hearing takes place.

Initially a researcher is appointed to gather all facts related to the claim. The researcher then files a report, which is relied on by RECO in determining whether or not the matter should proceed to a hearing or whether it can be disposed of immediately or through the mediation process.

Once a matter is referred to the discipline committee, that committee is empowered to reach a formal decision. The committee members are made up primarily of salespeople and brokers from the profession, who bring years of experience and understanding to their work. At least three members sit on each discipline panel. All members are also conscious of their duty to the public and to the profession in general, to ensure that serious violations are dealt with in a manner that will foster confidence in the system. A Notice of Hearing is given to the salesperson against whom the complaint is made, at least 45 days before the hearing. The salesperson will be given the opportunity to review all evidence compiled by RECO for use in the hearing. This is similar to the discovery process in a legal proceeding, but is much less formal. The initial complainant, whether a consumer or another salesperson, will also have to attend the discipline hearing in person in order to give evidence.

The hearing is conducted in front of the committee similar to a trial, with each party bringing their witnesses and the other side being given the opportunity to cross-examine any of the witnesses. Although there are grounds to appeal a decision, no new facts may be introduced on appeal. The salesperson would have to prove that there was a denial of natural justice, meaning that perhaps the committee was biased against him for personal or other reasons, in order to have a chance to succeed. There have been very few successful appeals. However, there have been cases in which the penalty given to the salesperson has been reduced on appeal. In most cases where there is any possibility of a conflict of interest, such as if the committee member works in the same area as the salesperson being complained of, the committee member will declare the conflict in advance and not sit on that particular hearing.

The hearing could be avoided if the parties agree on a joint statement of facts with a recommended penalty. Although the committee is not bound to accept the recommended penalty, they do accept it in the majority of cases.

It is interesting to note that although a salesperson who initiates a complaint against another salesperson will have to appear as a witness at the hearing itself, this salesperson will not be identified in the decision that is posted on the RECO website. He or she is just referred to as "the buyer's salesperson," or "buyer broker," as the case may be. This is done so as not to discourage salespeople from bringing complaints in the first place for fear of appearing in any subsequent written decision. If the salesperson or member of the public that made the complaint fails to attend in person for the hearing, this may in fact lead to the case not being proven to the satisfaction of the committee. It is an element of the fairness of the proceedings themselves that the salesperson should have the opportunity to challenge, by way of cross-examination, the evidence that is being presented by the complainant. If that person refuses to appear in person and thus denies the defending salesperson this opportunity, then the salesperson will have a very good chance of succeeding in his defence.

Notwithstanding the foregoing, I do not advise a salesperson to try to spend substantial resources and time defending a position in the hopes that the complainant will not appear at the discipline hearing. This is much different than hoping that the policeman who gave you a traffic ticket does not show up for the trial. You now know all procedural steps that are involved in a RECO proceeding. Do your best to avoid the proceeding in its entirety by practising safely and following your applicable Code of Ethics. If, however, proceedings are commenced against you, it is advisable to follow the step-by-step guidelines in this chapter on how to deal with the process.

My advice, should you become involved in a RECO hearing, is the same as with legal proceedings in general. Use the initial response as your best opportunity to have this matter dealt with as soon as possible. Treat this very seriously and try to answer all allegations as clearly as possible. Be cooperative with any researcher who may be assigned to collect information. If you can resolve the situation by attending education courses, that is a great result. You can then put the matter behind you immediately.

If that is not the case, try to resolve the matter through mediation and the ADR process. This should result in a negotiated settlement that, while not ideal, still serves the purpose of having the matter finalized quickly while not having your name publicized negatively on the RECO website.

Should the matter be set down for hearing, again I suggest that you try to settle through an agreed upon statement of facts with a recommended penalty, rather than go through the uncertainty of a hearing. Always listen to your legal adviser's recommendation regarding your chances for success.

The costs associated with a discipline committee proceeding should also be considered. In every case that I have referred to where a salesperson is found to have been liable, they have had to pay the costs of the RECO prosecutor, which have ranged in the decisions from about $1,000 to $2,000. The salesperson must also pay for their own legal costs in defending themselves before the RECO discipline committee. It is interesting to note that in a few of the cases where the salesperson succeeded in the matter, the salesperson asked for RECO to pay the salesperson's legal costs. In most instances, the committee has declined to make this payment, so the net effect is that the salesperson in almost all cases will have to pay their own legal costs as well, which can amount to $5,000 or even $10,000. These costs will likely not be covered by your insurance policy, a further incentive to avoid being the subject of RECO proceedings.

PRIVACY ACT PROCEEDINGS

Although the Privacy Act is relatively new and we have seen few cases involving real estate firms in general, we must continue to take the privacy issues outlined in this book very seriously. As discussed in Chapter 4, a complaint can be made to the Privacy Commissioner's office very easily. It does not cost a consumer anything to file one. The result of any complaint can be a very time-consuming, stressful audit. It can even result in federal fines, penalties, and subsequent civil proceedings by a consumer.

It is thus important for your organization to take seriously any complaint received from a client or customer. View this as an opportunity, not an aggravation. If you are able to solve a client's complaint, not only will you defuse a potential embarrassing situation, you will be able to establish guidelines in your office so that these kinds of complaints never occur again. Furthermore, the client is likely to remain even more loyal to your organization in the future and will be more likely to refer your company to others.

If you are not able, however, to solve the concern and the complaint is forwarded to the Privacy Commissioner's office, cooperate immediately with the commissioner's representatives. Take great care in preparing any response to allegations made. Try to give the commissioner's office the time to interview any applicable people in your organization, and ensure that your own privacy policy is available for the commissioner's office to review.

As we all become more familiar with this legislation, it is important for us to remember that the Privacy Commissioner's office will try, to the extent possible, to mediate the situation between a salesperson and a consumer who has lodged a complaint. One of the best ways to resolve the matter is to demonstrate that you have taken the steps to ensure that this kind of behaviour will not recur, through the more complete incorporation of a privacy policy as well as educational requirements in this regard by all of your salespeople and administrative staff.

Weisleder's Wisdom on . . . RISK MANAGEMENT

1. If you ever receive a notice that a complaint may be made against you, whether verbal or written, let your broker know immediately.

2. The next step is to inform your insurer about the facts and circumstances to avoid any situation where the insurer may try to deny liability.

3. If the opportunity arises to settle a claim, remember that "The worst settlement is still better than the best lawsuit."

4. If you are contacted by RECO for any discipline matter, cooperate fully.

5. Be ready to demonstrate that you understand why the complaint was made and, more importantly, that you have taken steps to ensure this kind of complaint never arises again.

6. In any Privacy Act proceeding, remember to respond in a timely manner to any inquiry by any client or by the Privacy Commissioner's office.

Forewarned Is Forearmed: The 14 Steps of Success

The goal of any real estate professional is to create long-lasting, satisfied clients who return to use your services in the future, and recommend you to their friends. By following the principles set out in this book, not only will you stay out of potentially negative legal, discipline, or Privacy Act proceedings, you will also achieve your main objective of loyal client relationships.

Here is a short summary of some basic principles to remember in your everyday real estate practice in order to avoid disciplinary or legal actions and increase your success.

1. Practise Full Disclosure

In everything that you do, remember the principle of full and complete disclosure no matter who you are representing. Disclose everything to your client and encourage your client to disclose everything material to the other party to the transaction. Be wary of any client who is not willing to disclose matters that you suspect will cause problems for buyers. Your disclosure obligation begins as soon as you meet your client and continues right up until the property is sold and the transaction is completed.

2. Be Prepared at Your First Client Meeting

There is a lot of truth to how much you can gain on a first impression with someone, whether in your personal or business relationships. Whether it is a listing presentation or a buyer representation meeting, being properly prepared serves many purposes. First, it ensures that you obtain all the required information to get started on your representation relationship. Second, it helps your client understand your relationship and what services you will be providing. Third, it helps your client begin to trust you, seeing that you consider them to be important and are treating them accordingly.

3. Get the Contact Numbers

At your initial client meeting, obtain all contact numbers for the client, including phone, cell phone, fax, and e-mail addresses. Insert these immediately into your own contact list. This will make it easier for you to reach this client and to have a record of any important communication.

4. Listen to Your Client

No two clients are alike. All have different needs, whether they are sellers or buyers. Everyone has emotional as well as physical needs in a typical home purchase. You must begin to understand all of these needs right away. The best way is to ask a lot of open-ended questions and then just listen. It's not important to impress your clients with how much knowledge you have about the business; they expect this. Rather, it is important that you listen to their needs. This demonstrates immediately that you care, and it will be very unlikely for a client to try to cheat you out of a commission later if you have treated them this way from the beginning of the relationship.

Make notes as to what the client wants. For example, the seller may not want to have traditional open houses or market their property over the Internet, and the buyer may only want to live in a particular area. Do not judge anyone as a result of any request. Besides writing the notes down, repeat back to the client what it is that you heard. This further demonstrates that you are listening to their concerns.

5. Take Notes and Confirm All Instructions and Conversations
Whenever something is very important, it is advisable to try to confirm the instructions via e-mail, as it can be done very quickly and then printed later for a permanent record. It is critical for you to make notes in your diary, daily planner, or personal digital assistant of all such conversations as well. Document everything. These will be extremely helpful should disputes arise later.

6. Follow Through with All Commitments
Once you make a commitment to a client, you must follow through with it. This can include checking the zoning on a property, the ability to obtain a building permit, the quality or quantity of water from an existing well, or concerns about septic systems. What's more, you should then let the client know that you have completed the task. Try to get confirmation from the client that the commitment has been fulfilled and then make a note of it.

7. Be Careful
Take your time when completing offers or listings. Most errors occur as a result of working too quickly and carelessly. Obtain written confirmation where possible for every important fact that is to be included on the MLS listing. Ensure that you look at a copy of the deed itself to verify ownership, check a current tax bill to verify the taxes, and find a current survey to confirm the lot measurements. Fill out the SPIS form with your seller. Review the lawyer's reporting letter for any other defects in the property and then disclose them to any buyer. As a buyer

salesperson, always review the SPIS form with your buyer if it is available. Be careful when drafting any condition to ensure that your client is properly protected.

8. Keep Track of All Important Dates

Ensure that all important dates in a transaction are noted, especially condition waiver dates, as these are usually critical to the legal enforceability of the transaction.

9. Keep Your Clients Regularly Updated and Informed

Follow up with your clients regularly. This practice permits you to convey the impression that they are important to you and also enables you to hear if anything new has arisen that may affect the listing or the transaction.

10. Do It the Same Way Every Time

Once you set up your own process as to how you sign up and explain the documents to your clients, be sure to do it the same way every time. Following the same pattern will also be invaluable to you as proof that you did do something if it is later disputed.

11. Refer to Others for Advice, When Needed

Never hesitate to refer your clients to a lawyer or other professional for advice, at any stage in the transaction. Many discipline proceedings have gone in favour of salespeople who have been able to demonstrate that when an issue arose that affected the transaction materially, they advised the client to seek independent legal counsel. The fact, in some cases, that the client refused to follow this advice did not hurt the salesperson's position.

12. Stock Training Materials

Ensure that there is a proper training manual in your office, with guidelines for all important office procedures, including advertising guidelines.

13. Establish a Mentor System

Try to establish a mentor system for every new salesperson so that there is proper supervision on everything they work on for at least the first six months of their practice.

14. Live Your Brand

Your personal reputation is your own brand image. Protect it at all costs as it is the source of all your referral business. Treat all clients, fellow salespeople, and office staff respectfully and professionally.

Seller Property Information Statement

OREA Ontario Real Estate Association   **Seller Property Information Statement**   **Form 220**
Residential   for use in the Province of Ontario

ANSWERS MUST BE COMPLETE AND ACCURATE This statement is designed in part to protect Sellers by establishing that correct information concerning the property is being provided to buyers. All of the information contained herein is provided by the Sellers to the brokerage/broker/salesperson. Any person who is in receipt of and utilizes this Statement acknowledges and agrees that **the information is being provided for information purposes only and is not a warranty as to the matters recited hereinafter even if attached to an Agreement of Purchase and Sale.** The brokerage/broker/salesperson shall not be held responsible for the accuracy of any information contained herein.

BUYERS MUST STILL MAKE THEIR OWN ENQUIRIES Buyers must still make their own enquiries notwithstanding the information contained on this statement. Each question and answer must be considered and where necessary, keeping in mind that the Sellers' knowledge of the property may be inaccurate or incomplete, additional information can be requested from the Sellers or from an independent source such as the municipality. Buyers can hire an independent inspector to examine the property to determine whether defects exist and to provide an estimate of the cost of repairing problems that have been identified. **This statement does not provide information on psychological stigmas that may be associated with a property.**

For the purposes of this Seller Property Information Statement, a "Seller" includes a landlord or a prospective landlord and a "buyer" includes a tenant, or a prospective tenant.

PROPERTY: SELLER(S):		SELLER(S) TO INITIAL EACH APPLICABLE BOX		
GENERAL:	**YES**	**NO**	**UNKNOWN**	**NOT APPLICABLE**
1. **(a)** I have owned the property for...............................years.				
(b) I have occupied the property from...........................to............................				
2. Does any other party have an ownership, spousal, or other interest in the property?				
3. Is the property subject to first right of refusal, option, lease, rental agreement or other listing?				
4. If the Seller owns adjoining land, has a consent to sever been obtained within the last 2 years?				
5. Are there any encroachments, registered easements, or rights-of-way?				
6. **(a)** Is there a plan of survey? Date of survey...				
(b) Does the survey show the current location of all buildings, improvements, easements, encroachments and rights-of-way?				
7. Are there any disputes concerning the boundaries of the property?				
8. What is the zoning on the subject property?..				
9. Does the subject property comply with the zoning? If not, is it legal non-conforming?..				
10. Are there any pending real estate developments, projects or applications for rezoning in the neighbourhood?				
11. Are there any restrictive covenants that run with the land?				
12. Are there any drainage restrictions?				
13. Are there any local levies or unusual taxes being charged at the present time or contemplated? If so, at what cost? .... Expiry date..................................				
14. Have you received any notice, claim, work order or deficiency notice affecting the property from any person or any public body?				

INITIALS OF BUYER(S): ⬭

GENERAL (continued):	YES	NO	UNKNOWN	NOT APPLICABLE
15. Are there any public projects planned for the immediate area? Eg: road widenings, new highways, expropriations etc.				
16. Is the property connected to municipal water and sewer? If not, Schedule 222 to be completed.				
17. (a) Are there any current or pending Heritage designations for the property?				
(b) Is the property in an area designated as Heritage?				
18. Are there any conditional sales contracts, leases, or service contracts? eg: furnace, alarm system, hot water tank, propane tank, etc. Are they assignable or will they be disharged?....................................				
19. Are there any defects in any appliances or equipment included with the property?				
20. Do you know the approximate age of the building(s)? Age.. Any additions: Age..				
21. Are there any past or pending claims under the Tarion Warranty Corporation (formerly ONHWP)? Tarion Warranty Corporation/ONHWP Registration No...				
22. Will the sale of this property be subject to GST?				

ADDITIONAL COMMENTS:..

....

....

ENVIRONMENTAL:	YES	NO	UNKNOWN	NOT APPLICABLE
1. Are you aware of possible environmental problems or soil contamination of any kind on the property or in the immediate area? eg: radon gas, toxic waste, underground gasoline or fuel tanks etc.				
2. Are there any existing or proposed waste dumps, disposal sites or land fills in the immediate area?				
3. Is the property subject to flooding?				
4. Is the property under the jurisdiction of any Conservation Authority or Commission?				
5. Are you aware of any excessive erosion, settling, slippage, sliding or other soil problems?				
6. Does the property have any abandoned well(s)?				
7. Does the property have a buried swimming pool?				
8. (a) Is there a fuel oil tank on the property? If yes, complete the following: ☐ Underground. Date for required upgrading or removal... ☐ Aboveground. Age of tank.......................... Date of last inspection............................				
(b) Does the fuel oil tank comply with the Technical Standards and Safety Authority requirements and any other requirements for fuel to be delivered?				
9. Has the use of the property ever been for the growth or manufacture of illegal substances?				

ADDITIONAL COMMENTS:..

....

....   **INITIALS OF BUYER(S):** ⬭

Form 220   2008   **Page 2 of 3**

IMPROVEMENTS AND STRUCTURAL:	YES	NO	UNKNOWN	NOT APPLICABLE
1. Are you aware of any structural problems?				
2. (a) Have you made any renovations, additions or improvements to the property?				
(b) Was a building permit obtained?				
(c) Has the final building inspection been approved or has a final occupancy permit been obtained?				
3. To the best of your knowledge have the building(s) ever contained ureaformaldehyde insulation?				
4. Is there vermiculite insulation on the property? If yes, has it been tested for asbestos?..				
5. (a) Are you aware of any deficiencies or non-compliance with the Ontario Fire Code?				
(b) Is your property equipped with operational smoke detectors?				
(c) Is the property equipped with operational carbon monoxide detectors?				
6. (a) Is the woodstove(s)/chimney(s)/fireplace(s)/insert(s) in good working order?				
(b) Is the wood energy system **WETT** certified? (Wood Energy Technology Transfer)				
7. Are you aware of any problems with the central air conditioning or heating system?				
8. Are you aware of any moisture and/or water problems?				
9. Are you aware of any damage due to wind, fire, water, insects, termites, rodents, pets or wood rot?				
10. Are you aware of any roof leakage or unrepaired damage? Age of roof covering if known..				
11. (a) Are you aware of any problems with the electrical system? Size of service................................				
(b) Type of wiring: ☐ copper ☐ aluminium ☐ knob-and-tube ☐ other.................................	▓	▓	▓	
12. Is the owner responsible for the maintenance/replacement of any hydro poles/equipment?				
13. Are you aware of any problems with the plumbing system?				
14. Is the outdoor lawn sprinkler system in working order?				
15. Is there any lead or galvanized metal plumbing on the property?				
16. Are you aware of any problems with the swimming pool, sauna, hot tub or jet bathtub?				
17. What is under the carpeting?...	▓	▓	▓	
18. Is there a home inspection report available? Date of report...				

ADDITIONAL COMMENTS:...
....
....

Schedule(s) attached hereto and forming part of this Statement include:...
The Sellers state that the above information is true, based on their current actual knowledge as of the date below. Any important changes to this information known to the Sellers will be disclosed by the Sellers prior to closing. Sellers are responsible for the accuracy of all answers. Sellers further agree to indemnify and hold the Brokerage/Broker/Salesperson harmless from any liability incurred as a result of any buyer relying on this information. The Sellers hereby authorize the Brokerage to post a copy of this Seller Property Information Statement into the database(s) of the appropriate MLS® system and that a copy of this Seller Property Information Statement be delivered by their agent or representative to prospective buyers or their agents or representatives. The Sellers hereby acknowledge receipt of a true copy of this statement.

.... DATE............................   .... DATE............................
(Signature of Seller)   (Signature of Seller)

I acknowledge that the information provided herein is not warranted and hereby acknowledge receipt of a copy of the above information including any applicable Schedule(s).

....   DATE...
(Signature of Buyer or Authorized Representative)

....   DATE...
(Signature of Buyer)

    Form 220   2008   **Page 3 of 3**

OREA Ontario Real Estate Association

Seller Property Information Statement
Schedule for Condominium

Form 221
for use in the Province of Ontario

This Schedule is attached to and forms part of the Seller Property Information Statement for:

PROPERTY:..

SELLER(S)...

CONDOMINIUM CORPORATION:	YES	NO	UNKNOWN	NOT APPLICABLE
1. **(a)** Condominium maintenance fee $..				
(b) Condominium fee includes:				
(c) Cost for amenities not included in maintenance fee $.................................... Details				
2. Are there any special assessments approved or contemplated?				
3. Have you received any written notice of lawsuit(s) pending?				
4. Have you been informed of any notices, claims, work orders or deficiency notices affecting the common elements received from any person or any public body?				
5. **(a)** Has a reserve fund study been completed? Date of Study....................				
(b) Approximate amount of reserve fund as of last notification $........................				
6. **(a)** Are there any restrictions on the use of the property? e.g. pets, renovations				
(b) Are there any restrictions on renting the property? e.g. minimum term				
7. **(a)** If any renovations, additions or improvements were made to the unit and/or common elements, was approval of the Condominium Corporation obtained?				
(b) Is approval of any prospective buyer required by the Condominium Corporation?				
(c) Are any other approvals required by the Condominium Corporation or Property Manager? If yes, specify:				
(d) Name of Property Management Company				
8. Are there any pending rule or by-law amendments which may alter or restrict the uses of the property?				
9. Is the condominium registered?				
10. Parking: Number of Spaces .... ☐ Owned ☐ Exclusive Use ☐ Leased or Licensed				
11. Locker:... ☐ Owned ☐ Exclusive Use				
12. **(a)** Amenities: ☐ Pool ☐ Sauna ☐ Exercise Room ☐ Meeting/Party Room ☐ Boat Docking ☐ Guest Parking ☐ Other................				
(b) Are you aware of any problems with any of the common element amenities? If yes, specify:				

ADDITIONAL COMMENTS:...

....

....

....

....

....

OREA Ontario Real Estate Association

Seller Property Information Statement
Schedule for Water Supply, Waste Disposal, Access and Shoreline

Form 222

for use in the Province of Ontario

This Schedule is attached to and forms part of the Seller Property Information Statement for:

PROPERTY: ....

SELLER(S) ....

WATER SUPPLY AND WASTE DISPOSAL:	YES	NO	UNKNOWN	NOT APPLICABLE
1. (a) What is your water source? ☐ Municipal ☐ Drilled ☐ Bored ☐ Dug ☐ Lake ☐ Community ☐ Shared ☐ Other..........				
(b) If your water source is Community/Shared, is there a transferrable written agreement?				
(c) Are you aware of any problem re: quantity of water?				
(d) Are you aware of any problems re: quality of water?				
(e) Do you have any water treatment devices?...				
(f) Is your water system operable year round? Heated lines? ☐ Yes ☐ No				
(g) Date and result of most recent water test......................................				
(h) Are any documents available for the well? If yes, specify				
(i) Does the property have any abandoned well(s)?				
2. (a) What kind of sewage disposal system services the property? ☐ Municipal ☐ Septic tank with tile bed ☐ Holding tank ☐ Other..........				
(b) Are you aware of any problems with the sewage system? Date septic/holding tank last pumped................... Age of system...........				
(c) What documentation for the sewage system is available? ☐ Use Permit ☐ Location Sketch ☐ Maintenance Records ☐ Inspection Certificate ☐ Other				
3. Are the well(s), water line(s) and waste disposal system(s) within the boundaries of the subject property?				

ACCESS AND SHORELINE:	YES	NO	UNKNOWN	NOT APPLICABLE
1. (a) Is property access by municipal road? If yes; ☐ Open all year ☐ Seasonally open				
(b) Is the property serviced by a private road? Cost $.................................. per year.				
2. If your access is across private property, access is: ☐ Right of way ☐ Deeded ☐ Other .... Cost $.............................. per year				
3. (a) If water access only, access is: ☐ Deeded ☐ Leased ☐ Other..........				
(b) Water access cost of: Parking $.................... Dock $.................. per year				
4. (a) Is the original Shore Road Allowance owned?				
(b) Are there any pending applications for shoreline improvement?				
(c) Are there any disputes concerning the shoreline or improvements on the shoreline?				
(d) Are there any structures or docks on the original Shore Road Allowance?				
(e) Is the original Road Allowance included in the lot size?				
5. Does the boundary of the property extend beyond the water line? If yes, explain				

ADDITIONAL COMMENTS:...
....
....
....

Realty Company
Salesperson Survey

Q 1 Using a scale of 1 to 10, where 1 means poor performance and 10 means excellent performance, how would you rate the service you received from the real estate salesperson from the time you entered into your listing/buyer representation agreement until your transaction was completed?

_____

Q 1a Please tell me the reasons for your rating.

_____

_____

_____

Q 2 Using the same 1–10 scale, evaluate the service specifically provided by the real estate salesperson with respect to

	Rating
a. the manner in which the listing/buyer representation process was conducted	_____
b. the display of courtesy, respect, and professionalism at all times	_____
c. the overall marketing of your property	_____

d. the conduct of any open houses   _____

e. answering any inquiries in a timely manner   _____

f. the ability to deal with any issue you had   _____

g. explaining the Agreement of Purchase and
Sale   _____

h. not pressuring you at any time   _____

i. the amount of time spent with you   _____

j. negotiating the Agreement of Purchase and
Sale   _____

k. the follow-up for any waivers, conditions,
mortgage verification   _____

l. assistance with any closing matters   _____

Q 2a Please tell me which of these attributes the salesperson performed best and the reason for your rating.

_____

_____

_____

Q 2b Please tell me which of these attributes require improvement and why.

_____

_____

_____

Q 3 What is the likelihood that you would come back to this real estate salesperson the next time you are buying or selling a home?

Rating _____

Q 3a What are your reasons for that rating?

_____

_____

_____

Q 4 What is the likelihood that you would recommend the real estate salesperson to your relatives, friends, and colleagues?

Rating _____

Q 4a What are your reasons for that rating?

_____

_____

_____

May we have your permission to use any of your responses to assist us in continuing to improve the way we serve and market to our customers?

Yes_____

Thank you very much for your time and comments.

Sample Privacy Policy

"Privacy Policy"
(Firm Name)

Policy on the Collection, Use, and Disclosure of Personal Information

1. Objective and Scope of Policy

(Firm Name) is committed to respecting your privacy and has prepared this Policy to inform you of our policy and practices concerning the collection, use, and disclosure of Personal Information.

This Policy governs Personal Information collected from and about:

(a) individuals who are or may become Clients of (Firm Name), and

(b) individuals or organizations with whom (Firm Name) works.

Using contractual or other arrangements, (Firm Name) shall ensure that agents, contractors, or third-party service providers, who may receive Personal Information in the course of providing services to (Firm Name) as part of our delivery of real estate services, protect that Personal Information in a manner consistent with the principles articulated in this Policy.

This Policy does not cover aggregated data from which the identity of an individual cannot be determined. (Firm Name) retains the right to use aggregated data in any way that it determines appropriate.

In the event of questions about (i) access to your Personal Information; (ii) (Firm Name)'s collection, use, management, or disclosure of Personal Information; or (iii) this Policy, please contact:

(Name or Title, address, e-mail address, telephone number)

_____

_____

_____

_____

2. The Collection, Use, and Disclosure of Personal Information
For the purpose of this Policy:

"Client" means an individual who may purchase or has purchased (Firm Name) real estate or services to buy real estate;

"Personal Information" means any information, recorded in any form, about an identified individual, or an individual whose identity may be inferred or determined from such information. Your provision of Personal Information to (Firm Name) means that you agree and consent that we may collect, use, and disclose your Personal Information in accordance with this Privacy Policy. If you do not agree with these terms, you are requested not to provide any Personal Information to (Firm Name) or a broker or sales representative working with (Firm Name). Unfortunately, certain services can only be offered if you provide Personal Information, and consequently, if you choose not to provide us with any required Personal Information, (Firm Name) may not be able to offer you those services.

This office only collects Personal Information necessary to effectively market and sell the property of sellers; to locate, assess, and qualify properties for buyers; to market the successful sale of property completed on behalf of sellers and buyers; and to otherwise provide professional and competent real estate services to Clients.

(Firm Name), Brokers, or sales representatives may use Personal Information for commission management purposes (e.g., commission financing, commission dispute resolution).

(Firm Name)'s use of Personal Information is limited to these purposes. (Firm Name) does not sell, trade, barter, or exchange for consideration any Personal Information it has obtained. Unless permitted by Law, no Personal Information is collected about an individual without first obtaining the consent of the individual to the collection, use, and dissemination of that information.

Personal Information will be collected, to the extent possible, directly from the individual concerned.

(Firm Name) does not knowingly collect Personal Information from anyone under the age of 18, especially children under 13, and does not use such information if (Firm Name) discovers that it is being provided by a minor.

Personal Information may also be transferred to another company in the event of a change of ownership of all or part of (Firm Name).

(Firm Name) may disclose Personal Information of Clients to organizations that perform services on its behalf. This will only be done if such organizations agree to use such information solely for the purposes of providing services to (Firm Name) and, with respect to that information, to act in a manner consistent with this Policy.

Please note that there are circumstances where the use and/or disclosure of Personal Information may be justified or permitted or where (Firm Name) is obliged to disclose information without consent. Such circumstances may include:

(a) where required by law or by order or requirement of any court, administrative agency, or other governmental tribunal;
(b) where (Firm Name) believes, upon reasonable grounds, that it is necessary to protect the rights, privacy, safety, or property of an identifiable person or group;
(c) where it is necessary to establish or collect monies owing to (Firm Name);
(d) where it is necessary to permit (Firm Name) to pursue available remedies or limit any damages that (Firm Name) may sustain; or
(e) where the information is public.

Where obliged or permitted to disclose information without consent, (Firm Name) will not disclose more information than is required.

3. Accuracy

(Firm Name) endeavours to ensure that any Personal Information provided by Clients and in its possession is as accurate, current, and complete as necessary for the purposes for which (Firm Name) uses those data. Information contained in files that have been closed is not actively updated or maintained.

4. Retention

(Firm Name) retains Personal Information as long as (Firm Name) believes it is necessary to fulfill the purpose for which it was collected and (Firm Name)'s legal or business requirements.

5. Security

(Firm Name) endeavours to maintain adequate physical, procedural, and technical security with respect to its offices and information storage facilities so as to prevent any loss, misuse, unauthorized access, disclosure, or modification of Personal Information.

(Firm Name) further protects Personal Information by restricting access to it to those Employees and Contractors that the management of (Firm Name) has determined need to know that information in order that (Firm Name) may provide services to Clients.

6. Access to Personal Information

(Firm Name) permits access to and review of Personal Information held by (Firm Name) about an individual by the individual concerned.

If an individual believes that any Personal Information concerning the individual is not correct, that person may request an amendment of that information by sending a request to the person indicated in Section 1 of this Policy. (Firm Name) reserves the right not to change any Personal Information but will append any alternative text the individual concerned believes appropriate. An individual may also request that (Firm Name) delete an individual's Personal Information from (Firm Name)'s system and records where not required to be retained by (Firm Name). Personal Information may continue to reside in (Firm Name)'s systems after deletion. Individuals, therefore, should not expect that their Personal Information would be completely removed from (Firm Name)'s systems in response to an accepted request for deletion.

(Firm Name) reserves the right to decline access to Personal Information where the information requested:

(a) would disclose the Personal Information of another individual or of a deceased individual;

(b) would disclose confidential business information that may harm (Firm Name) or the competitive position of a third party;

(c) is subject to solicitor-client or litigation privilege;

(d) could reasonably result in: (i) serious harm to the treatment or recovery of the individual concerned; (ii) serious emotional harm to the individual or another individual; or (iii) serious bodily harm to another individual;

(e) may harm, or interfere with, law enforcement activities and other investigative or regulatory functions of a body authorized by statute to perform such functions;

(f) is not readily retrievable and the burden or cost of providing it would be disproportionate to the nature or value of the information; or

(g) does not exist, is not held, or cannot be found by (Firm Name).

Where information will not or cannot be disclosed, the individual making the request will be provided with the reasons for non-disclosure.

Where information will be disclosed, (Firm Name) will endeavour to provide the information in question within a reasonable time and no later than 30 days following the request.

(Firm Name) will not respond to repetitious or vexatious requests for access. In determining whether a request is repetitious or vexatious, it will consider such factors as the frequency with which the information is amended, the purpose for which the information is used, and the nature of the information.

To guard against fraudulent requests for access, (Firm Name) will require sufficient information to allow it to confirm the identity of the person making the request before granting access or making corrections.

7. Amendment of Practices and This Policy

This Policy statement is in effect as of (insert date). (Firm Name) will from time to time review and revise its privacy practices and this Policy. In the event of any amendment, an appropriate notice will be communicated to Clients and others in an appropriate manner.

Confidentiality Provisions When Giving Out Comparative Market Analysis

"Confidential Information" means information regarding the sale price of homes that will be used on a comparison basis only for the purpose of determining the value of the subject property being purchased/sold, as typically contained in a comparative market analysis.

During the course of the relationship between the salesperson and the client, the salesperson may disclose to the client Confidential Information solely for the purpose of the client determining the value to either list or put in an offer to purchase a subject property.

The client agrees to protect and safeguard the Confidential Information, not to disclose it to any third party other than financial or legal advisers of the client, and only to use it for the purposes outlined in this agreement.

The obligations under this agreement shall survive the termination of the listing/buyer representation agreement between the parties.

The client will indemnify the salesperson for any damages suffered by the salesperson caused by a breach of the client of their obligations under this agreement.

_____   _____
Witness   Client

Receipt of Privacy Policy

To: **Name of Real Estate Brokerage (the "Company")**

The undersigned acknowledges having received, reviewed, and accepted the terms of the Company Privacy Policy.

_____   _____
Witness   Client

Code of Ethics Regulation under the Real Estate and Business Brokers Act, 2002

O. Reg. 580/05

Contents

Interpretation

19. Properties that meet buyer's criteria
20. Seller property information statement
21. Material facts
22. Agreements with third parties
23. Steps taken by registrant
24. Conveying offers
25. Agreements relating to commission
26. Competing offers
27. Written and legible agreements
28. Copies of agreements
29. Delivery of deposits and documents
30. Business records
31. Certificate of registration: broker or salesperson
32. Certificate of registration: brokerage
33. Certificates of registration for brokers and salespersons kept by brokerage
34. Current forms
35. Financial responsibility
36. Advertising
37. Inaccurate representations
38. Error, misrepresentation, fraud, etc.
39. Unprofessional conduct, etc.
40. Abuse and harassment
41. Duty to ensure compliance

Procedures of Discipline Committee and Appeals Committee
42. Composition and appointment of committees
43. Assignment of discipline committee panels
44. Parties: discipline committee
45. Notice of hearing
46. Disclosure of evidence
47. Disclosure from closed hearing
48. Notice of decision to complainant
49. Notice of appeal rights

Interpretation

1. (1) In this Regulation,

"buy" means acquire or seek to acquire an interest in real estate, and "buyer" has a corresponding meaning;

"buyer representation agreement" means a representation agreement between a brokerage and a buyer;

"material fact" means, with respect to the acquisition or disposition of an interest in real estate, a fact that would affect a reasonable person's decision to acquire or dispose of the interest;

"seller representation agreement" means a representation agreement between a brokerage and a seller, and includes a listing agreement that is a representation agreement.

(2) A person is related to another person for the purposes of this Regulation if,

(a) one person is associated with the other person within the meaning of section 1(2) of the Act; or

(b) one person is related to the other person by blood, adoption or conjugal relationship.

(3) For the purposes of this Regulation,

(a) a person is related to another person by blood if,
(i) one is the child or other descendant of the other, or
(ii) one is the brother or sister of the other;

(b) a person is related to another person by adoption if,
    (i) neither is related to the other by blood, and
    (ii) one would be related to the other by blood if all adopted children were deemed to be the natural children of their adoptive parents; and

(c) a person is related to another person by conjugal relationship if,
    (i) one is married to the other or to a person who is related by blood or adoption to the other, or
    (ii) one lives in a conjugal relationship outside marriage with the other or with a person who is related by blood or adoption to the other.

Obligations of Registrants

Brokers and salespersons

2. (1) A broker or salesperson shall not do or omit to do anything that causes the brokerage that employs the broker or salesperson to contravene this Regulation.

(2) Subsection (1) does not apply to a contravention by the brokerage of section 32, 33 or 41.

Fairness, honesty, etc.

3. A registrant shall treat every person the registrant deals with in the course of a trade in real estate fairly, honestly and with integrity.

Best interests

4. A registrant shall promote and protect the best interests of the registrant's clients.

Conscientious and competent service, etc.

5. A registrant shall provide conscientious service to the registrant's clients and customers and shall demonstrate reasonable knowledge, skill, judgment and competence in providing those services.

Providing opinions, etc.

6. (1) A registrant shall demonstrate reasonable knowledge, skill, judgment and competence in providing opinions, advice or information to any person in respect of a trade in real estate.

(2) Without limiting the generality of subsection (1) or section 5,

> (a) a brokerage shall not provide an opinion or advice about the value of real estate to any person unless the opinion or advice is provided on behalf of the brokerage by a broker or salesperson who has education or experience related to the valuation of real estate; and
> (b) a broker or salesperson shall not provide an opinion or advice about the value of real estate to any person unless the broker or salesperson has education or experience related to the valuation of real estate.

Dealings with other registrants

7. (1) A registrant who knows or ought to know that a person is a client of another registrant shall communicate information to the person for the purpose of a trade in real estate only through the other registrant, unless the other registrant has consented in writing.

(2) If a broker or salesperson knows or ought to know that a buyer or seller is a party to an agreement in connection with a trade in real estate with a brokerage other than the brokerage that employs the broker or salesperson, the broker or salesperson shall not induce the buyer or seller to break the agreement.

Services from others

8. (1) A registrant shall advise a client or customer to obtain services from another person if the registrant is not able to provide the services with reasonable knowledge, skill, judgment and competence or is not authorized by law to provide the services.

(2) A registrant shall not discourage a client or customer from seeking a particular kind of service if the registrant is not able to provide the services with reasonable knowledge, skill, judgment and competence or is not authorized by law to provide the service.

Commissions

9. A registrant shall not indicate to any person, directly or indirectly, that commissions or other remuneration are fixed or approved by the administrative authority, any government authority, or any real estate board or real estate association.

Information before agreements

10. (1) Before entering into an agreement with a buyer or seller in respect of trading in real estate, a brokerage shall, at the earliest practicable opportunity, inform the buyer or seller of the following:

1. The types of service alternatives that are available in the circumstances, including a representation agreement or another type of agreement.

2. The services that the brokerage would provide under the agreement.

3. The fact that circumstances could arise in which the brokerage could represent more than one client in respect of the same trade in real estate, but that the brokerage could not do this unless all of the clients represented by the brokerage in respect of that trade consented in writing.

4. The nature of the services that the brokerage would provide to each client if the brokerage represents more than one customer in respect of the same trade in real estate.

5. The fact that circumstances could arise in which the brokerage could provide services to more than one customer in respect of the same trade in real estate.

6. The fact that circumstances could arise in which the brokerage could, in respect of the same trade in real estate, both represent clients and provide services to customers.

7. The restricted nature of the services that the brokerage would provide to a customer in respect of a trade in real estate if the brokerage also represents a client in respect of that trade.

(2) The brokerage shall, at the earliest practicable opportunity and before an offer is made, use the brokerage's best efforts to obtain from the buyer or seller a written acknowledgement that the buyer or seller received all the information referred to in subsection (1).

Contents of written agreements

11. (1) A brokerage shall not enter into a written agreement with a buyer or seller for the purpose of trading in real estate unless the agreement clearly, comprehensibly and prominently,

> (a) specifies the date on which the agreement takes effect and the date on which it expires;
> (b) specifies or describes the method for determining,
>> (i) the amount of any commission or other remuneration payable to the brokerage, and
>> (ii) in the case of an agreement with a seller, the amount of any commission or other remuneration payable to any other brokerage;
> (c) describes how any commission or other remuneration payable to the brokerage will be paid; and
> (d) sets out the services that the brokerage will provide under the agreement.

(2) A brokerage shall not, for the purpose of trading in real

estate, enter into a written agreement with a buyer or seller that provides that the date on which the agreement expires is more than six months after the date on which the agreement takes effect unless,

>(a) the date on which the agreement expires is prominently displayed on the first page of the agreement; and
>(b) the buyer or seller has initialed the agreement next to the date referred to in clause (a).

(3) A brokerage shall ensure that a written agreement that is entered into between the brokerage and a buyer or seller for the purpose of trading in real estate contains only one date on which the agreement expires.

Copies of written agreements

12. If a brokerage and one or more other persons enter into a written agreement in connection with a trade in real estate, the brokerage shall ensure that each of the other persons is immediately given a copy of the agreement.

Seller representation agreements

13. If a brokerage enters into a seller representation agreement with a seller and the agreement is not in writing, the brokerage shall, at the earliest practicable opportunity and before any buyer makes an offer, reduce the agreement to writing, have it signed on behalf of the brokerage and submit it to the seller for signature.

Buyer representation agreements

14. If a brokerage enters into a buyer representation agreement with a seller and the agreement is not in writing, the

brokerage shall, before any buyer makes an offer, reduce the agreement to writing, have it signed on behalf of the broker-age and submit it to the buyer for signature.

Agreements with customers

15. If a brokerage enters into an agreement with a customer and the agreement is not in writing, the brokerage shall, at the earliest practicable opportunity and before any buyer makes an offer, reduce the agreement to writing, have it signed on behalf of the brokerage and submit it to the customer for sig-nature.

Disclosure before multiple representation

16. A brokerage shall not represent more than one client in respect of a trade in real estate unless it has disclosed the fol-lowing matters to the clients or prospective clients at the earliest practicable opportunity:

1. The fact that the brokerage proposes to represent more than one client in respect of the same trade.

2. The differences between the obligations the brokerage would have if it represented only one client in respect of the trade and the obligations the brokerage would have if it repre-sented more than one client in respect of the trade, including any differences relating to the disclosure of information or the services that the brokerage would provide.

Nature of relationship

17. If a registrant represents or provides services to more than one buyer or seller in respect of the same trade in real estate, the registrant shall, in writing, at the earliest practicable opportunity and before any offer is made, inform all buyers and sellers involved in that trade of the nature of the registrant's relationship to each buyer and seller.

Disclosure of interest

18. (1) A registrant shall, at the earliest practicable opportunity and before any offer is made in respect of the acquisition or disposition of an interest in real estate, disclose in writing the following matters to every client represented by the registrant in respect of the acquisition or disposition:

1. Any property interest that the registrant has in the real estate.

2. Any property interest that a person related to the registrant has in the real estate, if the registrant knows or ought to know of the interest.

(2) A brokerage shall, at the earliest practicable opportunity and before any offer is made in respect of the acquisition or disposition of an interest in real estate, disclose in writing the matters referred to in paragraphs 1 and 2 of subsection (1) to every customer with whom the brokerage has entered into an agreement in respect of the acquisition or disposition.

(3) A broker shall, at the earliest practicable opportunity and before any offer is made in respect of the acquisition or disposition of an interest in real estate, disclose in writing the matters referred to in paragraphs 1 and 2 of subsection (1) to every customer of the broker or salesperson with whom the brokerage that employs the broker or salesperson has entered into an agreement in respect of the acquisition or disposition.

(4) A registrant shall disclose in writing to a client, at the earliest practicable opportunity, any direct or indirect financial benefit that the registrant or a person related to the registrant may receive from another person in connection with services provided by the registrant to the client, including any commission or other remuneration that may be received from another person.

(5) A brokerage that has entered into an agreement with a buyer or seller that requires the buyer or seller to pay the brokerage a commission or other remuneration in respect of a trade in real estate shall not charge or collect any commission or other remuneration under another agreement entered into with another person in respect of the same trade unless,

> (b) the brokerage discloses at the earliest practicable opportunity to the other person, in writing, the terms of the agreement with the buyer or seller that require the payment of a commission or other remuneration; and
>
> (c) the brokerage discloses at the earliest practicable opportunity to the buyer or seller, in writing, the terms of the agreement with the other person that require the payment of a commission or other remuneration.

Properties that meet buyer's criteria

19. If a brokerage has entered into a representation agreement with a buyer, a broker or salesperson who acts on behalf of the buyer pursuant to the agreement shall inform the buyer of properties that meet the buyer's criteria without having any regard to the amount of commission or other remuneration, if any, to which the brokerage might be entitled.

Seller property information statement

20. If a broker or salesperson has a seller as a client and knows that the seller has completed a written statement that is intended to provide information to buyers about the real estate that is available for acquisition, the broker or salesperson shall, unless the seller directs otherwise,

(a) disclose the existence of the statement to every buyer who expresses an interest in the real estate; and

(b) on request, make the statement available to a buyer at the earliest practicable opportunity after the request is made.

Material facts

21. (1) A broker or salesperson who has a client in respect of the acquisition or disposition of a particular interest in real estate shall take reasonable steps to determine the material facts relating to the acquisition or disposition and, at the earliest practicable opportunity, shall disclose the material facts to the client.

(2) A broker or salesperson who has a customer in respect of the acquisition or disposition of a particular interest in real estate shall at the earliest practicable opportunity, disclose to the customer the material facts relating to the acquisition or disposition that are known by or ought to be known by the broker or salesperson.

Agreements with third parties

22. A registrant shall not, on behalf of a client of the registrant, enter into an agreement with a third party for the provision of goods or services to the client unless,

(a) the registrant has disclosed in writing to the client the subject-matter of the agreement with the third party and the identity of the person responsible for paying for the provision of the goods or services;

(b) the client has consented to the registrant entering into the agreement with the third party; and

(c) the registrant has disclosed in writing to the third party the identity of the person responsible for paying for the provision of the goods or services.

Steps taken by registrant

23. A registrant shall inform a client of all significant steps that the registrant takes in the course of representing the client.

Conveying offers

24. (1) A registrant shall convey any written offer received by the registrant to the registrant's client at the earliest practicable opportunity.

(2) A broker or salesperson shall establish a method of ensuring that,

(a) written offers are received by someone on behalf of the broker or salesperson, if the broker or salesperson is not available at the time an offer is submitted; and

(b) written offers are conveyed to the client of the broker or salesperson at the earliest practicable opportunity, even if the broker or salesperson is not available at the time an offer is submitted.

(3) Without limiting the generality of subsections (1) and (2), those subsections apply regardless of the identity of the

person making the offer, the contents of the offer or the nature of any arrangements for commission or other remuneration.

(4) Subsections (1) and (3) are subject to any written directions given by a client.

(5) Subsections (1) to (4) also apply, with necessary modifications, to,
> (a) written amendments to written offers and any other written document directly related to a written offer; and
> (b) written assignments of agreements that relate to interests in real estate, written waivers of conditions in agreements that relate to interests in real estate, and any other written document directly related to a written agreement that relates to an interest in real estate.

(6) Subsections (1) to (5) apply, with necessary modifications, if a brokerage and a customer have an agreement that provides for the brokerage to receive written offers.

(7) Subsections (1) to (5) apply, with necessary modifications, to brokers and salespersons employed by a brokerage, if the brokerage and a customer have an agreement that provides for the brokerage to receive written offers.

Agreements relating to commission

25. (1) If a brokerage has a seller as a client and an agreement between the brokerage and the seller contains terms that relate to a commission or other remuneration and that may affect whether an offer to buy is accepted, the brokerage shall disclose the existence of and the details of those terms to any person who makes a written offer to buy, at the earliest practicable opportunity and before any offer is accepted.

(2) Subsection (1) applies, with necessary modifications, to a brokerage that has a seller as a customer, if the brokerage and the seller have an agreement that provides for the brokerage to receive written offers to buy.

Competing offers

26. (1) If a brokerage that has a seller as a client receives a competing written offer, the brokerage shall disclose the number of competing written offers to every person who is making one of the competing offers, but shall not disclose the substance of the competing offers.

(2) Subsection (1) applies, with necessary modifications, to a brokerage that has a seller as a customer, if the brokerage and the seller have an agreement that provides for the brokerage to receive written offers to buy.

Written and legible agreements

27. (1) A registrant who represents a client in respect of a trade in real estate shall use the registrant's best efforts to ensure that,
>   (a) any agreement that deals with the conveyance of an interest in real estate is in writing; and
>   (b) any written agreement that deals with the conveyance of an interest in real estate is legible.

(2) Subsection (1) applies, with necessary modifications, if a brokerage and a customer have an agreement that provides for the brokerage to provide services to the customer in respect of any agreement that deals with the conveyance of an interest in real estate.

Copies of agreements

28. (1) If a registrant represents a client who enters into a written agreement that deals with the conveyance of an interest in real estate, the registrant shall use the registrant's best efforts to ensure that all parties to the agreement receive a copy of the agreement at the earliest practicable opportunity.

(2) Subsection (1) applies, with necessary modifications, if a brokerage and a customer have an agreement that provides for the brokerage to provide services to the customer in respect of any agreement that deals with the conveyance of an interest in real estate.

Delivery of deposits and documents

29. Except as otherwise provided by law, if a registrant is representing a client or providing services to a customer in connection with a trade in real estate, and the client or customer has entered into an agreement in connection with the trade that requires the registrant to deliver a deposit or documents, the registrant shall deliver the deposit or documents in accordance with the agreement.

Business records

30. In addition to the records required by Ontario regulation 579/05 (Educational Requirements, Insurance, Records and Other Matters) made under the Act, a brokerage shall make and keep such records as are reasonably required for the conduct of the brokerage's business of trading in real estate.

Certificate of registration: broker or salesperson

31. Every broker or salesperson shall carry his or her certificate of registration and, on the request of any person, shall show it to the person.

Certificate of registration: brokerage

32. (1) A brokerage shall ensure that every certificate of registration issued to the brokerage is kept at the office to which the certificate relates.

(2) A brokerage shall, on the request of any person, show to the person any certificate of registration issued to the brokerage.

Certificates of registration for brokers and salespersons kept by brokerage

33. (1) A brokerage shall ensure that all duplicate original certificates of registration given to the brokerage in respect of brokers and salespersons employed by the brokerage are kept in a safe place.

(2) A brokerage shall, on the request of any person, show the duplicate original certificate of registration given to the brokerage in respect of a broker or salesperson employed by the brokerage to the person.

Current forms

34. A registrant shall ensure that forms used by the registrant in the course of a trade in real estate are current.

Financial responsibility

35. A registrant shall be financially responsible in the conduct of business.

Advertising

36. (1) A registrant shall clearly and prominently disclose the name in which the registrant is registered in all the registrant's advertisements.

(2) A brokerage that identifies a broker or salesperson by name in an advertisement shall use the name in which the broker or salesperson is registered.

(3) A broker or salesperson shall not advertise in any manner unless the advertisement clearly and prominently identifies the brokerage that employs the broker or salesperson, using the name in which the brokerage is registered.

(4) A registrant who advertises shall,
  (a) use the term "brokerage", "real estate brokerage", "maison de courtage" or "maison de courtage immobilier" to describe any brokerage that is referred to in the advertisement;
  (b) use the term "broker of record", "real estate broker of record", "courtier responsable" or "courtier immobilier responsable" to describe any broker of record that is referred to in the advertisement;
  (c) use the term "broker", "real estate broker", "courtier" or "courtier immobilier" to describe any broker of record that is referred to in the advertisement;
  (d) use the term "salesperson", "real estate salesperson", "sales representative", "real estate sales representative",

"agent immobilier", "répresentant commercial" or "répresentant immobilier" to describe any salesperson who is referred to in the advertisement.

(5) Despite clause (4)(c), a registrant who advertises may, before April 1, 2008, use the term "associate broker", "associate real estate broker", "courtier associé" or " courtier immobilier associé" to describe any broker who is referred to in the advertisement.

(6) A registrant who advertises shall not use a term to describe any registrant that is referred to in the advertisement if the term could reasonably be confused with a term that is required or authorized by subsection (4) or (5).

(7) A registrant shall not include anything in an advertisement that could reasonably be used to identify a party to the acquisition or disposition of an interest in real estate unless the party has consented in writing.

(8) A registrant shall not include anything in an advertisement that could reasonably be used to identify specific real estate unless the owner of the real estate has consented in writing.

(9) A registrant shall not include anything in an advertisement that could reasonably be used to determine any of the contents of an agreement that deals with the conveyance of an interest in real estate including any provision of the agreement relating to the price, unless the parties to the agreement have consented in writing.

Inaccurate representations

37. (1) A registrant shall not knowingly make an inaccurate representation in respect of a trade in real estate.

(2) A registrant shall not knowingly make an inaccurate representation about services provided by the registrant.

Error, misrepresentation, fraud, etc.

38. A registrant shall use the registrant's best efforts to prevent error, misrepresentation, fraud or any unethical practice in respect of a trade in real estate.

Unprofessional conduct

39. A registrant shall not, in the course of trading in real estate, engage in any act or omission, that, having regard to all of the circumstances, would reasonably be regarded as disgraceful, dishonourable, unprofessional or unbecoming a registrant.

Abuse and harassment

40. A registrant shall not abuse or harass any person in the course of trading in real estate.

Duty to ensure compliance

41. (1) A brokerage shall ensure that every salesperson and broker that the brokerage employs is carrying out their duties in compliance with this Regulation.

(2) A broker of record shall ensure that the brokerage complies with this Regulation.

Procedures of Discipline Committee and Appeals Committee

Composition and appointment of committees

42. (1) The discipline committee and appeals committee shall each consist of at least five members, at least one of whom has never been a registrant or a shareholder, officer, director or employee of a registrant or former registrant.

(2) A person may be appointed under subsection 21 (3) of the Act as a member of both committees.

(3) A member of the board of the administrative authority shall not be appointed under subsection 21 (3) of the Act as a member of the discipline committee or the appeals committee.

(4) An appointment under subsection 21 (3) of the Act expires at the end of the day on the day before the second anniversary of the day the appointment took effect.

(5) If the term of office of a member of the discipline committee or appeals committee who has participated in a hearing expires before the hearing is completed or a decision is given, the term shall be deemed to continue, but only for the purpose of completing the hearing and participating in the decision and for no other purpose.

(6) The board of the administrative authority may at any time terminate an appointment under subsection 21 (3) of the Act for cause.

(7) Subsection (5) does not apply to a member whose appointment is terminated for cause under subsection (6).

(8) The board of the administrative authority shall appoint,

(a) from among the members of the discipline committee, one person as chair of the discipline committee and one person as vice-chair of the discipline committee; and

(b) from among the members of the appeals committee, one person as chair of the appeals committee and one person as vice-chair of the appeals committee.

(9) Subsections (4) and (6) apply, with necessary modifications, to an appointment under subsection (8).

(10) The vice-chair of a committee may exercise and perform the powers and duties of the chair on the request of the chair or if the chair is absent or unable to act.

(11) Every person appointed under subsection (8) or under subsection 21(3) of the Act as a chair, vice-chair or member of the committee shall, before beginning his or her duties, take and sign the following oath or affirmation in either English or French:

I solemnly swear (affirm) that I will faithfully, impartially and to the best of my skill and knowledge execute the duties of .... and that, except as I may be legally authorized or required, I will not disclose or give to any person any information or document that comes to my knowledge or possession by reason of my being ....

So help me God. (Omit this line in an affirmation.)

Assignment of discipline committee panels

43. (1) When a matter is referred to the discipline committee, the chair of the committee shall assign a panel in accordance with this section to hear and determine the matter.

(2) The panel has all the jurisdiction and powers of the discipline committee with respect to the hearing and determining the matter.

(3) Subject to subsection 4.2.(1) of the *Statutory Powers Procedure Act*, the panel must be composed of at least three members of the discipline committee.

(4) If the panel is composed of three or more members of the discipline committee,

> (a) at least two of the members of the panel must be registrants;
> (b) if a broker of record is the subject of the proceeding, at least one of the registrants must be a broker of record;
> (c) if a broker is the subject of the proceeding, at least one of the registrants must be a broker;
> (d) if a salesperson is the subject of the proceeding, at least one of the registrants must be a salesperson; and
> (e) at least one of the members of the panel must never have been a registrant or a shareholder, officer, director or employee of a registrant or former registrant.

Parties: discipline committee

44. The parties to a proceeding before the discipline committee are the registrant who is the subject of the proceeding, the administrative authority and any other person added as a party by the discipline committee.

Notice of hearing

45. Subject to section 6 of the *Statutory Powers Procedure Act*, the discipline committee shall give the parties to a proceeding at least 45 days notice of a hearing by the committee.

Disclosure of evidence

46. (1) A party who intends to tender evidence at a hearing before the discipline committee shall, not later than the date specified by subsection (3), disclose the following to every other party:

1. In the case of written or documentary evidence, a copy of the evidence.

2. In the case of oral evidence of a witness, the identity of the witness and a written statement containing the substance of the witness' anticipated oral evidence.

3. In the case of oral evidence of an expert, the identity of the expert and a copy of a written report signed by the expert containing the substance of the expert's anticipated oral evidence.

4. In the case of evidence that is not oral, written or documentary evidence, a written description of the evidence.

(2) A party who intends to tender written or documentary evidence, or other evidence that is not oral evidence, at a hearing before the discipline committee shall give every other

party a reasonable opportunity to examine the original evidence before the hearing.

(3) The date referred to in subsection (1) is,
    (a) in the case of evidence tendered by the administrative authority, the date that is 30 days before the date the hearing begins; and
    (b) in the case of evidence tendered by any other party, the date that is 15 days before the date the hearing begins.

Disclosure from closed hearing

47. If a hearing before the discipline committee is closed to the public, the committee may order that evidence given and submissions made at the hearing not be disclosed to any member of the public.

Notice of decision to complainant

48. If a proceeding before the discipline committee arises from a complaint by a person who is not a party to the proceeding, the committee shall send the person a copy of its final decision or order, including the reasons if any have been given, at the same time that it complies with section 18 of the *Statutory Powers Procedure Act.*

Notice of appeal rights

49. When the discipline committee sends a copy of its final decision or order to a party who participated in the proceeding, or the party's counsel or agent, under section 18 of the *Statutory Powers Procedure Act,* it shall also send a notice outlining the party's right to appeal under subsection 21(5) of the

Real Estate and Business Brokers Act, 2002, and the procedures applicable to an appeal.

Commencement of appeals

50. (1) A party may commence an appeal under subsection 21(5) of the *Real Estate and Business Brokers Act*, 2002, by delivering the following to the appeals committee within 30 days after the discipline committee sends notice, under section 18 of the *Statutory Powers Procedure Act*, of the order being appealed:

> 1. A notice of appeal that,
>> i. identifies the appellant and the other parties to the appeal,
>> ii. identifies the order being appealed,
>> iii. sets out the grounds for the appeal, and
>> iv. sets out the relief that is sought.
>
> 2. The fee for commencing the appeal, as set out by the administrative authority under clause 12 (1) of the *Safety and Consumer Statutes Administration Act*, 1996, payable to the administrative authority.

(2) The appellant shall, within the 30 day period referred to in subsection (1), deliver a copy of the notice of appeal referred to in paragraph 1. of subsection (1),
> (a) to the other parties to the appeal; and
> (b) to the discipline committee.

(3) When a party commences an appeal under subsection 21 (5) of the *Real Estate and Business Brokers Act*, 2002, the discipline committee shall at the earliest practicable opportunity forward to the appeals committee the record compiled under section 20 of the *Statutory Powers Procedure Act*.

Assignment of appeal committee panels

51. (1) The chair of the appeals committee shall assign a panel in accordance with this section to hear and determine an appeal to the committee under subsection 21 (5) of the Act.

(2) The panel has all the jurisdiction and powers of the appeals committee with respect to hearing and determining the appeal.

(3) Subject to subsection 4.2.1 (1) of the *Statutory Powers Procedure Act*, the panel must be composed of at least three members of the appeals committee.

(4) If the panel is composed of three or more members of the appeals committee,
> (a) at least two of the members of the panel must be registrants;
> (b) if a broker of record is the subject of the proceeding, at least one of the registrants must be a broker of record;
> (c) if a broker is the subject of the proceeding, at least one of the registrants must be a broker;
> (d) if a salesperson is the subject of the proceeding, at least one of the registrants must be a salesperson; and
> (e) at least one of the members of the panel must never have been a registrant or a shareholder, officer, director or employee of a registrant or former registrant. O. Re. 580/05 s. 51(4).

(5) A person who was a member of the panel of the discipline committee that made the order being appealed must not be assigned to the panel of the appeals committee that hears and determines the appeal.

Parties: appeals committee

52. The parties to a proceeding before the appeals committee are the appellant, the other persons who were parties to the proceeding before the discipline committee, and any other person added as a party by the appeals committee.

Application of ss. 45 to 48

53. Sections 45 to 48 apply, with necessary modifications, to proceedings before the appeals committee.

Index